THE UNIVERSITY OF LIVERPOOL   4A

ARTS READING ROOM

CONDITIONS OF BORROWING

Students registered for primary degrees etc. — 6 volumes
for 14 days or for the vacation.

Members of Council, teaching and administrative staffs,
and higher degree students — 20 volumes for one month.

All other readers — 6 volumes for one month.

Books may be recalled after one week for the use of
another reader.

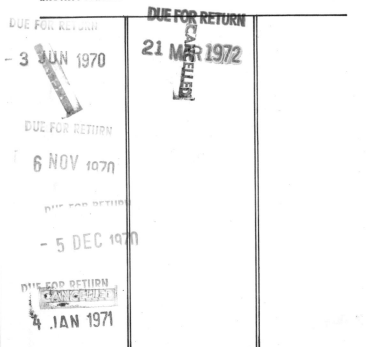

CAPITAL BUDGETING
AND THE USE OF
DCF CRITERIA IN THE
CORPORATION TAX REGIME

CAPITAL BUDGETING AND THE USE OF DCF CRITERIA IN THE CORPORATION TAX REGIME

G. H. LAWSON, M.A. (ECON.), A.A.C.C.A.
Professor of Business Studies, University of Liverpool

D. W. WINDLE, B.SC., PH.D.
Lecturer in Applied Mathematics, University of Sheffield

OLIVER & BOYD
EDINBURGH AND LONDON

OLIVER AND BOYD LTD

Tweeddale Court
Edinburgh 1

39A Welbeck Street
London W.1

First published 1967

Printed in Great Britain at
The University Press, Aberdeen

G 89263

PREFACE

Whilst successive U.K. Governments had, over a period of about two decades, actively pursued a policy of stimulating industrial investment with capital allowances, there emerged evidence in 1964 strongly and disturbingly suggesting that businessmen generally ignored both investment inducements and taxation in their investment planning. At the same time other research revealed the widespread use of (crude) criteria which, as analysis shows, tend to understate the profitability of investment.* Such a situation has serious implications from the standpoint of the economy in general and the investing public in particular.

If the *incidence* of investment inducements and measures of taxation is ignored by company decision-makers in investment planning, one result can be nothing less than a substantial weakening of conventional weapons of economic policy. Second, the use of crude investment criteria which understate the profitability of investment is in direct conflict with a major objective of economic policy itself: the encouragement of a higher level of investment. In addition, in that company shareholders are able to increase consumption or personal investment from a taxed residue of profit only, profits net of taxes (and investment incentives) are the index of economic efficiency. The use of an index expressed gross of taxes (and investment incentives) will, because of the rather complicated relationship between *net* and *gross*, generally result in a pattern of investment and net profitability which deviates significantly and adversely from the pattern resulting from indices (i.e., computations) correctly allowing for taxation and investment incentives with a consequent effect on shareholders' wealth.

In 1965 the NEDC in its paper, *Investment Appraisal*, exhorted businessmen to employ correct investment criteria and stressed the importance of investment computations which accurately allow for the incidence of taxation and fiscal inducements. Since that date major

* See the empirical studies cited in the bibliography on p. 239.

revisions to both the system of company taxation and structure of investment incentives have rendered details, but not of course principles, in the original NEDC pamphlet obsolete. From a capital budgeting standpoint, these changes have necessitated new quantitative analysis. The computational treatment of the corporation, income and capital gains taxes and investment incentives in long term company financial planning is the primary concern of this book.

CONTENTS

CORRIGENDUM

Contents page, Appendix C. $v_{\overline{n}|-r} = (1-r)^n$ should be $=(1-r)^{-n}$.

Page 59, Table 8. Headings of columns should be "project F" and "project G".

Page 70, Last word "follows" should be "above".

Page 89, Last number 0·369 should be 0·3697.

Page 99, 2nd term on right side of equation (*b*) should be $c(1-W)x_1$.

Note. As and when changes in the rate of corporation tax alter the values of Appendix E, up-to-date copies of the latter may be obtained from the authors.

INTRODUCTION

With the passing of the 1965 Finance Act, the publication of the White Paper on Investment Incentives, and the revelation of the rate of Corporation Tax in the 1966 Budget, it is now possible to take account of the effect of the new tax regime on the investment computations of companies in the private (as opposed to public) sector of the economy. The general objects of financial management are clearly no way affected in principle by these changes, rather is it the numerical values of certain variables which ought to be taken into account in the financing and appraisal of capital projects which have been altered by the new tax environment. This book is designed to achieve the purposes discussed below.

To set out (in Chapter 1) normative rules for capital budgeting; by this is meant that we begin from the assumption that business in general ought to be motivated by objectives which can be readily translated into financial and economic terms. We first attempt to settle these objectives and thereafter enumerate the decision-making rules which are logically implied in their attainment.

The collection of rules referred to here can in turn be translated into two sets of quantitative techniques which, though based upon the same financial mathematics, serve separate purposes. The one is concerned with the evaluation of the return on investment to companies net of corporation tax as relieved by the new system of investment induce-ments resulting from the White Paper of 17th January, 1966.* At first sight the impact of taxation and fiscal inducements on investment results in somewhat complicated investment computations and rather tedious arithmetic prior to the economic evaluation of investment *per se*. However, as is described in Chapter 3, using elementary algebra, simple formulae may be derived from which tabular values can be calculated which, in turn, considerably reduce the computational time required for investment evaluation. Appendix E is a set of tabulations for short-cut rate of return and present value calculations

* As amended in December, 1966 and subsequently.

which automatically allow for the incidence of corporation taxation and investment incentives.

The second set of quantitative techniques is applied to the determination of cut-off rates for capital budgeting, that is, the standards with which the (corporation) taxed earnings of a company need to be compared in judging whether the latter are adequate. Cut-off rates therefore need to reflect the rate of interest a company finds it necessary to pay (or offer) in order to attract finance. They also need to reflect the fact that a new programme of capital expenditure may well be financed from a variety of sources each of which is at a different rate of interest.* Thus, the *proportions* in which the next increment of finance is to be raised is a further determinant of a company's cut-off rate. Finally it is necessary to take into account that the new system of corporation taxation draws a clear line of demarcation between the income of companies and individuals. But, in so far as companies employ equity finance, the return to which attracts both income (including surtax) and capital gains taxes, the return on investment to a company will always be higher than the ultimate return to shareholders because of tax leakages on the payment of dividends and on the realisation of capital gains on the transfer of shares. Hence, if a company defines its financial objectives (as we argue it should) in terms of some given net of all taxes return to shareholders, an *equity* cut-off rate must embody some allowance for the income and capital gains taxes on investment.

Chapter 4 constructs a model from which equity cut-off rates can be calculated and, in this chapter, the assumptions on which the cut-off rate model is based are examined in turn in judging its general reliability at the practical level. Appendix F contains the equity cut-off rates which are derived from this formulation.

Chapter 2 is concerned with the arithmetic of capital budgeting and, among other things, explains the use of DCF tables contained in Appendices A and B.

* Hereafter we prefer the more general term " cost of finance " rather than " rate of interest ".

Chapter 1

THE GENERAL OBJECTIVES OF CAPITAL BUDGETING

In discussing the general objectives of capital budgeting in this chapter the argument is first conducted in a no-tax world. This assumption is relaxed towards the end by way of introduction to the subsequent chapters.

Capital budgeting may be regarded as an apparatus designed to promote the achievement of business objectives defined in financial terms and thus embodies the fundamental strategy of business policy. Notions of strategy as such are however only meaningful after the objects towards which it is directed have been clearly defined.

The traditional positive economic theory of the behaviour of the business firm proceeds from the assumption that firms attempt to maximise profits. As a normative rule for resource allocation this assumption is unsatisfactory at the practical level for a number of reasons of which two are of particular relevance in the present context. First, it does not adequately take account of the time factor whereas in reality all anticipations need to be carefully related to a time-scale for the fundamental reason that expectations are not timeless and that finance has a time-value. Second, the firm as an organisation in economic theory does not approximate to the real life company form of organisation which may have a mixed proprietorship of say equity interests, preference share interest and the interests of creditors providing long term finance.

Given a mixture of proprietary interests it is evidently necessary to determine whose interests are paramount and hence whose interests should be maximised and, furthermore, the conditions which must be complied with to satisfy the remaining proprietorship. The first issue which needs to be resolved in capital budgeting is therefore the precise obligations of a company to its proprietorship. In the remainder of this discussion we first attempt to settle this problem for a mixed capital structure and conclude by adducing the arguments to support the position taken in the remainder of this book, namely, that a company's optimal financing arrangement indeed constitutes a mixed proprietorship.

The obligations of a company to the providers of long term debt finance (hereafter, for convenience, referred to as debenture holders) are in general exhaustively defined in the deed creating a debenture. The fundamental status of a debenture holder is one of a creditor who is entitled to a fixed annual interest payment. Generally debentures are redeemable and the failure of a company to meet its debenture interest obligations will usually entitle the debenture holders to foreclose for the payment of arrears of interest and the repayment of capital, which may or may not be secured on assets of the company by way of a fixed or floating charge, prior to redemption. Clearly debenture rights may vary considerably from one company to the next; in any specific case they are, however, exhaustively defined and from the general standpoint of financial management in a going concern, the vehicle of primary interest to capital budgeting, they constitute a preferential charge on company income at a fixed rate of interest. So long as the net income of a going concern (i.e., income net of other trading claims) is adequate to service an issue of debentures and to permit their ultimate redemption,* the continuity of a business is by definition not threatened. The amount of debenture finance which can be expediently raised is a major consideration in capital budgeting on which external institutional factors may well impinge. Ultimately, it is the variability of a company's net income (as previously defined) which will determine the optimal volume of debenture financing.

Company obligations to preference shareholders can be similarly approached. Again, there may be variations from one company to the next but a company's constitution, found in its articles and memorandum of association, will exhaustively define the rights of preference shareholders whose capital may be redeemable, whose fixed annual dividends may be cumulative and may even be extended to further participation in company net income after an agreed initial participation by equity shareholders. In practice none of these variations give rise to difficulties in calculating the ultimate extent of preference share interests in company net income even when the eventuality of redemption is taken into account. Generally speaking in a company which,

---

* This by no means implies that a company needs to set aside specific amounts annually for eventual debenture redemption although such a condition may incidentally be embodied in a debenture deed.

in addition to preference shares, also has debentures and equities in issue, debenture holders are the first participants in net income followed by preference shareholders and finally equity holders.

If it can be said that the interests of equity shareholders are definable at all, it is in the negative sense that the equity interest amounts to the residue after the prior claims of debenture-preference shareholders have been serviced. The equity shareholders are thus the ultimate owners of a company and once the interests of the preferential proprietorship (debentures and preference shares) have been translated into fixed financial targets, a profit maximising company is by definition one which seeks to maximise equity interests through its financing and investment policies.

This fundamental principle which crystallises the paramount objective of financial management (capital budgeting) is readily illustrated in simple numerical terms.*

Illustrations

(i) Assume that the financial position of a company (which possesses no reserves) is as shown in Example 1 and that it expects to earn

Example 1

	(1)	(2)	(3)
	finance employed	division of expected profit	expected annual return in perpetuity
	£	£	%
6% debentures	800	48	6·00
7% preference shares	1200	84	7·00
equity at par	1500	218	14·53
	£3500	£350	10·00%

* The concept of maximising equity interests is illustrated numerically in the following example solely to clarify basic principles.

At the practical level this idea needs to be translated into the whole structure of equity returns obtainable throughout the entire capital market. Thus for any given class of equity investment there will be a tendency for equity returns to equate themselves. In terms of capital budgeting therefore, a company faced with the difficult problem of measuring the cost of equity finance should seek quantitative guidance in the approach outlined in Chapter 4.

At this stage we would merely add that if a company feels that it should aim to give shareholders say 9% p.a. in monetary terms, then, tax complications aside, 9% should measure the cost of equity finance. Once measured the other principles outlined here are logically implied and applicable.

net income of £350 p.a. in perpetuity. If for simplicity it is assumed that the three classes of finance in the company's capital structure are irredeemable, the respective perpetual returns are as in column (3).

(ii) Assume further that the company has the opportunity to undertake a programme of capital expenditure costing £1500 which promises a return of £195 p.a. in perpetuity. Such a project thus promises a rate of return of 13% p.a.*

(iii) In order to undertake this project the company floats a further equity issue of £1500 and the position shown in Example 2 emerges.

Example 2

	(1) finance employed	(2) division of expected profit	(3) expected annual return in perpetuity
	£	£	%
6% debentures	800	48	6·00
7% preference shares	1200	84	7·00
equity at par	3000	413	13·77
	£5000	£545	10·90%

In the foregoing illustration the company has succeeded in raising the overall rate of return on total capital employed but in the process has lowered the income *per unit* of equity finance. Such a policy evidently conflicts with the principle deduced earlier, namely, that investment and financing policy should be aimed at the maximisation of equity interests. Clearly the return on total investment cannot be looked at in isolation, the mode of financing needs to be concurrently taken into account. Assuming that finance for the new project could have been obtained from the three sources in the proportions and costs obtaining in Example 1, the resulting position would have been as in

---

* Although it may not appear so this 13% p.a. is, in fact, a DCF rate of return but one taken to infinity. It is calculated from the formula:

$$1500 = \frac{195}{1+r} + \frac{195}{(1+r)^2} + \ldots + \text{ad inf.}$$

which reduces to:

$$r = \frac{195}{1500} = 13\%.$$

Example 3. As can be seen, such a policy would simultaneously have raised the returns both on total capital employed and on equity finance. Furthermore, other things being equal, it is probable that the value of the equity finance would ultimately rise once the investing public became aware of the increased return to equity shareholders resulting from the new programme of capital expenditure.

Example 3

	(1) finance employed	(2) division of expected profit	(3) expected annual return in perpetuity
	£	£	%
6% debentures	1143	68·58	6·00
7% preference shares	1714	119·98	7·00
equity at par	2143	356·44	16·63
	£5000	£545·00	10·90

Had it not been possible to tap the three sources in the proportions and costs ruling in Example 1 it is clearly necessary from a capital budgeting standpoint to determine the maximum additional amount of equity, given the respective costs and amounts of the other two sources, which the company can raise whilst at least maintaining equity interests. The answer to this problem is almost intuitively obvious. The highest rate of interest which should be paid to finance a project promising a rate of return of 13% is evidently 13%. Hence additional finance raised, for example, in the proportions 2/3 equity at 14·53% and 1/3 preference shares at 7% would give a weighted average cost of

$$(2/3 \times 14\cdot53\%) + (1/3 \times 7\%) = 12\cdot02\%$$

and such a policy of financing would raise the return on both equity and overall capital employed as shown in Example 4.

Further examples are probably unnecessary; the two general inferences which can be drawn are firstly that investment should only be undertaken if it promises a return above the weighted average cost of the next increment of finance a company is capable of raising. In the extreme case equity finance may need to be used entirely because a company is unable to tap other sources; if so, the anticipated return on existing equity sets the cost of finance and the lower limit to an acceptable return on investment. Should a company be in a position to tap (cheaper) sources other than equity, the objective of financing policy should be seen as the minimisation of the weighted average cost of finance.

Example 4

	(1) finance employed	(2) division of expected profit	(3) expected annual return in perpetuity
	£	£	%
6% debentures	800	48	6·00
7% preference shares	1700	119	7·00
equity at par	2500	378	15·12
	£5000	£545	10·90

A DIGRESSION ON THE COST OF RETAINED EARNINGS

As is well known U.K. companies are heavily dependent upon retained earnings for investment financing; for practical purposes the foregoing analysis therefore requires an appendage handling their impact on financial policy and suggesting the cost which should be imputed to retentions for decision-making purposes.

Retained earnings can be regarded as withheld equity dividends—the property of equity shareholders which, under the present U.K. system of company law, is controlled by a company's directorate. The power to determine maximum rates of dividend with which company directorates are endowed can be used to sentence shareholders to the enforced saving of a significant proportion of equity earnings. It is not to be denied that equity shareholders may believe saving to be eminently desirable and indeed, even before buying shares can perhaps readily infer their prospective stream of future dividends from a company's past dividend record.

From a financial standpoint reinvested profits can be regarded as an additional injection of finance from existing equity shareholders; internal reinvestment is tantamount to a short-circuiting of the cumbersome process of distributing profits to the hilt and then inviting equity shareholders to subscribe for new shares. Once this notion is accepted it follows that the retention of profits is only justified if such retentions in turn promise a stream of future returns of sufficient magnitude to induce subscription in an external equity issue. The prospective return to shareholders subscribing for an external issue must clearly bear some relation to the returns in alternative equity investment in other companies if a flotation is to be successful. In short, the retention of profits is only justified if a company directorate can hold out the prospect that their redeployment will result in the returns which would be universally sought on comparable external equity issues; that is to say, a company contemplating the financing of capital expenditure with retained profits should begin from the premise that the cost of retentions (internal equity finance) is the same as the cost of an external equity issue. As we argue in Chapter 4 a company which aims to give its shareholders 9% net of all taxes would need to set a cut-off rate approximating $12\frac{1}{2}$ or 13% on external equity finance; likewise $12\frac{1}{2}$ or 13% should be the *starting point* in fixing the internal equity cut-off rate.* We emphasise the word " starting point " because the precise opportunity cost ascribable to retained earnings is a contestible issue. There are in fact two distinct schools of thought on this problem. We do not wish to enter this discussion in detail in Chapter 1 (which is concerned with a no-tax world) because the cleavage of opinion centres largely on the impact of taxation on the cost of retained earnings and the extent to which dividend taxes are saved when companies retain profits.

In its simplest form the argument of the one school is that a pound of retained earnings costs shareholders only £1 $(1-0\cdot4125)$, i.e., because of tax a pound distributed would be worth only £0·5875 to shareholders. Consequently (for simplicity of exposition we ignore capital gains taxes here) a company seeking to give shareholders a gross of taxes return of 12·5% on *external* equity finance could afford to lower the cut-off rate on *internal* equity finance to $58\cdot75\% \times 12\cdot5\% = 7\cdot344\%$. That is to say, the 12·5% *gross* return shareholders could have obtained on a net dividend of £0·5875 is exactly the same as a *gross* return of 7·344% which the company seeks on £1·0000.

Thus,

$$7\cdot344\% \times £1 = 7\cdot344\% \quad \text{(company)}$$
$$12\cdot5\% \times £0\cdot5875 = 7\cdot344\% \quad \text{(shareholders)}$$

* Once this principle is accepted it can then be argued that a company about to undertake an equity-based capital expenditure programme (promising returns at least equal to the cost of equity finance) should, if faced with the option, always prefer internal equity to external equity on the grounds that this action obviates the time and costs involved in the floating of an external issue.

2

Adherents to this school of thought must, if they are logically consistent, also argue that issue costs, which are obviated when retentions are preferred to external equity, should also be taken into account when setting a cut-off rate for retained earnings and that the cut-off rate should, in consequence, be further reduced.

The other school of thought subscribes to the view that the " opportunity cost " of retained earnings is not measured by the return that *shareholders* can earn elsewhere but rather by the return that a company itself can earn by investing in the equity of other companies. In a no-tax world these two schools of thought would lead to the same prescription; in the corporation tax regime they do not. A company can always do better with a pound of retained earnings than its shareholders.* The second school of thought therefore concludes that the return obtainable by a company measures the correct opportunity cost of retentions and that consequently the latter should never be used to finance projects promising a return below this opportunity cost. Hence reason suggests that any retentions surplus to the requirements of dividend and internal investment policy should be invested in the equity of other companies.

An apparent extension of the argument of the latter school results in what might be called " the capital gearing paradox ". Thus, if it is argued that the introduction of gearing lowers the weighted average cost of finance, a geared company obtaining finance more cheaply than an ungeared counterpart, can, at first sight, always invest finance (using the figures shown on p. 9 for illustration) at 12% having paid only 10·5% to obtain it. Hence, it can be argued that there is never any justification for accepting projects promising a return between 10·5% and 12·0%, because the latter rate can always be obtained elsewhere. We return to the capital gearing paradox in Chapter 5, and our own position on the opportunity cost of retained earnings in Chapter 4.

THE THEORY OF CAPITAL GEARING

Unavoidably and necessarily the discussion in the penultimate section introduced the notion of capital gearing or, to use the American term, leverage. A geared company is one which introduces fixed interest financing into its capital structure and, in so doing, the company in

---

* This argument is illustrated on pp. 116–17.

effect splits its future net income into two streams, a fixed amount paid preferentially and a residual amount subject to variation with possible variations in the total. These two streams are of different quality, i.e., inherent degree of risk. Thus the total income of a company may vary considerably with no effect upon the preferential income stream (see Example 5); because the residual equity stream is prone to variation the equity income is of lower quality, i.e., higher risk.

Example 5

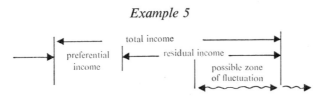

A leading principle explaining the behaviour of investors is that high returns are necessary to compensate for high risks relatively speaking. It is in fact of this principle that a company takes advantage in splitting its income into two components of differing quality; the return given by the preferential income component on fixed interest finance inducing investment in the latter is lower than the return given by the residual (equity) stream inducing equity investment. In effect by splitting its total income into two components a company succeeds in obtaining finance from two different sources at different rates of interest.

A simple way of illustrating the advantages of gearing is to compare two companies with identical assets and identical earning power but which differ in that the one is ungeared whilst the other has introduced leverage into its financial structure. The position * is usually argued as follows: the ungeared company A needs to offer a prospective return of (say) 12% p.a. to induce equity investment. Company B can obtain a certain proportion of its finance (say) 30% at 7% p.a. by floating an issue of debentures and is able to obtain the other 70% at the same equity rate as company A. The respective costs of finance to A and B are therefore

Company A 12·0%   p.a.
Company B $(0·3 \times 7\%) + (0·7 \times 12\%) = 10·5\%$ p.a.

---

* An alternative position to the one taken here can be suggested but it produces a similar outcome. The present explanation is modified later to take account of the alternative approach.

Company B not only obtains its finance cheaper but, if both companies decide to increase their assets, can take its investment to a level at which the marginal rate of return is 10·5 % p.a. compared to A's marginal rate of return of 12 % p.a. Not only will company B expand further, it will obtain a higher net return on every unit of investment undertaken

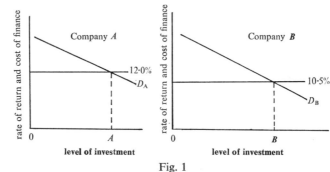

Fig. 1

assuming that additional finance can be raised in the respective proportions 0·3 and 0·7. This result can be illustrated diagrammatically as Fig. 1.*

The above description is perhaps an over-simplification of the advantages of leverage and should be regarded only as a departure point for more rigorous analysis.

We introduced the concept of gearing by stating that a company is able to obtain finance at two different rates of interest by splitting its total expected income into two streams of different quality. Clearly

* The two downward sloping investment demand curves labelled D are arrived at by the simple process of aggregation shown below (column (4)). (For ease of draftsmanship they are drawn here as linear functions.) For example, suppose that a company is confronted by the following array of investment proposals ranked by rate of return

(1) project	(2) capital cost £	(3) rate of return %	(4) cumulative capital costs £
a	1000	25	1000
b	1100	24	2100
c	700	22	2800
d	900	21	3700
etc.	etc.	etc.	etc.

The downward sloping curves are obtained by plotting column (3) (vertical axis) against column (4) (horizontal axis).

the line of demarcation separating the two streams cannot be drawn with indifference and, as the proportion of the preferential income in any given total increases, it is to be expected that there will be a resulting effect upon the respective rates a company will need to offer to induce investment. Thus as the preferential component increases, the residual component declines and the quality of both streams will tend to decline accordingly. That is to say, the larger the proportionate amount of the preferential income the more the latter approaches the possible

Example 6

debt proportion	debt cost	equity proportion	equity cost	weighted average cost
0	—	1·0	12%	12·0%
0·1	7%	0·9	12%	11·5%
0·2	7%	0·8	12%	11·0%
0·3	7%	0·7	12%	10·5%
0·4	8%	0·6	14%	11·6%
0·5	9%	0·5	17%	13·0%

zone of income fluctuation and the more risky is that preferential income. Likewise, the smaller is the residual component, the longer is the queue in which the equity shareholders must wait before they receive any return and the greater is the effect of income fluctuation on the residual income stream. The principle that capital gearing enables a company to minimise the cost of finance is one which might therefore be expected to assert itself in the manner illustrated in Example 6. It is emphasised that the figures used are chosen simply for illustrative purposes and that it should not necessarily be inferred that beyond the " optimal capital gear ratio " (in this case 30% gearing) the respective costs of finance would increase concurrently; one of them may indeed have begun to rise even before the optimal ratio had been reached, e.g., at the 30% gear ratio the costs may well have been:

$$(0.3 \times 7\%) + (0.7 \times 12.5\%) = 10.85\%$$

An alternative way of illustrating the theory of capital gearing is as in Fig. 2.

The basic theory briefly outlined above * illustrates the nature of the capital budgeting problem on the financing side, namely, the manner in

---

* The theory described here seems highly consistent with financial policies recently exhibited by many quoted companies; it should however be contrasted with the Modigliani-Miller hypothesis (examined in detail elsewhere) which denies that the introduction of gearing affects the cost of finance.

which in financing capital expenditure, a company should attempt to minimise the cost of finance. This objective is merely an alternative way of stating the premise, initially deduced, that in a company organisation the interests of equity shareholders should be held to be paramount.

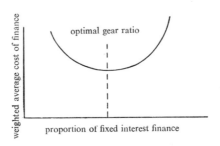

Fig. 2

CONVENTIONAL ANALYSIS OF GEARING IN PRACTICE *

The purpose of the normative theory outlined above is pre-eminently to facilitate a clear statement of financial objectives. Such a theory does not of itself provide an immediate answer to such quantitative questions as the respective costs of fixed interest and equity finance † nor does it indicate the numerical magnitude of the proportion of fixed interest finance constituting an optimal capital gear ratio. In practice acceptable standards of capital gearing are usually expressed in terms of the ratios of investment analysis, the two most important of which for present purposes are:

(i) the ratio of long term debt to net worth. For this purpose net worth would normally include equity capital plus reserves and preference shares, i.e., preference shares are excluded from fixed interest finance and regarded as part of the equity of the company. For a manufacturing or distributive firm a gear ratio such that long term debt constituted between (say) 30% and 50% of net worth would be considered practical.

---

* A comprehensive treatment of this subject is to be found in Merrett and Sykes, *The Finance and Analysis of Capital Projects* (Longmans Green and Co. Ltd.), Chapter 4.

† The meaning of the cost of finance is treated in detail in Chapter 4.

(ii) the cover for annual fixed interest payments (including lease payments): taxed profits (excluding fixed payments) equal to at least 5 or 6 times the net of tax fixed annual payments would generally be regarded as acceptable cover for the latter.

It should, however, be emphasised that intrinsically it is both the earning power of a company's assets *and* their piece-meal realisable value which really determine a financially expedient degree of capital gearing. The former provides the cover for annual fixed interest payments and the latter the security for long term creditors' capital to which conventional accounting written down values (original cost minus depreciation to date) have small relevance. Consequently, a company seeking to introduce gearing would be well-advised first to adjust asset values measured on a historical cost basis where these are patently out of line with piece-meal market prices. Thus, for gearing calculations, *net worth* should provide a reasonable measure of the realisable value of a company's net assets, i.e., total assets minus *all* liabilities.

Clearly gearing can also be defined as a long term debt-assets ratio, i.e., the ratio of long term debt to the value of a company's assets minus all claims other than the long term debt itself; the two ratios are best illustrated with a balance sheet example. Assume that the balance sheet of a company is:

balance sheet as at:

	£		£
equity capital and reserves (net worth)	825	fixed assets as revalued	1000
long term debt	275	net current assets	100
	£1100		£1100

In the foregoing balance sheet the ratio of long term debt to net worth is 1 : 3 whilst the long term debt-asset ratio is 1 : 4. Hence, to recapitulate slightly, an acceptable long term debt-net worth ratio at the 50% limit previously suggested would constitute a long term debt-assets ratio of 33%.

In suggesting that gearing ought to be defined in terms of asset values realistically calculated it is however necessary to make two qualifications. First, although a company may possess a balance of net current assets, i.e., an excess of current assets over current liabilities, the *ratio* of current assets to current liabilities should itself conform to a conventionally acceptable standard. In general a minimum requirement would constitute a current asset-current liability ratio of about 1·5 : 1.

Second, a qualification is needed to cover the eventuality that a company's assets may include financial investments in other companies. For example, assume that the balance sheet of a company which is about to undertake a large programme of capital expenditure stands as follows:

balance sheet as at:

	£		£
equity capital and reserves	2000	fixed assets (as revalued)	1000
		net current assets*	200
		other liquid balances	800
	£2000		£2000

Further details of the company's capital expenditure and financial proposals are:

(i) a dividend distribution of £350,

(ii) capital expenditure amounting to £920,

(iii) the introduction of gearing amounting to 30% of the value of assets, minus all liabilities (excluding the long term debt itself) and the flotation of a debenture issue for this purpose,

(iv) the external investment of any resulting surplus funds in the equity of the other companies.

It is suggested that the size of the debenture issue should be based primarily on the value of fixed plus net current assets (as above) *plus* the new programme of capital expenditure, i.e., the company should float a debenture issue of:

$$0{\cdot}3 \times (£1000 + £200 + £920) = £636.$$

* The net current assets are assumed to include an allowance for liquidity requirements in the forthcoming operating period including the necessary working capital for the new programme of capital expenditure and, for illustrative purposes, the resulting current asset-current liability ratio is taken to be adequate.

After paying the dividend and undertaking the capital expenditure, the balance sheet would appear:

balance sheet as at:

	£			£
equity capital and reserves	2000	fixed assets		1000
less dividend	350	*plus* expenditure		920
	——	net current assets		200
	1650	liquid balances	800	
debentures	636	*plus* debenture issue	636	
			1436	
		less dividend	350	
		capital ex-		
		penditure	920	1270
		surplus to be invested in		
		equities		166
	£2286			£2286

Now it might be objected that the debenture issue of £636 does not represent 30% of assets as previously defined for this purpose: £2286 (30% thereof = £686). We would argue that, as above, financial investments ought to be ignored in calculating the 30% long term debt-assets ratio because external equity investment would in general be deployed in other companies which are themselves already geared or likely to become geared in the future. That is to say, the inclusion of financial investments in the equity of other companies in the capital gearing calculation could result in disguised over-gearing. However, if in this case the £166 is invested in a number of companies with an aggregate long term debt-assets ratio of 30% whose *aggregate* balance sheet is thus:

aggregate balance sheet as at:

	£		£
equity shares (purchased by		sundry net assets	237
investing company)	166		
fixed interest finance	71		
	£237		£237

the consolidation of the latter with the balance sheet of the investing company would lead to a cancellation of the inter-company investment and a resulting aggregate long term debt-asset ratio of 30%.

consolidated balance sheet as at:

	£		£
investing company		*investing company*	
equity finance	1650	fixed assets	1920
debentures	636	net current assets	200
	2286		
investee companies		*investee companies*	
fixed interest finance	71	sundry net assets	237
	£2357		£2357

Capital gear ratio:

fixed interest finance: total assets (as in above consolidated balance sheet)

£636 + £71: £2357

£707: £2357

aggregate ratio 3 : 10

Clearly the aggregate long term debt-assets ratio would have been raised above 30% had the investing company initially included the financial investments in its capital gearing calculation; had such a result occurred it would, in effect, have amounted to the introduction of gearing above the desired level by the investing company with all the attendant financial implications.

As we argue again later, surplus retentions should always be deployed in external equity investments if not to be distributed as dividends; they should never be invested in fixed interest securities because, as can readily be inferred from the foregoing illustration, such a policy would amount to a lowering of the " optimal " capital gear ratio of the investing company.

So long as financial investment in equities is left out of gearing calculations such investments have a neutral effect upon a company's capital gear ratio. Hence we underline our earlier premise; that is to say, gearing calculations should be based pre-eminently on the value of a company's trading and productive assets.

The importance of conventional gearing standards, which might be expected to vary somewhat from industry to industry (or even from one company to the next) because of inherent risk differences, depends upon the extent to which their operation can in practice be enforced.

Whilst it is not intended to pursue this question here, the matter is primarily one residing in the institutional organisation of the capital market, the demand for fixed interest securities, and government control through the Capital Issues Committee, etc. At the time of writing it is difficult not to say impossible for private companies to obtain long term fixed interest finance on any scale at, or even well above, market interest rates.*

As regards public companies a flotation of fixed interest finance will generally be underwritten by Issuing Houses which at present adopt the policy of placing the greater proportion of such an issue among their lists of institutional investors; it was estimated in 1964 † that about 79% of quoted debentures resided in the portfolios of institutions. The crux of the matter is that the organisation and handling of long term fixed interest finance in the capital market is such that the adherence to conventional gearing standards will typically be the order of things. Thus the great problem for small companies is not so much whether they can plunge themselves into dangerously high capital gear ratios but, rather, whether in the foreseeable future they can, with the exception of relatively small renewable bank overdrafts, obtain any long term finance at all. For large companies able to make full use of the capital market the acceptable conventions of gearing must in present conditions be regarded as a strong factor militating against the possibility that gearing can be pushed to dangerous levels. Finally, it is perhaps worth observing that hitherto U.K. companies have typically tended to be undergeared compared with their counterparts elsewhere.‡ At the aggregate level there would appear to be some not inconsiderable slack to be taken up although, judging from the relative flood of fixed interest issues in the twelve or eighteen months up to the time of writing, the new system of taxation has apparently persuaded many companies that debenture finance is now, in the new tax regime, much cheaper than equity. Consequently we may now be experiencing

* This statement is based upon impression, enquiry and recent experience.
† See, J. G. Blease, " Institutional Investors and the Stock Exchange ", *District Bank Review*, September, 1964.
‡ A. J. Merrett, " Company Finance—Too Much Equity ". *The Banker*, **113**, 391–9, 1963.

a period in which the previously existing gearing potential is gradually being filled out by public companies able to enter the capital market.

THE IMPACT OF TAXATION ON CAPITAL BUDGETING

The foregoing discussion implies that two of the main objectives of capital budgeting which need to be taken together amount to the calculation of the return *per se* on programmes of capital expenditure and the minimisation of the cost of finance; if the former exceeds the latter then, aside from such considerations as the degree of risk and uncertainty inherent in the investment projects, the profitability, and hence adoption, of a project is indicated. In calculating the return on investment, mathematically correct investment criteria, of which the DCF present value and rate of return variants are the best known methods, clearly need to be used; in Chapter 2 we explain the principles of DCF arithmetic.

Throughout this chapter we have studiously avoided reference to taxation and fiscal inducements to investment. In reality the stream of cash-flows anticipated from an investment project is subject to taxation; the burden of the latter is however somewhat ameliorated by investment incentives. Investment returns to a company must be looked at net of company taxation for the evident reason that the return to proprietors can only be paid out of a taxed residue in the hands of a company. In a sense, company taxation is a cost which needs to be allowed for like any other operating cost. At this juncture it is important and necessary to emphasise the clear distinction, made by the new system of taxation, between the taxable income of companies and the taxable income of individuals, some of which may be derived from companies.

Company income is now subject to corporation tax at the rate of 40%, the capital allowances to which a company may be entitled reduce the burden of corporation tax only. The prospective net of tax return to a company on an investment project is thus a return net of corporation tax and investment incentives. A practical objective of capital budgeting is therefore the measurement of these net of tax returns thus defined. But corporation tax alone does not exhaust the taxation on investment in the private sector of the economy; the proprietors of a company suffer personal taxation on a distribution of (corporation) taxed company income. Hence, from a capital budgeting standpoint it is necessary to determine whether, and how, this further (personal) taxation should be accounted for in investment computations. Our recommendations for dealing with this problem is that an allowance for personal taxation, the *amount* of which depends upon a company's dividend policy (pay-out ratio) and the frequency with which shareholders realise capital gains, should be embodied in the numerical value reflecting the cost of finance. As described in Chapter 4, this problem centres largely upon the measurement of the cost of equity finance.

The distinction between the income of companies and the income of individuals is thus one which can be conveniently adopted from the computational standpoint of capital budgeting, and which basically draws the line of demarcation between the contents of Chapters 3 and 4. In the former we first illustrate the impact of corporation taxation and investment incentives in detailed computational form, and thereafter, short-cut DCF methods which, relying upon the precomputed tables presented in Appendix E automatically take account of corporation tax and investment incentives. In Chapter 4 we formulate an equity cut-off rate model from which numerical values reflecting the cost of equity finance, and embodying an allowance for personal taxation, can be calculated.

Chapter 2

Basic DCF Arithmetic

The principles of DCF arithmetic can be conveniently illustrated by concentrating on the demand side of capital budgeting, i.e., on the evaluation of capital investment proposals. Although relatively straightforward, it may be found that the manipulation of DCF arithmetic in symbolic terms is rather off-putting and, for this reason, illustration in this chapter largely, though not entirely, takes the form of numerical examples.

At least three investment criteria can be derived from the so-called DCF formula which is a practical application of basic principles of financial arithmetic. In this chapter we describe the two best known DCF variants: the present value method; and the rate of return criterion which is described elsewhere as internal rate of return, interest rate of return, investors' method, yield and marginal efficiency of capital. Both these DCF variants are well-known in the literature of economics and can be found there as far back as the turn of the century.

THE DCF RATE OF RETURN

A DCF rate of return can be defined formally as the value of r which satisfies the equation:

$$C = \frac{a_1}{1+r} + \frac{a_2}{(1+r)^2} + \frac{a_3}{(1+r)^3} + \ldots + \frac{a_n}{(1+r)^n}$$

where C is a proposal's acquisition cost; $a_1, a_2, a_3, \ldots, a_n$, is the prospective stream of end-year cash-flows generated by the proposal commencing end-year 1; n is the life of the proposal in years; and r is the interest rate (DCF rate of return) expressed as a percentage of unity, e.g., 15% would be stated as 0·15, which discounts the right-hand side of the equation to equality with the capital cost, C.

Impressive though the DCF rate of return may appear when defined in symbolic terms it amounts to nothing more than the rate of interest calculated on an outstanding balance in a double-entry account in the manner in which say a building society calculates interest on a mortgagee's outstanding balance. The purpose of the ensuing paragraphs is to demonstrate that this is so.

In ordinary business language it might be said that capital expenditure is worthwhile if it promises to generate a stream of cash-flows covering the initial outlay after making due allowance for interest on the capital tied up in the project. In addition to covering interest charges and all other operating cash-outflows, a businessman will of course ordinarily require a margin of profit. A precondition to the evaluation of an investment proposal is thus a statement of all cash-outflows and inflows resulting from the proposal.

Consider the following simple example:

A factory manager is advised that a new labour-saving device costing £800 which can be installed immediately is estimated to reduce total factory costs (cash-outflows) by £492 p.a. The machine has an estimated life of two complete years.* The relevant data can be stated as follows:

outlay	cash-flows (cost savings)	
beginning year 1	end year 1	end year 2
£800	£492	£492

Clearly the decision whether to invest in the new machine cannot be based solely on the fact that the total cost savings, £984, exceed the acquisition cost, £800, by £184. Aside from the risk that the project may not pay off as estimated, it must be explicitly recognised that the profile of cash-(in)flows spans a period of time and that money has a time-value.

£800 invested in a bank deposit account at 5% p.a. (interest calculated annually) with a withdrawal of £492 at the end of the 1st year would earn £57·4 in interest after two years as shown:

* This example raises a number of other issues highly relevant to capital budgeting, e.g., the reliability of both the life and cost estimates, the basis of the costing calculations, etc. These matters are referred to later (see pp. 75–80); at this stage we are primarily concerned with arithmetic only.

Illustration 1

deposit account

beginning-year 1	To deposit	£800·0	end-year 1	By withdrawal	£492·0
end-year 1	To interest @ 5% p.a.	40·0	end-year 1	By balance c/d	348·0
		£840·0			£840·0
beginning-year 2	To balance b/d	£348·0	end-year 2	By balance c/d	£365·4
end-year 2	To interest @ 5% p.a.	17·4			
		£365·4			
beginning-year 3	To balance b/d	£365·4			

Total interest received £40·0 + £17·4 = £57·4

Similarly, if the factory borrows £800 from the bank at 5% p.a. to finance the project but repays £492 and £365·4 at the end of years 1 and 2 respectively interest charges of £57·4 will be incurred.

Now if the factory possesses £800 of its own with which the machine can be financed this does not mean that interest on capital can be ignored.   In deciding the " cost of capital " management must take into account the best rate of return which can be earned elsewhere at equal risk for, evidently, if the cost savings cannot absorb interest charges equal to such a rate, management can make better use of its funds by investing elsewhere.*   Assuming again that such a rate is 5% p.a. the profitability of the project can be viewed as follows:

Illustration 2

investment project account

beginning-year 1	To acquisition cost	£800·0	end-year 1	By cash-(in)flows	£492·0
end-year 1	To interest @ 5% p.a.	40·0	end-year 1	By balance c/d	348·0
		£840·0			£840·0
beginning-year 2	To balance b/d	£348·0	end-year 2	By cash-(in)flow	£492·0
end-year 2	To interest @ 5% p.a.	17·4			
end-year 2	To surplus (or profit)	126·6			
		£492·0			

* This principle is known in economics as the opportunity cost rule which, as a little reflection might suggest, will effect the best use of financial and other resources if applied universally.

That is to say, given cash-(in)flows of £492 at the end of years 1 and 2 respectively, the cost savings can cover interest charges of 5% p.a. and, in addition, provide a profit of £126·6.

Should we wish to measure the profitability of the project in terms of its rate of return, we must calculate the highest rate of interest which the project can bear without showing a deficit. This can be done by trial and error with, or without, the use of tables specially designed for the purpose. For a project having only a two-year life it is relatively simple to calculate the rate of return without tables but for longer lives it will be found that tables become indispensable. In Illustration 2, it can be seen at a glance that the project could bear a rate of interest of 10% p.a. and still leave a profit. At a rate of 15% p.a. costs (including interest) are equated with the total cash-(in)flows hence the project gives a return of 15% p.a. (see Illustration 3) and if, as we assumed earlier, finance can be obtained at a rate of interest of 5% p.a., is clearly a highly profitable proposition.†

† An alternative way of presenting Illustration 3 is as below (the two cash-flows can be split into capital and interest components).

	interest £	capital £	total £
end-year 1	120·0	372·0	492·0
end-year 2	64·2	427·8	492·0
	£184·2	£799·8	£984·0

The DCF rate of return thus allows for the full recovery of capital and provides (in the above case), an interest rate of return of 15% p.a. which exceeds the 5% p.a. interest payable.

Illustration 2 is amenable to similar treatment and shows again that the recovery of capital and interest are automatically provided for in the DCF methods themselves.

	interest £	capital £	profit £	total £
end-year 1	40·0	452·0	—	492·0
end-year 2	17·4	348·0	126·6	492·0
	£57·4	£800·0	£126·6	£984·0

The foregoing statement is much more significant than may be at first apparent; it means however, that in the computation of cash-flows it is cash-(in)flows and -(out)flows which must be accounted for and *not* such notional charges as depreciation. When DCF methods are applied the inclusion of depreciation charges as operating costs would amount to the double counting of capital costs for, as we have just shown, the recovery of capital cost is automatically provided for in the use of DCF criteria.

3

Illustration 3

investment project account

beginning-year 1	To acquisition cost	£800·0	end-year 1	By cash-(in)flow	£492·0
end-year 1	To interest @ 15% p.a.	120·0	end-year 1	By balance c/d	428·0
		£920·0			£920·0
beginning-year 2	To balance b/d	£428·0	end-year 2	By cash-(in)flow	£492·0
end-year 2	To interest @ 15% p.a.	64·2			
		£492·2			

In using DCF tables to calculate an investment proposal's rate of return the problem is however viewed from a different angle. In the above examples interest is calculated on unrecovered investment in the case of a project having a two-year life which produces cash-flows at the end of years 1 and 2 respectively. The manipulation of the figures to facilitate the use and preparation of tables is illustrated most simply with the example of a project generating a single cash-flow.

Assume that two projects W and Z, both costing £800, generate cash-flows as follows:

	Cash-flows	
Project	end-year 1	end-year 2
W	£928	—
Z	—	£1039·68

Project W gives a rate of return of 16% and project Z 14%, i.e.,

$$\text{project } W \quad £800 + (16\% \times £800) = £928 \tag{1}$$

$$\text{project } Z \quad £800 + (14\% \times £800) + 14\%[£800 + (14\% \times £800)]$$
$$= £1039·68 \tag{2}$$

Equation (1) can be rewritten:

$$£800(1 + 0·16) = £928 \tag{3}$$

and equation (2) as:

$$£800(1 + 0·14) + 0·14[£800(1 + 0·14)] = £1039·68$$

or

$$£800(1 + 0·14)(1 + 0·14) = £1039·68$$

or

$$£800(1 + 0·14)^2 = £1039·68. \tag{4}$$

Dividing both sides of equation (4) by $(1 + 0·14)^2$ we obtain:

$$800 = \frac{1039·68}{(1 + 0·14)^2}. \tag{5}$$

Dividing both sides of equation (3) by $(1+0.16)$ we obtain:

$$800 = \frac{928}{(1+0.16)}. \tag{6}$$

From equations (5) and (6) it is easy to formulate a general rule with regard to the calculation of the rate of return of a proposal producing a single future cash-flow. Thus, converting the rate of return into decimal form and representing it with the symbol r, if the single payment arises one year hence the rate of return is the value of r in the divisor $(1+r)$. If the payment arises two years hence the divisor is $(1+r)^2$, if three years hence $(1+r)^3$, and n years hence $(1+r)^n$.

Returning to Illustration 3 in which the proposal costing £800 generates £492 at the end of years 1 and 2 respectively; it would seem to follow that the first year's cash-flow should be divided by $(1+r)$ the second by $(1+r)^2$ and that the proposal's rate of return is the value of r satisfying the equation:

$$800 = \frac{492}{1+r} + \frac{492}{(1+r)^2}. \tag{7}$$

That 15% p.a. is the proposal's DCF rate of return can be confirmed arithmetically as follows:

$$800 = \frac{492}{1+0.15} + \frac{492}{(1+0.15)^2}. \tag{8*}$$

In general if a DCF equation contains n terms, and n is greater than 2, it is not possible to express r explicitly (at least in simple form) in terms of the known parameters, $a_1 a_2, \ldots, a_n$, C and n, in which case, were it

* A more rigorous proof is as follows: the calculation embodied in Illustration 3 can, ignoring the negligible error in rounding interest to the nearest whole number, be written as:

$$[800(1+0.15)-492](1+0.15)-492 = 0,$$

simplifying and rearranging

$$800(1+0.15)^2 = 492(1+0.15)+492,$$

dividing both sides by $(1+0.15)^2$

$$800 = \frac{492}{1+0.15} + \frac{492}{(1+0.15)^2}.$$

Thus, as stated at the outset we arrive at the rate of return of a proposal which promises a succession of cash-flows $a_1, a_2, \ldots, a_n$, which are assumed to arise at the end of years $1, 2, \ldots, n$ by finding the solution value of r in the equation:

$$C = \frac{a_1}{1+r} + \frac{a_2}{(1+r)^2} + \cdots + \frac{a_n}{(1+r)^n},$$

where C; $a_1, a_2, \ldots, a_n$; n and r are defined as previously.

not for the existence of tables, the determination of r would involve excessive calculation.

Referring back to equation (7); it is clear that if we possessed values of $1/(1+r)$ and $1/(1+r)^2$ for an extensive range of interest rates it would require about two or three multiplication sums to demarcate the range in which the precise value of r must lie, and probably one further calculation to arrive at an accurate value of r (see Illustration 4).

Illustration 4

		rate of interest (discount)			
row		0·05	0·10	0·15	0·20
1	$\dfrac{1}{1+r}$	0·952 381	0·909 091	0·869 565	0·833 333
2	$\dfrac{1}{(1+r)^2}$	0·907 029	0·826 446	0·756 143	0·694 444
3	$\dfrac{1}{1+r}+\dfrac{1}{(1+r)^2}$	1·859 410	1·735 537	1·625 708	1·527 777

In solving for the value of r in equation (7) using the values reproduced in Illustration 4 it is in effect necessary to find the value of r satisfying

$$800 = 492\left(\frac{1}{1+r}\right)+492\left[\frac{1}{(1+r)^2}\right].\tag{9}$$

As is shown arithmetically, only the value $r = 0{\cdot}15$ satisfies the equation, i.e.,

$$800 = 492\left(\frac{1}{1+0{\cdot}15}\right)+492\left[\frac{1}{(1+0{\cdot}15)^2}\right]$$
$$= (492 \times 0{\cdot}869\ 565)+(492 \times 0{\cdot}756\ 143).\tag{10}$$

Illustration 4 and equation (9) also underline the extreme usefulness of tables when an investment proposal is estimated to generate a constant cash-flow. For example equation (9) can be rewritten:

$$800 = 492\left[\frac{1}{1+r}+\frac{1}{(1+r)^2}\right].\tag{11}$$

Now as row 3 in Illustration 4 gives values of the function

$$\left[\frac{1}{1+r}+\frac{1}{(1+r)^2}\right]$$

at various rates of interest, it is evidently unnecessary to solve for the value of r in the manner shown in equation (10).

If we now divide both sides of equation (11) by 492, i.e.,

$$\frac{800}{492} = \frac{1}{(1+r)} + \frac{1}{(1+r)^2} \qquad (12)$$

we arrive at the value of

$$\left[\frac{1}{1+r} + \frac{1}{(1+r)^2} \right] = 1 \cdot 626\,016$$

and it is then only necessary to locate the value $1 \cdot 625\,708$ in row 3 of Illustration 4 in order to read off the proposal's rate of return of 15% p.a. (approximately).

It is useful to mention at this juncture that, as in Appendices A and B, the tables usually cover a range of interest rates from 1% to 50% at 1% interest intervals over time periods from one year, i.e., $1/1+r$ to 50 years, i.e., $1/(1+r)^{50}$ at annual intervals. In addition, two types of (discount) tables are available: firstly for the rate of return calculations on proposals which do not have constant cash-flow streams (Appendix A), and secondly for those which in fact do (Appendix B). The former are usually labelled $\dfrac{1}{(1+r)^n}$ (or what is mathematically the same thing

$(1+r)^{-n}$) and the latter $\dfrac{1 - \dfrac{1}{(1+r)^n}}{r}$ or $\dfrac{1 - (1+r)^{-n}}{r}$*.

---

* It can be readily inferred from Illustration 4 that Appendix B can be constructed from Appendix A simply by adding successive tabular values in the latter. As indicated, Appendix A is a series of tabular values for the function $\dfrac{1}{(1+r)^n}$ in which case Appendix B is calculated from the function $a_{n/r} = \dfrac{1}{1+r} + \dfrac{1}{(1+r)^2} + \dfrac{1}{(1+r)^3} + \cdots + \dfrac{1}{(1+r)^n}$.

Appendix B does not, however, bear this function as a label because using simple algebra it can be reduced to $\dfrac{1 - (1+r)^{-n}}{r}$.

For example let:

$$P = \frac{1}{1+r} + \frac{1}{(1+r)^2} + \frac{1}{(1+r)^3} + \cdots + \frac{1}{(1+r)^n}. \qquad (i)$$

[continued over

Examples

Using tables calculate the respective rates of return of two proposals
A and *B* from the following data:

proposal	cost	cash-flows (end-year)		
		year 1	year 2	year 3
	£	£	£	£
A	800	380	380	380
B	900	509	450	400

As described above the rate of return of proposal *A* can, by using
tables, be calculated with little difficulty; the data can be stated as:

$$800 = 380\left[\frac{1}{1+r}+\frac{1}{(1+r)^2}+\frac{1}{(1+r)^3}\right]$$

or

$$800 = 380\left[\frac{1-(1+r)^{-3}}{r}\right]$$

whence

$$\frac{800}{380}=\left[\frac{1-(1+r)^{-3}}{r}\right] = 2 \cdot 1053.$$

It is now only necessary to look along year 3 of Appendix B, the tables
designed for evaluating proposals with constant cash-flows, until the
value 2·1053 (or some value closely approximating it) is found.   Once
the value is located the proposal's rate of return can be read off;
proposal A is found to give a rate of return of 20 % (approximately).

Proposal *B* is not so simple to evaluate: when cash-flows are irregular
but do not fluctuate widely, an approximate guide to the rate of return

---

Multiply both sides of (i) by $1+r$
whence:

$$P(1+r) = 1+\frac{1}{1+r}+\frac{1}{(1+r)^2}+ \cdots +\frac{1}{(1+r)^{n-1}}. \tag{ii}$$

Subtract (i) from (ii), whence:

$$P[(1+r)-1] = 1-\frac{1}{(1+r)^n} = 1-(1+r)^{-n}.$$

Hence:

$$P = \frac{1-(1+r)^{-n}}{r}.$$

can be obtained by dividing the *average* annual cash-flow into the capital cost. This will then provide a starting point for the calculation of the exact rate of return. Thus in the case of proposal B:

Average cash-flow $(509+450+400) \div 3 = 453$ (say) 450.

Capital cost $\div$ average cash-flow $= \dfrac{900}{450} = 2 \cdot 000.$

That is to say, 2·000 is the " discount factor " for a proposal costing £900 with a three-year cash-flow of £450 p.a., and, from Appendix B, it can be seen that such a proposal gives a rate of return of 23% p.a. The exact rate of return can now be determined using Appendix A as follows:

Illustration 5*

	cash-flows	discount factors at rates of			discount factor × cash-flows at rates of		
	£	23%	24%	25%	23%	24%	25%
end year 1	509	0·813 008	0·806 451	0·800 000	414	410	407
end year 2	450	0·660 982	0·650 364	0·640 000	297	293	288
end year 3	400	0·537 384	0·524 487	0·512 000	215	210	205
					£926	£913	£900

As the aggregate discounted cash-flow of proposal B is equal to its capital cost at a 25% rate of discount, this rate is the proposal's rate of return. An alternative way of describing a proposal's rate of return is the rate of interest which discounts the future cash-flows to equality with its cost.

LINEAR INTERPOLATION

If in the previous case it was guessed that the rate of return might be about 26% such a discount rate could have been used as a datum line for calculating the correct rate of return in the following manner:

* Because the cash-flows of this proposal B are irregular and slightly concentrated into years 1 and 2, it is clear that its rate of return will exceed 23% p.a.; consequently, in determining the precise rate of return subsequent discounting will need to be at higher rates.

capital cost	end-year cash-flows			
	1	2	3	
£900	£509	£450	£400	(1)
discount factors @ 26%	0·793 651	0·629 881	0·499 906	(2)
present value @ 26%	£403·97	£283·45	£199·96	(1)×(2)

total present value of cash-flows discounted @ 26%: £887.

As the present value of the cash-flows discounted at 26% is less than the capital cost of the project, i.e., £887<£900, 26% is too high a rate of discount and must therefore be lowered because we are seeking the rate which discounts the cash-flows to *equality* with the project's capital cost.   If we now try a 23% discount rate the present value of the cash-flows is shown to be £926.

capital cost	end-year cash-flows			
	1	2	3	
£900	£509	£450	£400	(1)
discount factors @ 23%	0·813 008	0·660 982	0·537 384	(2)
present value @ 23%	£413·82	£297·44	£214·95	(1)×(2)

total present value of cash-flows discounted @ 23%: £926.

As the present value of the cash-flows discounted at 23% exceeds the capital cost of the project, i.e., £926>£900, the DCF rate which equates the cash-flows with the capital cost must lie somewhere between 23% and 26%.   The correct DCF rate of return is interpolated as in the following calculation:

	£
present value of cash-flows @ 23%	926
present value of cash-flows @ 26%	887
difference	39
present value of cash-flows @ 23%	926
capital cost of project	900
difference	26

Therefore the rate of return is given by:

$$23\% + \frac{26}{39} \times 3 = 25 \cdot 0\% \text{ (to one decimal place).}$$

It should be noted that the fraction 26/39 is multiplied by 3 because the DCF rate of return is interpolated over a 3% interest interval.

Before leaving the DCF rate of return concept, passing reference can be made to the possibility that a proposal may give more than one rate of return. There has been considerable discussion in the literature of this phenomenon, which is entirely a mathematical property, and largely of academic interest. Multiple rates of return are possible when there are multiple " sign changes " in a proposal's cash-flows, e.g., an initial out-flow(s) followed by inflow(s) and a further subsequent outflow(s) in that order.*

PRESENT VALUE CALCULATIONS

As mentioned earlier, rate of return is a measure of the degree of profitability after fully allowing for the time-factor. The present value criterion described below also allows for the time-factor and may be described as a measure of a proposal's value in " absolute " terms where the word " absolute " is used in the sense described later.

The present value of an investment proposal is defined symbolically as the value, V, given by:

$$V = \frac{a_1}{1+i} + \frac{a_2}{(1+i)^2} + \ldots + \frac{a_n}{(1+i)^n}$$

where $a_1, a_2, \ldots, a_n$ is the stream of end-year cash-flows defined as previously; n is the proposal's life in years, and i is the discount rate reflecting the cost of finance to a business. If the capital cost C is less than V an investment project is profitable.

Satisfactory elaboration of the concept of present value probably succeeds numerical illustration and we can first usefully proceed with examples of present value calculations.

The present value of a proposal is a function of the rate of interest (discount) selected for the calculation but this is not meant to imply that the rate should, or indeed can, be chosen with indifference. The appropriate discount rate is a reflection of a company's " cost of finance " which should be calculated in the manner discussed in Chapter 4.

Using the data of the previous example (p. 28) the present values of Projects A and B at interest (discount) rates of 10% p.a., 11% p.a. and 12% p.a. are calculated as in Illustration 6.

* See pp. 44–45 for further discussion of this phenomenon.

Illustration 6

project A

life (years)	constant end-year cash-flow	discount factors from Appendix B at 10% p.a.	11% p.a.	12% p.a.	present value of cash-flows 10% p.a.	11% p.a.	12% p.a.
3	£380	2·4869	2·4437	2·4018	£945	£929	£913
		less project cost			800	800	800
		net present values			£145	£129	£113

project B

	cash-flows £	discount factors from Appendix A at 10% p.a.	11% p.a.	12% p.a.	cash-flows × discount factors at 10% p.a. £	11% p.a. £	12% p.a. £
end-year 1	509	0·909 091	0·900 901	0·892 857	463	459	454
end-year 2	450	0·826 446	0·811 622	0·797 194	372	365	359
end-year 3	400	0·751 315	0·731 191	0·711 780	301	292	285
		present value of cash-flows			1136	1116	1098
		less project cost			900	900	900
		net present values			£236	£216	£198

The significance of a proposal's present value should be clearly understood.   Consider the present value of project *A* in Illustration 6 at the 10% p.a. discount rate, £945.   If we assume that finance for this project can be obtained at 10% p.a. (interest calculated annually), the profit computation can be drafted accounting-wise as below. Note, however, that instead of showing the project's cost, £800, as the first entry we have entered its present value of £945.

From the investment account it follows that £945 is the maximum sum which can be paid for project *A* if the " cost of finance " is 10% p.a.; present value thus has a meaningful economic interpretation. As the project's acquisition cost is however less than its present value at a 10% rate of discount (i.e., £945 > £800) it is clearly an economic

proposition.   We showed earlier that project A gives a 20% p.a. rate
of return and if money can be obtained at 10% to finance it then,
clearly we must conclude that it is a profitable proposal.   Similarly,

investment project account

	£			£
beginning-year 1	945	end-year 1	By cash-flow	380
end-year 1 To interest @ 10% p.a.	95	end-year 1	By balance c/d	660
	1040			1040
beginning-year 2 To balance b/d	660	end-year 2	By cash-flow	380
end-year 2 To interest @ 10% p.a.	66	end-year 2	By balance c/d	346
	726			726
beginning-year 3 To balance b/d	346	end-year 3	By cash-flow	380
end-year 3 To interest @ 10% p.a.	35			
	381			

in the above case, if the cost of finance were 11% or 12% p.a., the
maximum costs a firm could afford to pay for project A are £929 and
£913 respectively.   We can sum up at this juncture as follows:

(i) Ignoring the complications which may arise because there are
multiple sign changes in a proposal's cash-flow stream, it can be
stated that provided a consistent assumption is made about the
cost of finance the DCF rate of return and present value criteria
will give the same answer to the relatively simple question of
whether a proposal is profitable or not.   That is to say $V > C$
when $r > i$ and vice versa where:

V is proposal's present value at a cost of finance, i;
C is proposal's acquisition cost;
r is proposal's rate of return.

(ii) In using the present value method to evaluate investment
proposals the firm's cost of finance should be taken as the
minimum rate of discount.

EXCEPTIONS TO THE GENERAL CASE

Exceptions to the basic situation implied in the above rules are very typical in practice; probably the most common investment complication arising in business results from the incidence of mutually exclusive proposals, i.e., the problem of deciding which of a number of possible alternative ways of undertaking an investment ought to be adopted. Cases do arise in which it is found that two projects, *A* and *B*, both satisfy the two variants of the DCF formula individually but are ranked by them in a conflicting order, i.e., they may be ranked first *A* and second *B* using the present value method and first *B*, second *A* by rate of return. The question which must then be asked is which criterion can be relied upon to select the most profitable proposal from a number of alternatives where only one is required.   We deal with this complication under the next sub-heading.

A further practical complication is the capital rationing problem, a discussion of which succeeds the next section.

MUTUALLY EXCLUSIVENESS

The acceptance of one of a group of mutually exclusive proposals automatically signals the rejection of all others *in the mutually exclusive group*.   To take a concrete example; a firm may contemplate the construction of a new building of a certain size and may well find that, constructed of a certain combination of materials, the building may have relatively high capital costs but very low maintenance costs thereafter.   Construction from alternative materials may result in considerably lower (initial) capital costs but subsequently in much higher costs.*   Leaving aside aesthetic and considerations other than those of economic expediency, the firm should choose the building which is the more profitable where profitability is measured in terms of the criteria defined previously.

As stated in the previous section the situation is not so simple as it may first appear because the ranking of relative profitability by the present value method may conflict with a ranking by rate of return as exemplified in Illustration 9, p. 41.   Given such a conflict as in Illustration 9 it is natural to ponder its practical significance and to

---

* A choice from such alternatives is apparently not uncommon in building construction.

question whether doubts are cast upon the reliability of either or both of the methods themselves. These questions can be best answered with some preliminary numerical examples.

Example

Consider two proposals D and E costing £2 and £200 respectively. Proposal D produces £8 two years hence and therefore gives a rate of return of 100% p.a., i.e., $2+2+4 = 8$ or, $2 = 8/(1+1)^2$. E produces £288 two years hence giving a rate of return of 20% p.a. Discounted at 10% p.a. the respective net present values of D and E are:

$$(8 \times 0.826\ 446) - 2 = £4.6 \qquad\qquad D$$
and $\qquad (288 \times 0.826\ 446) - 200 = £38.0 \qquad E$

Other things being equal, in the above case proposal E is clearly to be preferred for the following reason.

The situation described here is exactly analogous to one in which a business might have to choose between a very small turnover and high gross profit percentage, say 75% (and consequently a gross profit which is very low in absolute terms); and, a much larger turnover at lower percentage gross profit but with considerably higher gross profit in absolute terms. From these examples it can be clearly inferred that, notwithstanding the uses which rates of gross profit, return, etc., may have for certain purposes, they need to be used with care in other cases. A logical inference is the assertion that a firm wishing to maximise net present value, i.e., future wealth in absolute terms, should adopt the present value method as its decision-making rule in cases of mutually exclusiveness. We return to this rule presently and digress slightly at this stage to explain the basis of the possible conflict between the two criteria which, it should be emphasised, does not necessarily arise.

In the two examples already referred to in this section the conflict between the DCF rate of return and net present value method seemingly arises because of differing capital commitments. A capital differential as between two projects may not be the only reason for conflicting results. As is shown in Illustration 7 even where two (or more) mutually exclusive projects have identical capital costs and the same lives, the DCF rate of return and present value criteria may still be in conflict.

Illustration 7

project	cost	cash-flows end-year 1	end-year 2	present value at 10% p.a.	DCF rates of return p.a.
	£	£	£	£	
A'	1000	100	1820	1595	40%
B'	1000	1000	750	1529	50%

The basis of the conflict shown in Illustration 7 is best seen in a case where projects are ranked equally by DCF rate of return but unequally by present value. Consider the projects *P* and *Q* in Illustration 8 below:

Illustration 8

project P

	(1) cash-flows £	(2) discount factors at 10% p.a.	(1)×(2) £
end-year 1	1000·0000	0·909 091	909·09
end-year 2	5940·0000	0·826 446	4909·09
		present value	5818·18
		cost	4000·00
		net present value	£1818·18

project Q

	(1) cash-flows £	(2) discount factors at 10% p.a.	(1)×(2) £
end-year 1	4659·2592	0·909 091	4235·69
end-year 2	1000·0000	0·826 446	826·45
		present value	5062·14
		cost	4000·00
		net present value	£1062·14

The calculation of the respective DCF rates of return of projects *P* and *Q* in Illustration 8 which happen to be equal could be written:

	cost £	discounted cash-flows end year 1 end year 2

project P $\quad 4000 = \dfrac{1000 \cdot 0000}{1+0 \cdot 35} + \dfrac{5940 \cdot 0000}{(1+0 \cdot 35)^2}$ $\qquad$ (13)

$\qquad\qquad\quad = 740 \cdot 74 + 3259 \cdot 26.$ $\qquad\qquad\qquad$ (13a)

project Q $\quad 4000 = \dfrac{4659 \cdot 2592}{1+0 \cdot 35} + \dfrac{1000 \cdot 00000}{(1+0 \cdot 35)^2}$ $\qquad$ (14)

$\qquad\qquad\quad = 3451 \cdot 30 + 548 \cdot 70.$ $\qquad\qquad\qquad$ (14a)

Likewise, the present value calculations in Illustration 8 could be stated as:

	present value £	discounted cash-flows end-year 1 end-year 2

project P $\quad 5818 \cdot 18 = \dfrac{1000 \cdot 0000}{1+0 \cdot 1} + \dfrac{5940 \cdot 0000}{(1+0 \cdot 1)^2}$ $\qquad$ (15)

$\qquad\qquad\quad = 909 \cdot 09 + 4909 \cdot 09.$ $\qquad\qquad\qquad$ (15a)

project Q $\quad 5062 \cdot 14 = \dfrac{4659 \cdot 2592}{1+0 \cdot 1} + \dfrac{1000 \cdot 0000}{(1+0 \cdot 1)^2}$ $\qquad$ (16)

$\qquad\qquad\quad = 4235 \cdot 69 + 826 \cdot 45.$ $\qquad\qquad\qquad$ (16a)

As noted earlier and as seen again in equations (13) and (14), a project's DCF rate of return may be defined as the rate of interest which discounts the cash-flows to equality with a proposal's acquisition cost. Now if a project gives a rate of return above the cost of finance, the DCF present value calculation results, in effect, in a lowering of the discount rate. In the example illustrated in equations (13) to (16) inclusive, the rate of discount is lowered from 35% p.a. to 10% p.a. However, as between one year and the next the discount factors applied to a proposal's cash-flows vary in a geometric progression, e.g., $(1+r)^{-1}$, $(1+r)^{-2}$, etc.; in the case of proposals P and Q in equations (13) and (14) the cash-flows for years 1 and 2 are divided by $1 \cdot 35$ and $1 \cdot 35^2$ ($= 1 \cdot 8225$) respectively but, if the rate of discount is lowered to 10%, the divisors fall by the respective amounts $0 \cdot 25$ and $0 \cdot 6125$ to $1 \cdot 10$ and $1 \cdot 21$ respectively. The effect of this is to increase the difference between the present values of the second year cash-flows by more than the increase in the difference between the two first year cash-flows, i.e., the increase in the difference between the two first year cash-flows is:

project	Q	P
present value of end-year 1 cash-flow at 10%	4235·69	909·09
present value of end-year 1 cash-flow at 35%	3451·30	740·74
	£784·39	£168·35
increase in difference (1st year)		£616·04

whilst the increase in the difference between the two second year cash-flows is:

project	P	Q
present value of end-year 2 cash-flow at 10%	4909·09	826·45
present value of end-year 2 cash-flow at 35%	3259·26	548·70
	£1649·83	£277·75
increase in difference (2nd year)		£1372·08

Increase in present value of project P over present value of project Q (discount rate reduced from 35% to 10%):

$$£1372·08 - £616·04 = £756·04$$

The general inference which emerges from Illustration 8 (and the succeeding calculations) is that if two projects, like P and Q, give the same rate of return but project P has a bigger cash-flow in the second year than project Q, project P must give a larger DCF present value when both are discounted at the same rate below the mutual DCF rate of return. Similarly, for mathematical completeness it can be stated that if these projects were discounted at a common rate *above* the mutual rate of return, the project with the greater cash-flow in the second year, i.e., P, would give a smaller DCF present value than the other. In this case an increase in the rate of discount raises the second year's divisor by a greater amount than the first year's and the project with the greater cash-flow in the second year is more heavily penalised, so to say. The conclusion which follows from the above discussion is that even where the lives and capital costs of two or more proposals with a mutual rate of return are equal, they will be ranked unequally by present value if there is any difference, no matter how small, in the time pattern of the respective cash-flows. It would also follow that if the lives of projects (of equal capital costs and same DCF rate of return) are different, they will be ranked unequally. Such a case of course reduces to the one discussed previously, namely, the situation in which the respective time-patterns of cash-flows differ.

A corollary to the above explanation, which also can be demonstrated arithmetically, is that any group of investment proposals which are ranked *equally* by the DCF net present value method when discounted by a common rate of interest, will be ranked unequally by their respective rates of return if there are differences in either or all of capital costs, the time patterns of cash-flows and, as we have just stated, what amounts to the same thing as the latter, differences in project lives.

We can now return to a question raised earlier: does the possible conflict in rankings of projects by the DCF present value and rate of return criteria respectively, cast doubt upon the reliability of these methods? The foregoing explanation of the basis of a possible conflict between the two criteria shows that this is not a capricious state of affairs but, when arising, is simply an arithmetical result which must necessarily follow.

An alternative way of illustrating this possible conflict is to draw a simple graph plotting a curve of net present value as a function of a range of discount rates. If such a chart is drawn for projects *A* and *B* on p. 36 (Illustration 7) the picture in Fig. 3 emerges.

On what basis should selection from a group of mutually exclusive proposals proceed? As we have already implied the answer to this question depends upon the profit-making aims of a business. Should a business wish to maximise net present value then it must evidently use the DCF present value method as its rule for resource allocation. If, on the other hand, the aim is to maximise the rate of return on capital, the DCF rate of return criterion is logically implied. As net present value can be taken as a measure of profitability in absolute terms and rate of return a measure in relative terms, it seems intuitively more reasonable to assume that the maximisation of net present value (absolute profits) is universally a more appropriate objective, and that the DCF net present value method should be used as the tool of selection from a group of mutually exclusive proposals. This statement implicitly assumes that the proposals in a mutually exclusive group are equally risky and *ipso facto* that the same rate of discount

4

is appropriate for each. In practice this condition may not hold in which case the problem then becomes one of adjusting respective rates of discount to allow for differential risk. We return to this problem

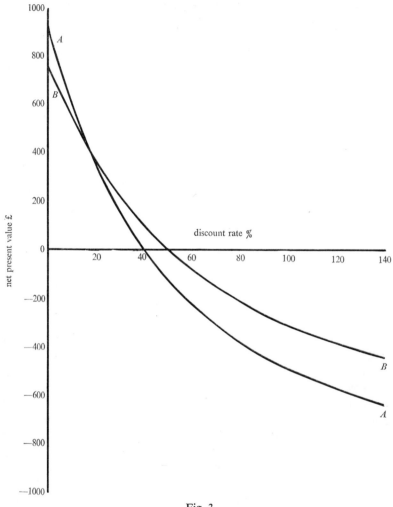

Fig. 3

presently; at this stage we would mention that with modified use the DCF rate of return will give the same results as the DCF net present value method in many mutually exclusive situations.

MODIFIED USE OF THE DCF RATE OF RETURN IN MUTUALLY EXCLUSIVE
SITUATIONS

The modification referred to has been described in capital budgeting
literature as the *incremental yield* approach but has long been known
in economics as " Fisher's rate of return over cost". Risk considerations aside, it is the rate of interest at which two mutually exclusive
options would be equally profitable, i.e., the rate of discount at which
two such projects give the same net present value.

The situation postulated in Illustration 8 in which two mutually
exclusive projects *P* and *Q* have identical capital costs and equal lives,
and cash-flows which vary in opposite directions is useful as an illustration of the principles of DCF arithmetic but can only be regarded as
a very special case at the level of practical business. The most typical
incidence of mutually exclusiveness is probably characterised by projects
which have capital costs and cash-flow streams which differ in a manner
exemplified in Illustration 9.

Illustration 9

proposal	cost	life (years)	annual cash-flow	DCF rate of return p.a.	DCF present and net present values at 7% p.a. PV	NPV
	£		£	%	£	£
F	1004	10	200	15	1405	401
G	1560	10	288	13	2023	463
G–F	556	10	88	9·4	618	62

In Illustration 9 there is a conflict between DCF rate of return and
NPV but as the projects have different capital costs, it might be argued
that they are not therefore strictly comparable. Arithmetical com-
parability can however be made possible by deducting the capital cost
of *F* from the capital cost of *G* and likewise the annual cash-flow of *F*
from the annual cash-flow of *G*. The capital cost difference can
then be related to the annual cash-flow difference and both a DCF
rate of return and NPV can be calculated on the differences as shown.

It is important to consider precisely what has been done in this
incremental calculation; deducting proposal *F* from *G* to cancel out
of the calculation the values which are arithmetically common to both

leaves only the need for an appraisal of the differences in determining which of the two proposals is superior.

This said it is however necessary to refer again to the question of the degree of risk inherent in each of a group of mutually exclusive proposals. Just as it was argued that the same rate of discount is only applicable to each individual proposal in a mutually exclusive group if it can be tolerably assumed that there is risk equality throughout the entire group, it is for consistency necessary to argue that to deduct the capital cost, etc., of one project from the capital cost, etc. of another is an admissible procedure when the degree of risk inherent in the respective values cancelled out is the same for all projects and when the rate of return promised by the least (capital) costly project is satisfactory after allowing for a risk premium. In some cases such an assumption may be eminently reasonable, in particular when the mutually exclusive alternatives display close technological features and even where there are significant differences in scale. The differential risk inherent in scale differences which give rise to different outputs, and hence different cash-flows, would be essentially the consideration handled in the incremental yield interpretation explained in the next paragraph. If the degrees of risk inherent in the respective capital costs, etc., cancelled out are not equal then the cash-flows of *all* projects in the group should, in theory, first be corrected to establish risk equality. Thereafter the incremental yield requires a further corrective for risk and can be used directly for selecting from a mutually exclusive group in the following manner.

Subject to the foregoing qualifications the data in Illustration 9 can be interpreted as follows; proposal G promises all that proposal F is estimated to give and on an additional capital outlay will give a rate of return of 9·4%. If, as we have assumed, finance can be raised at 7% p.a., the incremental investment is worthwhile (assuming the risks inherent in the incremental investment in proposal G are deemed to be covered by a margin of 2·6%) and investment in proposal G is therefore indicated.

When the number of proposals in a mutually exclusive group is not limited to two, the procedure to be applied is an extension of the one outlined above and is, in effect, a process of elimination which begins by comparing the mutually exclusive alternative of the lowest capital cost with the proposal with the next lowest capital cost. The proposal judged to be superior in this couple is then used as the basis of comparison with the next most costly (in terms of capital cost) and so the process continues until all proposals but one have been eliminated.

One further observation on the incremental yield approach which should now be made is that it is not *per se* a separate computational method but merely a useful mode of interpretation for administrative purposes which adds nothing to the net present value method from a mathematical standpoint. If the projects in a mutually exclusive group are profitable *per se* the incremental yield method will always give the same answer as the net present value method in the mutually exclusive case. An incremental yield above the cost of finance is not of itself a sufficient condition to indicate which of a group of mutually exclusive projects ought to be accepted and for this reason it is necessary to issue the following caveat about the use of the incremental yield method.

Before an incremental yield comparison is made it must be ensured that all projects in a mutually exclusive group are profitable *per se*; if an incremental yield comparison is attempted before individual project evaluation, an incremental yield above the cost of finance may result which, in turn, might tempt an analyst to suggest the inclusion of one of a number of mutually exclusive alternatives in a capital budget when in fact none of the group may be worthy of inclusion. This point is exemplified in Illustration 10.

Illustration 10

project	capital cost	life (years)	annual cash-flow
R	£2500	10	£356
S	2000	10	272
R–S	£500		£84

The incremental yield is the value of r satisfying:

$$£500 = £84\left[\frac{1-(1+r)^{-10}}{r}\right]$$

whence

$$r = 10\cdot8\%.$$

Aside from risk considerations, if the cost of finance is 8% the incremental yield is adequate but neither project is profitable; project R promises a return of 7% and project S a return of 6%.

Finally, it should be mentioned that although the incremental yield method will, if correctly used, provide not only the correct prescription but also a useful means of interpretation for a multiplicity of cases of mutually exclusiveness there is one particular occasion when the method requires very careful interpretation. This is when a series of incremental cash-flows is characterised by more than one sign-change; for example, an incremental capital outlay (negative), followed by incremental cash-(in)flows (positive), followed by an incremental out-flow(s) (negative), i.e., two sign changes.* In such cases as this there may be multiple real positive roots of r, i.e., multiple values of r in a DCF rate of return calculation. In other cases of multiple sign-change the value of r may be indeterminate. A third variation of the complication caused by multiple sign-changes is the possibility of obtaining a unique value of r; there are in turn, two variations of this possibility. The multiple sign-change phenomenon is thus a *necessary*, but not of itself a *sufficient* condition for multiple rates of return.

The multiple sign-change complication is not of course a possibility restricted only to incremental yield comparisons but may also characterise individual projects appraised as independent ventures. We discuss this subject under the next sub-heading.

THE IMPLICATIONS OF MULTIPLE SIGN-CHANGES—THE INTERPRETATION OF MULTIPLE AND UNIQUE YIELDS FROM A SERIES OF CASH-FLOWS CHARAC-TERISED BY MULTIPLE SIGN-CHANGES

This subject is primarily of academic interest for the reason that investment projects characterised by cash-flows with multiple sign-changes are a rare occurrence in practice which do not in any case present an intractable problem in capital budgeting. That is to say, the present value method will always give a meaningful economic interpretation of situations in which the sign-change complication is present whether individual projects are examined in isolation or in a mutually exclusive group. (As we have just explained, in the latter

* A simple example of such a case is as follows:

	acquisition cost	end-year cash-(in)flows 1	2	3	4	5
project U	−3000	+874	+874	+874	+874	+874
project V	−2709	+600	+700	+800	+900	+1100
U—V	−291	+274	+174	+74	−26	−226

We refer to this example again in the context (see p. 45).

case the most (or more) profitable project is indicated by the highest *net* present value at the firm's cost of finance.) Furthermore, even when there are multiple sign-changes a meaningful economic interpretation can always be given to the rate (or rates) which discount a series of cash-flows to a zero net present value although, in many cases, the correct interpretation may differ from the " normal rule " that investment is profitable when it gives a rate of return above the cost of finance. It should however be emphasised that because the incidence of multiple sign-changes is so rare in practice, the " normal " interpretation of the DCF rate of return must always remain a decision-making rule of extensive application.

A detailed analysis of the implications of multiple sign-changes in cash-flows is a specialist problem in mathematics *; our primary purpose in drawing attention to the phenomenon in this book is to give the reader a general awareness of the problem that it might be kept within sensible perspective at the practical level. If on an exceptional occasion the multiple sign-changes complication should present itself the problem should be clearly recognised for what it is; in such circumstances the safest recommendation is, as just stated, to employ the DCF present value criterion—the universally correct decision-making rule for all capital budgeting problems.†

We now present three cases in which the normal interpretation of the DCF rate of return does not hold but for which alternative economically meaningful interpretations can be substituted.

Multiple Sign-changes and Multiple Rates of Return

In the example in the footnote on p. 44 the line $U - V$ gives the series:

end-year	0	1	2	3	4	5
	-291	$+274$	$+174$	$+74$	-26	-226

which has two sign-changes. The necessary condition for multiple rates of return is thus present and, according to Descartes' rule of signs,

* Readers who are interested in further treatment should consult, for example, Bierman and Smidt, *The Capital Budgeting Decision* (MacMillan Company, New York, 1960), Chapter 3; and Merrett and Sykes, *The Finance and Analysis of Capital Projects* (Longmans Green & Co., London, 1963), Chapter 5.

† This recommendation is perhaps too restrictive. Where multiple sign-changes arise for no other reason than the time-lag between the earning of a terminal cash-flow and the payment of the taxation thereon, the multiple rates of return problem does not present itself—provided the net present value of the complete series is positive at a zero rate of discount.

there *can* be as many as two rates of return, which can be readily calculated by plotting the net present value of the series against the rate of discount as shown in Fig. 4(a).

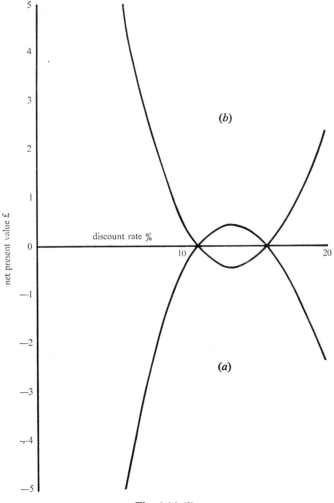

Fig. 4 (*a*) (*b*)

An indication of the behaviour of the net present value of this series can also be obtained from Table 1. The fact that we reproduce the calculation at only six rates of discount should not lead to the inference that the curve in Fig. 4(a) has been plotted from so few points; for mathematical rigour many more points are necessary.

Fig. 4(a) shows that the series has a present value of zero at discount rates of 11·2% and 15·9%, i.e., these are its two rates of return. As Table 1 shows the series has a net present value of −£21 at a discount rate of zero which rises to −£6·78 at 5% and to a zero net present value at 11·2%. Between its two rates of return (11·2% and 15·9%) the series has a positive net present value but after the 15·9% discount rate it again becomes negative and declines steadily with successive increases in the discount rate.

TABLE 1

(cash-flows illustrated in Fig. 4(a))

| | present value at discount rates of | | | | | |
	0%	5%	10%	15%	20%	50%
end-year 0	−291	−291·00	−291·00	−291·00	−291·00	−291·00
end-year 1	+274	+260·95	+249·09	+238·26	+228·33	+182·67
end-year 2	+174	+157·82	+143·80	+131·57	+120·83	+77·33
end-year 3	+74	+63·92	+55·60	+48·66	+42·82	+21·93
end-year 4	−26	−21·39	−17·76	−14·87	−12·54	−5·14
end-year 5	−226	−177·08	−140·33	−112·36	−90·82	−29·76
NET PRESENT VALUE	−21	−6·78	−0·60	+0·26	−2·38	−43·97

The rates of return of 11·2% and 15·9% respectively are not economically meaningless, and in this case should be interpreted as the limits to the cost of finance at which the project is economic. At first sight it may seem illogical to suggest that a project is uneconomic if finance costs only 10% p.a. but that it is profitable if the cost of finance is between 11·2% and 15·9%. It might be objected that this argument is tantamount to suggesting that if a businessman can obtain finance at 10% he should insist on paying between 11·2% and 15·9% to obtain it! The definition of the cost of finance to a firm is however a little more subtle than this objection allows. The cost of finance is not only the rate a firm pays, but also the rate at which it can invest and insistence upon the payment of a higher rate than the current market price would clearly not confer an attendant right to *invest* above the market rate of interest. The series in the line $U - V$ could in fact be interpreted as an outlay of £291 followed by inflows of £274, £174 and £74 with two terminal liabilities of £26 and £226 respectively.   Only if the business can provide for these two liabilities by setting aside a sum of money *now*, equal to the present value of £26 and £226 discounted at a rate between 11·2% and 15·9%, which can then be accumulated at an interest rate between 11·2% and 15·9% is the project profitable (provided of course that the cash-(in)flows are discounted at the *same* rate). Any discount rate below 11·2% would not be high enough to reduce the present value of the two liabilities sufficiently and, likewise, any higher discount rate than 15·9% would " penalise " the cash-(in)flows too much.

If we now reverse all the signs in the series $U - V$ we obtain the following sequence of cash-flows:

TABLE 2

end-year	0	1	2	3	4	5
	+291	−274	−174	−74	+26	+226

The net present value of this series for a range of discount rates, r, is plotted in Fig. 4(b) and, as shown, the same two rates discount the net present value to zero.   For reasons similar to those given above the discount rates of 11·2% and 15·9% should be interpreted as limits to the cost of finance between which a project with the cash-flow characteristics of the project in Table 2 would be *uneconomic*, i.e., at a cost of finance not exceeding 11·2% the project is profitable and at a cost of finance *above* 15·9% it is also profitable.

Multiple Sign-changes and an Indeterminate Rate of Return

A rate of return cannot be calculated for the following series:

annual end-year cash-flows

0	1	2	3	4	5	6	7˙	8	9
+£900	−£60	−£180	−£1160	−£90	−£90	−£90	+£270	+£270	+£270

Indication of why the rate of return should be indeterminate in the above case is given in Fig. 5(a).   As is shown, a curve of present value plotted against successive discount rates never cuts the horizontal (rate of discount) axis and, in consequence, no rate can be determined which discounts the series to a zero net present value.

investment project account

		£			£
end-year 1	To cash	60	end-year 0	By cash	900
end-year 1	To balance c/d	930	end-year 1	By interest @ 10% p.a.	90
		990			990

end-year 2	To cash	180	beginning-year 2	By balance b/d	930
end-year 2	To balance c/d	843	end-year 2	By interest @ 10% p.a.	93
		1023			1023

end-year 3	To cash	1160	beginning-year 3	By balance b/d	843·0
			end-year 3	By interest @ 10% p.a.	84·3
			end-year 3	By balance c/d	232·7
					1160·0

beginning-year 4	To balance b/d	232·70	end-year 4	By balance c/d	345·97
end-year 4	To interest @ 10% p.a.	23·27			
end-year 4	To cash	90·00			
		345·97			

beginning-year 5	To balance b/d	345·970	end-year 5	By balance c/d	470·567
end-year 5	To interest @ 10% p.a.	34·597			
end-year 5	To cash	90·000			
		470·567			

beginning-year 6	To balance b/d	470·567 0	end-year 6	By balance c/d	607·623 7
end-year 6	To interest @ 10% p.a.	47·056 7			
end-year 6	To cash	90·000 0			
		607·623 7			

beginning-year 7	To balance b/d	607·623 70	end-year 7	By cash	270·000 00
end-year 7	To interest @ 10% p.a.	60·762 37	end-year 7	By balance c/d	398·386 07
		668·386 07			668·386 07

beginning-year 8	To balance b/d	398·386 07	end-year 8	By cash	270·000 00
end-year 8	To interest @ 10% p.a.	39·838 61	end-year 8	By balance c/d	168·224 68
		438·224 68			438·224 68

beginning-year 9	To balance b/d	168·224 68	end-year 9	By cash	270·000 00
end-year 9	To interest @ 10% p.a.	16·822 47			
end-year 9	To profit	84·952 85			
		270·000 00			

The present value of the profit in year 9 discounted at 10% p.a. is £84·952 85 × 0·424 098 = £36·03 i.e. the net present value of the project at a 10% rate of discount.

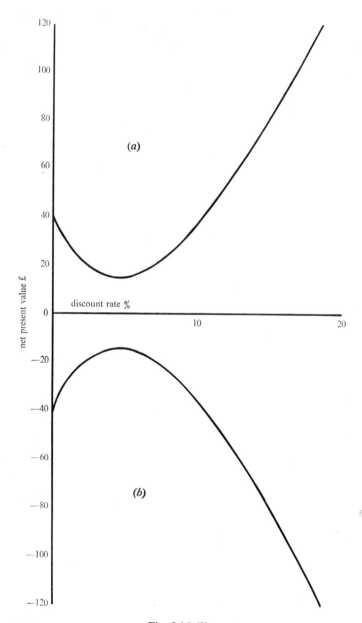

Fig. 5 (a) (b)

Because there is no determinate rate of discount, the only meaningful interpretation which can be given to this situation is provided by the net present value criterion; for example at 10% p.a. the net present value of the series is +£36·03 which is the present value (discounted at 10% p.a.) of the profit shown in the account above in which the above series is recorded accounting-wise.

A series characterised by such a curious time-pattern of sign-changes as the above could be a simulation of a case in which a businessman receives an advance payment on a contract to finance heavy expenditure in the early years followed by a series of completion payments in the terminal years of the contract. (Fig. 5(b) is arrived at by reversing the signs.)

Multiple Sign-changes and a Unique Rate of Return not Amenable to " Normal " Interpretation

If the graph of a project's net present value, plotted as a function of the discount rate, touches the discount rate axis once only there is a unique rate of discount which reduces the project's cash-flows to a zero net present value (see Fig. 6).

TABLE 3

(cash-flows illustrated in Fig. 6(a))

present value at discount rates of

	0%	5%	10%	15%	20%	50%
end-year 0	−291·44	−291·44	−291·44	−291·44	−291·44	−291·44
end-year 1	+274·00	+260·95	+249·09	+238·26	+228·33	+182·67
end-year 2	+174·00	+157·82	+143·80	+131·57	+120·83	+77·33
end-year 3	+74·00	+63·92	+55·60	+48·66	+42·82	+21·93
end-year 4	−26·00	−21·39	−17·76	−14·87	−12·54	−5·14
end-year 5	−226·00	−177·08	−140·33	−112·36	−90·82	−29·76
NET PRESENT VALUE	−21·44	−7·22	−1·04	−0·18	−2·82	−44·41

Moreover, as shown, such a curve may be tangential to the horizontal axis from either the positive (upper) or negative (lower) quadrant. If the curve is tangential from the positive quadrant as in Fig. 6(b) the project is profitable for any cost of finance except the " break-even " tangential rate of discount (in this case 13·46%). Tangency from the negative quadrant signals that the project is unprofitable at every discount rate except the tangential rate at which it would break even.

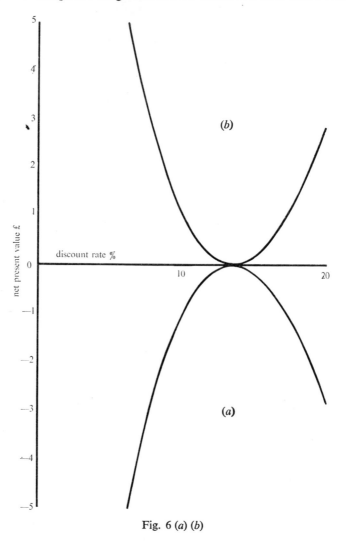

Fig. 6 (*a*) (*b*)

The curve in Fig. 6(a) is plotted from the series of net present values shown in Table 3.

Fig. 6(b) is obtained simply by reversing the signs in the cash-flows in Table 3.

Multiple Sign-changes and a Unique " Normally " Interpreted Rate of Return

We conclude this section by referring to the curve in Fig. 7(a) which is the net present value of the series in Table 4 as a function of the rate of discount.

TABLE 4

end-year cash-flows

0	1	2	3	4	5	6
−2689	+1560	+720	+690	+668	+651	−248

There is only one rate of discount which discounts the series in Table 4 to a zero net present value, namely 20·2%. Furthermore this rate is amenable to the normal DCF rate of return interpretation, i.e., the project in Table 4 would be profitable for any cost of finance less than 20·2%.

By reversing the signs of the cash-flows of Table 4 the curve drawn in Fig. 7(b) is obtained; the zero net present value at the 20·2% discount rate is the lowest cost of finance at which the project is profitable. Again, it should be emphasised that this interpretation only holds if the firm is also *able to invest* at 20·2%.

Summary

1. A " conventional " investment project defined as capital cost(s) (negative) followed by a series of cash-(in)flows (positive) gives a unique positive DCF rate of return if the sum of the undiscounted cash-flows exceeds the project's capital cost(s). That there can be but a single DCF rate of return in such a case results directly from the presence of only one sign-change. The unique DCF rate of return given by a " conventional " investment can always be given a normal interpretation, i.e., when the DCF rate of return exceeds the cost of finance profitability is indicated. In practice the vast majority of projects are amenable to " normal " DCF rate of return interpretation and the exceptional cases discussed in this section merely serve to prove the rule.

It is important to re-emphasise that the normal interpretation of the DCF rate of return variant must always remain a decision-making criterion of extensive application.

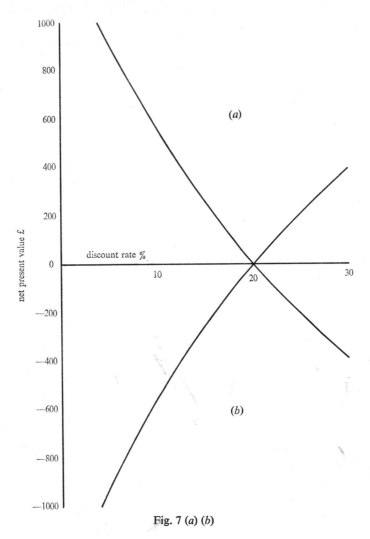

Fig. 7 (a) (b)

2. Where multiple sign-changes are caused by tax payments in the post-terminal year of a capital project it is safe to assert that multiple

rates of return will never result because of the relative magnitudes of the untaxed cash-flow and the taxation assessed thereon.

If, in cases other than the one just mentioned, the multiple sign-change complication should present itself the correct decision will always be signalled by the net present value criterion and, if desired, a complete picture of the behaviour of net present value as a function of the rate of discount can readily be obtained by preparing graphs similar to those illustrated in Figs. 3–7. From such charts meaningful interpretations of the discount rates which reduce a series of cash-flows to a net present value of zero can readily be inferred.

CAPITAL RATIONING

The resources available to a business for the financing of capital investment may be limited for a number of reasons; from a capital budgeting standpoint limited finance defines a situation in which less funds are available than is required to finance all investment proposals which have been shown to be profitable on either DCF criterion—given the cost of finance. The contradiction in this statement is more apparent than real; that is to say, although it would seem to follow *ex definitio* (once the market price has been defined) that as much finance as is desired may be obtained (at the market price), situations do nevertheless arise in which firms either cannot, or will not, go to the market or financial institutions to supplement internal sources. Consequently proposals which are clearly profitable when judged against the market price of finance are left unadopted. This is not the place to investigate the rationale of financial rationing in detail but it is useful to make one or two pronouncements which challenge the logic of " self-imposed " rationing.

As is evidenced by the extent to which companies rely on internally generated funds to finance capital expenditure there can be small doubt that many companies deliberately pursue policies of constraining growth within their profit-making abilities.* In such circumstances the level of capital investment is subject to a constraint which may often be an agreed proportion of profits plus depreciation provisions. Now correct analysis would dictate that the evaluation of investment proposals is the first stage in capital budgeting procedure, to be followed

* Categorical statements of this nature are occasionally observed in published accounts.

5

by a consideration of the ways in which the *volume* of funds necessary to finance all profitable proposals should be raised (whether internally or externally).

A second type of rationing is an essential feature of all unincorporated businesses and all others which do not have a stock exchange quotation: these undertakings do not have full access to the capital market and may frequently find it impossible to obtain further finance elsewhere on terms which are not severely restrictive. Thirdly, companies which are quoted but have gone through a period of low profit-making may find that despite their " free access " to the capital market the cost of finance has become prohibitive. Fourthly, the flow of commercially viable projects resulting from technological progress may outweigh the ability of even the giant corporation to raise or generate finance. Clearly there are recognisable cases of financial rationing and it is important to consider whether rationing, no matter how it arises, implies a re-appraisal of investment criteria.

When the supply of finance is restricted the investment objective must be seen as the optimal use of the limited finance and if, as is here the case, a business is unable to adopt some proposals which promise a prospective return above the market price of finance, the inference which should be drawn is that the opportunity cost of finance is not measured by its market price but rather by the rate of return on the marginal investment project, i.e., the one which just succeeds in getting into the budget. Once the cost of finance has been defined in this way, the problem then reduces to the general question of whether projects are profitable or not.

Two prescriptions can be suggested for calculating the rate of return on the marginal project and hence the most profitable combination of proposals fitting a financial constraint. (The procedure for dealing with a relatively simple case of financial rationing, i.e., one in which the mutually exclusive complication is absent and in which all capital outlays are undertaken in one budgetary period, is illustrated in Table 5.)

(i) Rank proposals in descending order by DCF rate of return and, beginning at the head of the ranking, work downwards accepting proposals until the limited funds are exhausted.

(ii) Using the DCF present value criterion find the rate of discount at which there are just enough profitable proposals to exhaust the limited finance, i.e., starting from the discount rate (reflecting the market price of finance) at which too many proposals are profitable raise the rate of discount until just enough profitable projects remain.

TABLE 5

proposal	cost	life (years)	constant annual cash-flow	NPV @ 10% p.a.	NPV @ 18% p.a.	rate of return % p.a.
	£		£	£	£	
a	1 601	8	481	+965	+360	25
b	2 500	20	632	+2881	+883	25
c	99	3	50	+24	+9	24
d	950	8	278	+533	+184	24
e	371	7	112	+174	+56	23
f	4 602	18	1 041	+3936	+887	22
g	1 726	3	832	+343	+83	21
h	1 151	6	355	+395	+91	21
i	3 200	9	794	+1373	+217	20
j	276	4	107	+63	+12	20
k	1 948	15	400	+1094	+89	19
l	1 802	6	515	+441	0	18
m	2 324	10	499	+742	−81	17
n	2 102	5	657	+389	−47	17
o	3 100	6	841	+563	−159	16
p	4 003	13	749	+1317	−326	16
q	4 500	14	786	+1290	−564	15
TOTAL	£36 255					

Note If available capital were limited to £20 226 proposals a to l (inclusive) could be accepted. If the constraint were £20 000, proposal j would, in practice, be omitted. It is evident that the rate of discount would need to be raised to 18% to eliminate all but enough proposals necessary to exhaust a constraint of £20 226.

These two prescriptions must signal the acceptance of the same combination of proposals for, as a little reflection will suggest, they are merely alternative ways of finding the minimum rate of discount needed to eliminate all but the proposals which will fit the constraint.*

* It should of course be recognised that because of the discreteness of capital costs it will generally not be possible to obtain a combination of proposals giving an aggregate capital cost exactly equal to the limited finance. This possibility will usually necessitate an adjustment at the margin (as suggested in the note to Table 5) to ensure that the maximum amount of finance is allocated to investment. Subject to this minor qualification the prescriptions suggested will provide the best allocation of limited finance in the circumstances illustrated by Table 5.

The question of a conflict between the two DCF variants (rate of return and net present value) does not therefore arise in the rationing situation unless, of course, the mutually exclusive complication is also present. To this problem we now turn.

The single-period capital rationing problem is only complicated by the presence of mutually exclusive proposals in so far as the rate of return-present value " conflict " is present where net present values

TABLE 6

proposal	cost £	life (years)	annual cash-flow £	DCF rate of return p.a.	DCF present and net present values at 10% p.a.	
					PV	NPV
X	1200	7	333	20%	£1621	£421
Y	1000	7	262	18%	1276	276

are initially calculated at the market price which would be paid if further finance were sought. If this is not the case all but one of the alternatives can be immediately eliminated leaving only one project to compete in the ranking of independent projects. For example, if projects X and Y in Table 6 are mutually exclusive X would be superior to Y at every rate of discount up to 20% * and can therefore be immediately preferred to Y.

TABLE 7

proposal	cost £	life (years)	annual cash-flow £	DCF rate of return p.a.	DCF present and net present values at 7% p.a.	
					PV	NPV
F	1004	10	200	15%	£1405	£401
G	1560	10	288	13%	2023	463

Suppose however, that the mutually exclusive projects are F and G as in Table 7. In a capital rationing situation it is by no means obvious which of these projects should be accepted to the exclusion of the other. If 7% is the market price that would be paid to obtain further finance, G is preferable to F *in the absence of a financial constraint*. If a financial constraint is imposed then, following the second prescription outlined

---

* This statement can be confirmed by calculating the net present values of X and Y at every discount rate up to 20% in the manner illustrated in Table 8.

above, the discount rate must be raised. Table 8 shows that for all discount rates up to and including 9 % G is superior to F; after 9·4 % F is preferable. Evidently the conclusion which should be drawn is that G should be included in the budget for all discount rates up to 9·4 % and that F should be included thereafter. This conclusion provides

TABLE 8

net present value of cash-flows, £

discount rate %	project A (annual cash-flow £200)	project B (annual cash-flow £288)	
0	+996	+1320	
1	+890	+1168	
2	+793	+1027	
3	+702	+897	
4	+618	+776	$G>F$
5	+540	+664	
6	+468	+560	
7	+401	+463	
8	+338	+373	
9	+280	+288	
9·5	+252	+248	
10	+225	+210	
11	+174	+136	
12	$F>G$ +126	+67	
13	+ 81	+3	
14	+ 39	−58	
15	0	−115	

the rule for dealing with the mutually exclusive complication in single period capital rationing situations; the clearest picture of the nature and mode of solving this problem is obviously provided by Table 8. Where the number of mutually exclusive alternatives is not limited to two the same approach can be adopted.

MULTIPERIOD COMPLICATIONS

We now refer to the complication presented by the operation of a financial constraint on each one of a succession of budgetary periods. If rationing is expected to persist throughout a significant proportion of the lives of the proposals adopted in the current budgeting period and results continuously in approximately the same level of limited finance, the above prescriptions are satisfactory even in multiperiod rationing.

Should, however, rationing in successive periods be characterised by _variable_ levels of available finance, the cost of finance is subject to variation in so far as by definition cost is measured by the rate of return on the marginal project. If such is the expectation of the future levels of available finance, then it follows that in using the DCF net present value method, the successive cash-flows of an investment proposal should be discounted at rates which vary as the respective levels of available finance vary.

A multiperiod problem of this nature is highly complicated for a number of reasons. First, the sequence of discount rates for the cash-flows of the proposals to be adopted in period one cannot be calculated until the rate of return on the marginal project in every period is known. Second, because there is now a different discount rate for every period the rate of return criterion breaks down in its application to marginal investment projects. Third, in planning a multiperiod investment programme the fact that the time-series of discount rates for proposals adopted in period one depends upon the programmes undertaken in every subsequent year might suggest that the programme should be planned backwards from the terminal period to the initial period. Unfortunately this approach encounters the further difficulty that the financial constraints ruling in the later periods of a multiperiod problem may be a function of the cash-flows of the projects undertaken in the earlier periods. Here then is a problem which is pervaded by some extremely complicated feed-backs and inter-relationships, and which can only be correctly stated and resolved by applying mathematical programming methods outside the scope of this book.*

It is perhaps wise to conclude this section by again questioning the rationale of capital rationing. The dubious logic of a self-imposed capital rationing situation is brought into sharp focus when a multiperiod rationing problem is held up to close scrutiny.

The imposition of a succession of financial constraints upon successive budgeting periods is to compromise the _raison d'être_ of business enterprise—the profit-making motive. Multiperiod self-imposed capital rationing is thus a policy of second best. The very notion of using sophisticated programming techniques to achieve the objectives

---

* Readers interested in an approach relying upon mathematical techniques should consult Baumol and Quandt, " Investment and Discount Rates Under Capital Rationing—A Programming Approach ". _The Economic Journal_, 1965, **75**, 317–29.

of a policy of second best is tantamount to setting the objective of doing the wrong things very well.*

APPENDIX TO CHAPTER 2: THE CALCULATION OF WORKING CAPITAL FOR CAPITAL INVESTMENT DECISIONS

A necessary adjunct to Chapter 2 is an appendix on the calculation of working capital—an important item of expenditure which in practice is frequently either ignored or incorrectly analysed. Where the need for it arises, working capital is as much a part of the total capital cost of any project as is the generally more readily recognisable " fixed " or " hard " acquisition cost, for example, the cost of an additional plant, etc. It is therefore important to be as right about working capital as about the other components of capital cost for the obvious reason that if working capital calculations are inaccurate then total capital costs, and hence in turn rate of return and present value calculations, will also be inaccurate.

The importance of the *distinction* between " working " and " fixed " capital costs resides in the fact that in a majority of cases the latter qualify for investment incentives whereas the former are never so eligible.† Furthermore, working capital is not even tax deductible for expenditure thereon will usually be contained in the value of closing inventories, etc., which, viewing the matter in profit and loss account terms, consequently cancel out an equivalent amount of expenditure on the debit side. However, in the terminal year of a project's life, the component of the cash-(in)flows resulting from the liquidation of inventories, etc., also escapes taxation in that, from a taxation standpoint, it is countervailed by the opening inventory balances at the beginning of the terminal year.

Whilst it is widely appreciated that the need for working capital often arises because it may, for example, become necessary: to increase

* An alternative analogy may be the case of the man who, before jumping from the top of a ten-storey building, ensures that the best team of surgeons in the country is ready to deal with him when he lands.
† This fact in turn suggests the possibility that a failure on the part of a company clearly to differentiate between working and fixed capital allied to a general failure to allow for investment incentives and taxation in investment computations (see Chapter 3) could leave the company indifferent between ostensibly equally profitable projects regardless of the composition of total capital costs when, in point of fact, there is a fiscal bias in favour of projects in which " fixed " capital expenditure predominates.

stocks of raw materials and finished goods; to give a period of credit to customers; to cover time-lags in production; to pay wages in advance of sales, etc., it is generally less well appreciated that each of these possibilities can be translated into their effects upon the cash-flows associated with a particular line of action, in this case an investment decision, and, indeed, the correct mode of allowing for working capital requirements for any particular investment proposal is not of itself a separate exercise but merely a cash-flow forecast in detailed form. The foregoing remarks are exemplified in the following illustration.

Illustration

Note The purpose of this example is pre-eminently to illustrate the principles of cash-flow accounting and the incidence of working capital expenditure; *it is not meant to be an accurate simulation of reality.*

In the appraisal of a capital expenditure proposal a company makes *inter alia* the following estimates:

(i) *Excluding* working capital the cost of the project (incurred in the year prior to the commencement of production) is £4256. [Such sum is assumed to be eligible for an initial allowance of 30% and annual allowances on a reducing balance basis at the rate of 15%. This fact can however be ignored until part xv of the illustration.] The estimated economic life of the project is 6 years.

(ii) The volume of sales will on average amount to 1200 units per annum, which is about 75% of the project's productive capacity, and is expected to show a uniform monthly level of 100 units except in the first month (of year 1) when, because of the initial time-lag in production a sales volume of only 60 will be achieved. It is assumed that in the terminal year 1200 units will be produced.

The sales forecast of year 1 is thus:

Month

	Jan.	Feb.	Mar.	Apr.	May	June	July	Aug.	Sept.	Oct.	Nov.	Dec.
Sales (units)	60	100	100	100	100	100	100	100	100	100	100	100

(iii) It will be necessary to build up raw material stocks from the outset to a level representing about 2 month's production requirements (say 200×5 lb) excluding the raw material requirements necessary for (iv).

(iv) It will be necessary to build up a finished goods inventory as soon as possible equal to about one month's sales (i.e., 100 units).

(v) The product specification based on a normal output of 1200 units per annum is:

	£	s	d
direct materials 5 lb @ 10/- lb	2	10	0
direct labour 3 hr @ £1 hr	3	0	0
variable costs (including power, etc.)	0	6	0
	£5	16	0

selling price = £7 per unit.

Under a special wage agreement the annual cost of a direct operative is £1800 (including national insurance) for an output not exceeding 2000 productive hours. The direct labour hourly rate in the foregoing specification is however based upon an assumed standard productive output of 1800 hours per operative. (For simplicity the selective employment tax is ignored.)

(vi) The new project will necessitate no addition to the indirect labour force but requires two direct operatives, i.e., $2 \times 2000 = 4000$ available direct labour hours (that is, an immediate capacity potential of 1333 units p.a. (say) 110 units per month).

(vii) The first year's production plan allowing for the finished goods inventory build-up to 100 units within the immediate potential capacity of 110 units per month (excluding overtime working) is thus:

Finished Goods Production (units)

						Months						
	1	2	3	4	5	6	7	8	9	10	11	12]
Opening Inventory	—	50	60	70	80	90	100	100	100	100	100	100
Production	110	110	110	110	110	110	100	100	100	100	100	100
Sales	60	100	100	100	100	100	100	100	100	100	100	100
Closing Inventory	50	60	70	80	90	100	100	100	100	100	100	100

(viii) The raw materials budget * based upon the foregoing production plan and " desired " level of material stocks would thus be:

Raw Materials (lb)

		Months										
	1	2	3	4	5	6	7	8	9	10	11	12
Opening Inventory	—	1000	1000	1000	1000	1000	1000	1000	1000	1000	1000	1000
Purchases	1550	550	550	550	550	550	500	500	500	500	500	500
Less Issues	550	550	550	550	550	550	500	500	500	500	500	500
Closing Inventory	1000	1000	1000	1000	1000	1000	1000	1000	1000	1000	1000	1000

(ix) If we assume that the suppliers of raw materials allow one month's credit, the time pattern of payments, assuming material to cost 10/- lb. would, in the first year, be:

		Months										
	1	2	3	4	5	6	7	8	9	10	11	12
Raw Materials (£)	—	775	275	275	275	275	275	250	250	250	250	250

(x) Assuming the two additional operatives are paid monthly the time-pattern of monthly wage payments $(2 \times £1800 \div 12) = £300$ would be:

		Months										
	1	2	3	4	5	6	7	8	9	10	11	12
Wages (£)	300	300	300	300	300	300	300	300	300	300	300	300

(xi) If, on average, customers are allowed (say) one month's credit, the time-pattern of sales revenue (selling price = £7 per unit) is:

		Months										
Sales (£)	1	2	3	4	5	6	7	8	9	10	11	12
Cash from customers	—	420	700	700	700	700	700	700	700	700	700	700

(xii) In order to establish the time-pattern of cash payments for the variable costs, some assumption about credit received is necessary.

* For ease of illustration the problem of minimising inventory costs by determining the optimum frequency and size of material deliveries is ignored. A bypassing of the inventory problem is admissible here as we are primarily concerned to illustrate the method of determining the time-pattern of cash receipts and payments but, in practice, efficient inventory policy would require the application of the techniques of inventory theory. The frequency and size of deliveries, subject to the agreed " safety " stock levels, would then of course influence the pattern of cash payments for material purchases.

Thus, assume that an average of three month's credit is received on this expenditure; on the basis of the production plan the accrued and cash expenditure would be:

Months

Variable Costs	1	2	3	4	5	6	7	8	9	10	11	12
Accrued Expenditure (£)	33	33	33	33	33	33	30	30	30	30	30	30
Cash Expenditure (£)	—	—	—	99	—	—	99	—	—	90	—	—

(xiii) (*a*) The cash-flows can now be collated as follows:

First year—Months

	1	2	3	4	5	6	7	8	9	10	11	12
Sales (£)	—	420	700	700	700	700	700	700	700	700	700	700
Less												
Wages (£)	300	300	300	300	300	300	300	300	300	300	300	300
Raw material (£)	—	775	275	275	275	275	275	250	250	250	250	250
Variable costs (£)	—	—	—	99	—	—	99	—	—	90	—	—
(£)	300	1075	575	674	575	575	674	550	550	640	550	550
(£)	−300	−655	+125	+26	+125	+125	+26	+150	+150	+60	+150	+150

Net cash-flow=+£132

(*b*) Given that the project has a life of 6 years and that a uniform level of production and sales of 1200 units per annum is anticipated over the remainder of its life, the cash-flows of years, 2, 3, 4 and 5 would all be:

	£	
Sales (1200 × £7)		8400
	£	
Less: Wages (2 × £1800)	3600	
Material (12 × £250)	3000	
Variable Costs	360	6960
	Cash-flow £	1440

(*c*) In year 6 (the terminal year) stocks of raw materials would be used up with a resultant fall in the volume of raw material purchases, i.e.,

	units
Sales volume	1200
	lb
Raw material requirements for production (1200 × 5 lb) =	6000
Less stock of raw materials	1000
purchases (assumed to be 500 lb a month in each of the first 10 months)	5000

The payment for raw materials in year 6 allowing for one month's credit from suppliers would therefore be:

months lb price	£
10 ×500×10/-	2500
Plus the payment for 500 lb in the last month of the previous year	250
	£2750

The cash-flow for year 6 is thus:

		£
Sales (1200 × £7)		8400
Less: Wages (2 × £1800)	3600	
Material (as above)	2750	
Variable costs	360	6710
	Cash-flow	£1690

(*d*) There would, in addition to the cash-flow in the 6th year be the following overspill in year 7.

Sales	£	£
One month received one month in arrears	700	
Proceeds of finished goods inventory	700	
	—	1400
Less:		
Variable costs		90
Cash-flow in year 7		£1310

(xiv) Assuming that the capital cost of £4256 (excluding working capital) is incurred end-year 0, the cash-flows over the entire life of the project can be set out thus:

Cash-flows (end-year)

	0	1	2	3	4	5	6	7
(£)	−4256	+132	+1440	+1440	+1440	+1440	+1690	+1310

However, as the cash-flow in year 1 arises from cash deficits of £300 and £655 (total = £955) in months 1 and 2 respectively, followed by a series of monthly surpluses amounting to £1087 it would, for two reasons,* be more accurate to rearrange the cash-flows (with a

* First, it is more accurate in relation to end-year discounting, i.e., £955 is incurred at a point in time closer to end-year 0 than to end-year 1 whilst the bulk of £1087 arises in the second half of the year. Second, to state the cash-flow as £+132 and thereafter calculate corporation tax thereon would, in effect, be to treat working capital as being tax deductible which is not the case. Hence, for tax purposes, working capital should be separated out (as shown above) so that the first cash-flow corresponds more nearly to the first year's assessable profit.

similar adjustment for years 6 and 7) thus:

	0	1	2	3	4	5	6
(£)	−4256						
(£)	−955	+1087	+1440	+1440	+1440	+1440	+3000

whence the project's *gross* DCF rate of return is 18·7 % p.a. calculated
thus:

	cash-flow	discount factors at 17% p.a.	present value at 17% p.a.
	£		£
end-year 1	1087	× 0·8547	= 929·06
2	1440 ⎫		
3	1440 ⎪		
4	1440 ⎬ 1440 × 2·7432 × 0·8547		= 3376·24
5	1440 ⎭		
6	3000	× 0·3898	= 1169·40

Present value of cash(in)-flows @ 17%   £5474·70

Note £1440 × 2·7432 × 0·8547 is the present value of a four-year series of constant amounts which commences one year hence.

	cash-flow	discount factors at 19% p.a.	present value at 19% p.a.
	£		£
end-year 1	1087	× 0·8403	= 913·41
2	1440 ⎫		
3	1440 ⎪		
4	1440 ⎬ 1440 × 2·6386 × 0·8403		= 3192·79
5	1440 ⎭		
6	3000	× 0·3521	= 1056·30

Present value of cash(in)-flows @ 19%   £5162·50

Linear interpolation: £

present value at 17% = 5474·70
present value at 19% = 5162·50

difference   312·20

present value at 17% = 5474·70
capital cost   = 5211·00

difference   263·70

∴ DCF rate of return is $17\% + \dfrac{263 \cdot 70}{312 \cdot 20} \times 2 = 18 \cdot 7\%$ (to one decimal place.)

(xv) To calculate the project's rate of return net of corporation tax and investment incentives it is first necessary to work out the dimensions and incidence of the latter (30% initial allowance and 15% annual allowance). As the company's financial year-end has been taken as 31st December, there is a consequent time-lag of 12 months between the receipt of income and the payment of tax thereon. Likewise, assuming that the company has sufficient other taxable income to absorb capital allowances at the earliest possible date, the initial allowance and first annual allowance can be set against the tax assessment due for payment one year after the incurrence of the eligible capital cost.

(a) Schedule of capital allowances (assuming company elects to take balancing allowances and that, in this case, the project has no terminal value).

	£			value of capital
eligible acquisition cost	4256		tax	allowances
30% initial allowance 1277		£	rate	£
15% annual allowance 638	1915	(1915×0·40)	=	766 end-year 1
	2341			
15% annual allowance	351	(351×0·40)	=	140 end-year 2
	1990			
15% annual allowance	299	(299×0·40)	=	120 end-year 3
	1691			
15% annual allowance	254	(254×0·40)	=	102 end-year 4
	1437			
15% annual allowance	216	(216×0·40)	=	86 end-year 5
	1221			
15% annual allowance	183	(183×0·40)	=	73 end-year 6
	1038			
balancing allowance	1038	(1038×0·40)	=	415 end-year 7

The foregoing illustration shows the working capital, £955, which will be required in the early months of the above project. As illustrated, the need arises because of the different time-profiles and different dimensions of the cash in- and out-flows respectively. As suggested earlier, if investment projects are analysed on the basis exemplified above, working capital is automatically allowed for.

(b) DCF rate of return computation including taxation and capital allowances.

	0 £	1 £	2 £	3 £	4 £	5 £	6 £	7 £
(1) Gross cash-flows (end-year)	$\left.\begin{array}{r}-4256\\-955\end{array}\right\}$	+1087	+1440	+1440	+1440	+1440	$\left.\begin{array}{r}+2045\\+955\end{array}\right\}$*	
(2) Taxation at 40% (lagged 12 months)			−435†	−576	−576	−576	−576	−818*
(3) Tax " rebates " resulting from capital allowances (as in (a) above)		+766	+140	+120	+102	+86	+73	+415
(4) Net cash-flows (1)+(2)+(3)	−5211	+1853	+1145	+984	+966	+950	+2497	−403
(5) Present value at 12%		+1654·46	+912·79	+700·39	+613·91	+539·06	+1265·06	−182·30 = £+5503
(6) Present value at 15%		+1611·30	+865·78	+647·00	+552·31	+472·32	+1079·52	−151·50 = £+5077

Linear interpolation:

$$\begin{array}{lr} & \text{£} \\ \text{present value at } 12\% = & 5503 \\ \text{present value at } 15\% = & 5077 \\ \hline \text{difference} & 426 \end{array}$$

$$\begin{array}{lr} \text{present value at } 12\% = & 5503 \\ \text{capital cost} = & 5211 \\ \hline \text{difference} & 292 \end{array}$$

$$\therefore \text{ DCF rate of return} = 12\% + \frac{292}{426} \times 3 = 14\cdot1\% \text{ p.a. (to one decimal place)}$$

* The gross cash-flow of £3000 receivable end-year 6 is split into a taxable component of £2045, and an untaxable sum of £955 which is assumed to be working capital recovered; the taxation paid in year 7 is therefore £2045×40% = £818.

† (See following page.)

Year 1   Profit and loss account

		£	£
Total sales (11 × £700 + £420)			8120
Costs			
materials			
purchases (7300 lb @ 10/-)		3650	
less closing stock			
(1000 lb @ 10/-)		500	3150
wages (2 × £1800)			3600
overheads (2 × £99 + 2 × £90)			378
			7128
less value of finished goods			
inventory (100 × £5·8)			580
			6548
	accounting profit		£1572

		£	£
end-year 1	cash-flow		1087
	deduct		
	working capital		955
	original cash-flow		132
	add		
	increases in debtors	700	
	stocks:		
	materials	500	
	finished goods		
	(100 × £5·8)	580	1780
			1912
	less		
	increases in creditors:		
	overheads	90	
	suppliers	250	340
	accounting profit		£1572

† It is not strictly correct to base the first tax assessment (of £435) on the first cash-flow of £1087. In reality the first tax assessment would be raised on profits calculated on an accruals basis in which closing inventories are taken into credit and, consequently, cause the assessable profits to exceed the first cash-flow. As explained in the context hereafter, this inaccuracy can be countervailed to a significant degree. The initial cash-flow can be reconciled with the accounting profits as follows: above

A point perhaps worth emphasising is the fact already mentioned and to which effect is given in the foregoing illustration: that as expenditure on working capital is not tax deductible an equivalent sum will escape assessment to taxation in the terminal year of a project's life. This statement should however, be qualified by reference to the factor mentioned in footnote † of the foregoing example: that even after separating out the working capital in the first cash-flow, the adjusted end-year 1 figure (cash-flow) will generally understate the first year's assessable profits; consequently, the first tax payment will also be understated and the ultimate tax payment will be *overstated* by an equivalent amount. To base the first tax payment on the first year's cash-flow (modified as above) is to introduce a tendency to *overstate* the profitability of investment.

The obvious way of remedying this error and, at the same time, ensuring correct tax treatment in the terminal year is clearly to base both the first and ultimate tax payments on assessable profits. Our reason for not adopting this (correct) procedure resides first in the practical convenience of the assumption that the first (modified) cash-flow (rather than the first assessable profits) is the basis of the first tax payment; and, secondly, in the fact that the understatement of the first tax payment can be conveniently countervailed by treating the ultimate cash-flow as though it were *entirely* taxable.

The practical convenience to which we refer is concerned with the application of " effective net of tax factors " to a stream of untaxed cash-flows in reducing the latter to equivalent net amounts. This and other short cut methods are the subject of the following chapter throughout which it is assumed that, after separating out working capital outlays in the manner described above, the first and terminal cash-flows correspond to assessable profits; the ultimate cash-flow is thus regarded as being entirely taxable. For all practical purposes this assumption is accurate enough and will generally result in somewhat conservative calculations, i.e., in investment returns being very slightly understated.

6

PREFACE TO CHAPTERS 3 AND 4*

It is highly probable that in the fullness of time Appendices E and/or F, which contain present values of investment incentives and equity cut-off rates respectively, will be rendered obsolete by changes in either the levels and structure of investment incentives or in taxation. The purpose of Chapters 3 and 4 is pre-eminently to explain the basic methodology and principles underlying the formulae for deriving these appendices which are aids to short-cut DCF computational processes.

It will be found that the actual amount of computational time spent in preparing new editions of Appendices E and F (as and when required) is actually quite small and well worth the effort in terms of time ultimately saved.† In practice many companies find it unnecessary to extend Appendix E beyond a 30% rate of discount.

* See also the addendum to Appendix E, pp. 232–37.
† For any individual company, only four pages of Appendix E are relevant.

Chapter 3

MEASURING THE RETURN ON INVESTMENT NET OF CORPORATION TAX AND INVESTMENT INCENTIVES

INTRODUCTION—BASIC MEASUREMENT AND ALLOWANCES FOR DEVIATIONS IN THE ESTIMATES

In the foregoing chapter we have in effect stated that in order to measure the prospective return on an investment proposal it is necessary to obtain three separate pieces of information: the capital cost of the project, C; the anticipated stream of cash flows $a_1, a_2, \ldots, a_n$, arising in years $1, 2, \ldots, n$; and the estimated life of the project, n years.

In measuring capital costs it is necessary to make the distinction between acquisition cost which is eligible for investment incentives and working capital in the form of increased stocks, debtors, etc., which does not so qualify.

In estimating future cash-flows it is important to hold clearly in view that it is the net inflow of cash resulting from investment which is being measured. Consequently conventional income and cost accounting rules must be abandoned. Such notional charges as depreciation, and equitable apportionments of existing overheads are irrelevant in cash-flow accounting. It is cash payments and cash receipts alone which are the main preoccupation of cash-flow computation. Such distinctions as direct costs and overheads should be studiously avoided for in this context it is extra net cash-flows which must be compared with capital expenditure. The manner in which the extra net cash-flows arise depends primarily on the nature of an investment decision; in the case of a labour-saving device the net cash-flow may result from (cash) cost savings alone, whilst an extension of productive capacity to increase saleable output will give rise to increases in operating (cash) costs and, if the project is to be economically viable, to greater increases in operating (cash) revenue.

It may be extremely difficult to estimate the economic life of an investment project to a high degree of accuracy. Generally speaking, however, the informed judgement of individuals familiar with the technological features of an investment proposal will usually suffice to provide information on life estimates which is adequate for capital budgeting purposes.

The difficulty of forecasting also pervades the estimation of future cash-flows but in a large majority of cases informed judgement and the use of existing knowledge which in turn may only be located after careful searching and correction must, by definition constitute informa-tion which is better than no information at all. There are, in fact, systematic methods, including for example sensitivity analysis, of allowing for the imprecision in estimates; basically this is a question of considering the degree by which the best estimates could vary whilst the project remained viable and an important part of the tech-nique is to determine which variables in a calculation are critical and which are not. A pertinent point which may frequently prove to be the case is that the uncritical variables in a decision may be those which defy precise quantification. If so, an inaccurate numerical statement of such variables is largely a matter of indifference.

It is not intended to illustrate in detail the application of sensitivity analysis to the measurement of the return on investment but general indication of its application can be obtained from Figs. 8 and 9 which, in effect, are a means of calculating how much risk a project can bear when risk is interpreted as the contingency that each one of the actual values of the variables handled in an investment computation may subsequently deviate from the best estimates.

Fig. 8 is a sensitivity chart based upon the DCF present value method; the curves of cumulative present value are obtained in the following manner (which we illustrate with reference to the upper curve labelled " annual cash-flow = £10 000 "): the present value at 8% p.a. (the assumed cost of finance in this case) of a cash-flow of £10 000 p.a. is first computed for a 10-year life; the calculation is then repeated at 9 years, then 8 years, etc., to give a series of points from which the upper curve is drawn. This exercise is then repeated for annual cash-flows of £9000 to give the second curve labelled " annual cash-flow = £9000 " and so on until the whole family of curves is obtained.

The best estimates of the project considered in Figs. 8 and 9 imply a DCF rate of return of 15% p.a. which in relation to an assumed cost of finance of 8% p.a.* allows a margin for deviation of 7% p.a. (or,

* It is worth emphasising that a sensitivity analysis based upon the present value method should employ a discount rate reflecting a cost of finance unweighted for an individual project's risk premium. The object of the exercise is, as stated, to calculate the amount of risk a project can bear; hence, to discount at a rate embody-ing some allowance for the risk inherent in an individual project would amount to the double-counting of risk.

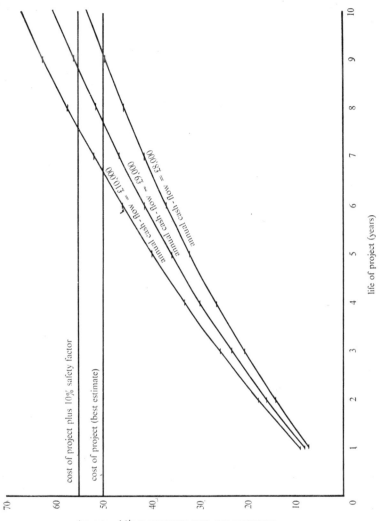

Fig. 8   Best estimates: aquisition cost   £50 188
                        life   10 years
                        cash-flow p.a.   £10 000
                        rate of return   15% p.a.
                        company's cost of finance   8% p.a.
                        present value at 8% p.a.   £67 100
                        net present value   £16 912

in terms of present value, a deviation of £16 912). Exactly where attention should be focused in appraising the project depends upon the respective degrees of confidence regarding the estimates which have been made. A sensitivity diagram allows each estimate to be isolated individually and gives the decision-taker the opportunity to concentrate his attention on the variable which, in the nature of the decision, is the most difficult to quantify. Should most argument

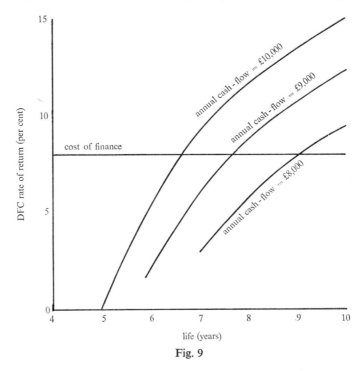

Fig. 9

centre upon the life-estimate, a directorate unwilling to stake everything on a 10-year conjecture may take great comfort from the fact that the project (analysed in Figs. 8 and 9) would need to have a life of only 6·7 years to allow fully for the recovery of total capital invested plus interest at 8% p.a. thereon. In other cases whilst there may be equal confidence about all estimates it may be felt desirable to allow for a safety factor amounting to an unfavourable deviation of 10% in each. As regards the project analysed in Figs. 8 and 9, a 10% increase in the capital cost above the best estimate, associated with a 10% decline in the annual cash-flow would still leave the project profitable and give a break-even life, again allowing for the full recovery of capital and interest, of 8·75 years.*

By way of contrast Fig. 9 is a sensitivity diagram which presents the same data in terms of the DCF rate of return criterion. This approach lacks one advantage of the present value basis: it requires a family of DCF rate of return curves for each probable level of capital expenditure whereas a single family of curves suffices for Fig. 8.

A further frequently applicable sensitivity approach is to begin with the variable(s) in the decisions which are objectively determined and from it (them) calculate the break-even values of the others. (By break-even we again mean the full recovery of capital after allowing for interest.) Thus if the capital cost of a project cannot conceivably deviate † the break-even cash-flows for each of a succession of life-estimates are automatically determined. Once calculated, such figures provide either a useful objectively determined bench-mark for judging estimates prepared elsewhere or, alternatively, if some individuals find it difficult to bring themselves to quantify anticipated benefits at all, they provide a standard with which favourable or unfavourable reactions may be elicited. Thus, such a question as, " Do you think you can achieve a sales level of £1000?" may readily stimulate an affirmative or negative response whereas the same respondent may, even with some prompting, have hesitated to suggest any figure at all. There can be small doubt that some individuals who do not hesitate to provide direct answers to direct questions will readily imply that a problem assumes intractable dimensions when asked in a less direct manner to provide the same information.

It is not idle to suggest that sensitivity analysis helps to remove some of the apprehension which may exist in the minds of decision-makers

---

* It is perhaps useful to give one further example. Assume that the project considered in Figs. 8 and 9 is an extension of capacity for the manufacture of a new product and that the scale of the new capacity is governed by technical factors. For illustrative purposes the major problem in the analysis of the project is taken to be the potential level of sales. (The annual cash-flows, a_i, are of course extra (cash-inflow) sales, b_i, minus extra (cash-outflow) operating costs, d_i.)

In such a case management should estimate a series of price-volume relationships within the new capacity and choose the turnover, b_i, which maximises the value of $(b_i - d_i)$. Thereafter if, as stated, b_i is the only value giving concern it can be recalculated for a number of alternative selling prices.

† Such may be the case because the entire installed capital cost of (say) a machine may be contractually determined.

and to the extent that it does so by presenting additional data in a systematic, comprehensible and objective manner it removes factors which might otherwise constitute a bias against much profitable investment.

ALLOWING FOR CORPORATION TAXATION AND INVESTMENT INCENTIVES

Consider a project costing £2689 of which £2000 is expenditure on manufacturing plant qualifying for a 25% cash grant with the remaining 75% eligible for annual allowances on a reducing balance basis at the rate of 25%; the balance of expenditure, £689, is taken to be working capital which does not qualify for investment incentives. The gross cash-flow of the project is £1000 p.a. arising at the end of each of 5 years and the company's cost of finance is 10% p.a. It is also assumed that there are respective time-lags (k and z) both of 12 months between the incurring of the expenditure and the receipt of the cash grant, and between the earning of cash-flows and the payment of tax thereon.*

Excluding taxation and investment incentives, the project's DCF rate of return is given by r in the equation:

$$2689 = 1000\left[\frac{1-(1+r)^{-5}}{r}\right]$$

whence

$$2 \cdot 689 = \frac{1-(1+r)^{-5}}{r}$$

using Appendix B

$$r = 25\%.$$

Again using Appendix B, the *net* present value of the project at 10% p.a. is:

$$(1000 \times 3 \cdot 7908) - 2689 = £1102.$$

* Equal time-lags of 12 months are assumed here for convenience of illustration. It has already been announced that initially there will be an 18 months time-lag before the receipt of cash grants on eligible expenditure. Eventually this period will be reduced to six months.

The second time-lag depends on the relationships of a company's financial year-end to the date upon which tax payments are due. The tables in Appendix E separately allow for time-lags of 9 months, 12 months, 18 months and 21 months. 9 months and 21 months represent minima and maxima; companies with other periods can interpolate as desired.

The time-lag k in Appendix E is 18 months in all cases where it occurs; in the addendum to Appendix E it is six months.

With corporation tax at the rate of 40% *detailed* net of tax rate of return and present value calculations on the above data can be set out as shown in Illustration 11(a) and (b).

Illustration 11(a)

Schedule of investment incentives (assuming company elects to take balancing allowances).

	£	value of investment incentives
eligible acquisition cost	2000	£
25% cash grant	500	500 end-year 1
	1500	tax rate
25% annual allowance	375	$(375 \times 0\cdot40) = 150$ end-year 1
	1125	
25% annual allowance	281	$(281 \times 0\cdot40) = 112$ end-year 2
	844	
25% annual allowance	211	$(211 \times 0\cdot40) = 84$ end-year 3
	633	
25% annual allowance	158	$(158 \times 0\cdot40) = 63$ end-year 4
	475	
25% annual allowance	119	$(119 \times 0\cdot40) = 48$ end-year 5
balancing allowance	356	$(356 \times 0\cdot40) = 142$ end-year 6

It can be seen from inspection that the following computation (p. 82) has three basic components namely a capital cost of £2689 which can be regarded as giving rise to a succession of five end-year cash-flows of £1000 subject to taxation, at the rate of 40%, and a series of tax rebates. The taxed cash-flows would, if tax were paid immediately, be worth £1000 $(1-0\cdot4)$, i.e., 60% of their gross value. Because in this example the payment of the tax on the cash-flows is delayed 12 months $(z=1)$*, the taxed cash-flow is thus equal to a gross cash-flow minus the present value of the tax paid one year later, i.e.,

$$£1000 - \frac{400}{1+i}$$

or

$$£1000\left(1 - \frac{0\cdot4}{1+i}\right)$$

* This time-delay z is defiined further on p. 87.

Illustration 11(*b*)

DCF Rate of Return Computation Including Taxation and Investment Incentives

	0	1	2	3	4	5	6
(1) Gross cash-flows (end-year)	−2689	+1000	+1000	+1000	+1000	+1000	
(2) Taxation at 40% (lagged 12 months)			−400	−400	−400	−400	−400
(3) Cash grant and tax saved by investment incentives		+650	+112	+84	+63	+48	+142
(4) Cash-flows (1)+(2)+(3)	−2689	+1650	+712	+684	+663	+648	−258
(5) Present value at 21%		1363·64	486·31	386·10	309·29	249·83	−82·21 = 2713
(6) Present value at 22%		1352·46	478·37	376·68	299·28	239·76	−78·25 = 2668
(7) Present value at 10%		1500·00	588·43	513·90	452·84	402·36	−145·63 = 3312

Linear interpolation:

$$\begin{array}{ll} \text{present value at } 21\% & = 2713 \\ \text{present value at } 22\% & = 2668 \\ \hline \text{difference} & 45 \end{array}$$

$$\begin{array}{ll} \text{present value at } 21\% & = 2713 \\ \text{cost} & = 2689 \\ \hline \text{difference} & 24 \end{array}$$

$$\therefore \quad r = 21\% + \frac{24}{45} \times 1 = 21 \cdot 5\% \text{ to one decimal place}$$

Note

The end-year 1 net cash-flow, £1650, exceeds the gross cash-flow, £1000, for two reasons. First, in this illustration the cash-grant of £500 is assumed to be received 12 months after the capital expenditure is incurred. Secondly, although the tax on the end-year 1 gross cash-flow is paid after a 12 months' time-lag, the first annual allowance can be claimed 12 months after the *capital expenditure* assuming, as have we, that the company in question has other taxable income. The assumption of a sufficiency of taxable income to absorb initial (where applicable) and annual allowances as and when they fall due, is adhered to throughout this chapter and Appendix E.

where i is the company's cost of finance. Clearly, if a company has to pay $i\%$ p.a. to obtain finance then a delay in the payment of tax obviates the raising of an equivalent amount of money for that period or, alternatively, provides the company with the opportunity to invest the ultimate tax payment for the 12 months prior to payment.

The present value Q of the taxed cash-flows in the above case can thus be stated as

discount factor from
Appendix B

$$Q = 1000\left(1 - \frac{0.40}{1+i}\right)\left[\frac{1-(1+i)^{-5}}{i}\right].$$

Assuming $i = 10\%$,

$$Q = 1000 \times 0.6364^* \times 3.7908$$
$$= £2412.47.$$

The cash grant and the series of tax rebates which in effect result from the annual allowances have a present value, S, given by

$$S = \frac{650}{1+i} + \frac{112}{(1+i)^2} + \frac{84}{(1+i)^3} + \frac{63}{(1+i)^4} + \frac{48}{(1+i)^5} + \frac{142}{(1+i)^6}.$$

When $i = 0.1$ (i.e., 10%)

$$S = 590.91 + 92.56 + 63.11 + 43.03 + 29.80 + 80.16$$
$$= £899.6.$$

The present value of the project at 10% after allowing for taxation and capital allowances is thus $£2412.5 + £899.6 = £3312$ (as is confirmed by reference to the detailed computation, line 7).

It is obvious that the project's rate of return could also be calculated using this method of splitting the cash-flows into two components. As stated earlier a DCF rate of return may be regarded as the rate which just discounts cash-flows to equality with a project's capital cost. Consequently in splitting the cash-flows it is necessary to find the rate of discount which equates the sum of the split cash-flows with the capital cost. Trying a 21% discount rate in determining the rate of return we obtain:

* Effective net of tax factor y, Appendix E, column (5), $z = 1$.

CAPITAL BUDGETING

present value of investment incentives discounting at 21%

$$S = \frac{650}{1+0\cdot21} + \frac{112}{(1+0\cdot21)^2} + \frac{84}{(1+0\cdot21)^3} + \frac{63}{(1+0\cdot21)^4} + \frac{48}{(1+0\cdot21)^5}$$

$$+ \frac{142}{(1+0\cdot21)^6}$$

$$= £754\cdot3$$

present value of taxed cash-flows at 21%

$$Q = 1000\left(1 - \frac{0\cdot4}{1+0\cdot21}\right)\left[\frac{1-(1+0\cdot21)^{-5}}{0\cdot21}\right]$$

$$= 1000 \times 0\cdot6694 \times 2\cdot9260$$

$$= 1958\cdot7$$

$S+Q = £2713$ (as shown in Illustration 11(b), line 5).

As the £2689 capital cost is less than £2713 we would then repeat the above calculation at a higher rate of discount and then interpolate the rate of return in the manner already shown. Whilst this procedure of splitting the cash-flow into the taxed cash-flow and series of tax rebates may at first sight appear to give rise to extra computation compared to the single discounting procedure shown in Illustration 11(b), it is a device which leads to a short-cut method for DCF present value and rate of return calculations.

In the foregoing example the present value S of the capital allowances on eligible expenditure of £2000 at a 10% discount rate is £899·6. Had the eligible expenditure been £1000 the present value would obviously have amounted to £449·8. £1 of eligible expenditure would thus give rise to a present value of 0·4498 when discounting at 10%. Had we known this value of 0·4498 *in advance* then to obtain the present value of the cash grant and series of tax rebates it would simply have been necessary to multiply £2000 by 0·4498 and to add the

result, £899·6, to $Q = £1000\left(1 - \frac{0\cdot40}{1+0\cdot1}\right)\left[\frac{1-(1+0\cdot1)^{-5}}{0\cdot1}\right]^* = £2412\cdot5.$

Thus, £899·6 + £2412·5 = £3312 (as in Illustration 11(b), line 7).

---

* As explained in Chapter 2, the value of the contents of the square brackets is obtained from Appendix B, 5 year line and 10% column.

Likewise, had we known in advance the present value of investment incentives on a principal of unity, *and* the value of $\left(1 - \dfrac{0\cdot4}{1+r}\right)$ at a series of discount rates covering a range extending over 21%, the rate of return could also have been calculated. Trying a 21% rate of discount the calculation is:

capital cost		present value of investment incentives, S (at 21%)
£2689	$\backsimeq$	(£2000 × 0·3697) *
		present value of taxed cash-flows (at 21%)
	+	(£1000 × 0·6694 × 2·9260)
	$\backsimeq$	£2698 (Illustration 11(b), line 5).†

The present value of investment incentives on £1 of eligible expenditure clearly depends upon three things.

(i) The category of the capital expenditure itself and whether or not the expenditure is incurred in a development area. The scales of allowances for which defined categories of plant and buildings are eligible are laid down in the recent White Paper.‡

(ii) The rate of discount reflecting the cost of finance to a company.

(iii) The project life over which the investment incentives are spread.

Consideration (i) is a question of fact; although the White Paper increases the number of eligible categories, though in some cases giving less favourable treatment than hitherto, it is not difficult to work out the present value per £1 of eligible expenditure for each of the new categories.

The rate of discount reflecting the cost of finance to a company (consideration (ii)) depends upon such considerations as gearing, etc., and may vary from one company to the next. This possibility is simply covered by calculating the present value of investment incentives over a wide range of discount rates.

---

* The value of 0·3697 representing the present value of investment incentives on £1 of eligible expenditure at a 21% discount rate is obtained from the formula which is derived on pp. 87–89. It should be noted that 0·3697 will not be found in any of the tables of present values of investment incentives on plant qualifying for cash grants in Appendix E for the reason that all such tables are based upon a time-lag of 18 months between the incurring of eligible capital expenditure and the receipt of the cash-grant. Moreover in the addendum to Appendix E, k is 6 months.

† The source of this difference of £2713 − £2698 = £15 is explained on pp. 89–91.

‡ *Investment Incentives*, op. cit.

As it happens (iii) is, in general, not a critical consideration; * the reason being that investment incentives are concentrated in the early years of a project's life. Consequently whether the life of a project is relatively short (say, 5 years) or infinite, the present value of the investment incentives is, for any given rate of discount, much the same. As will be seen, this fact simplifies the precalculation of the present values of investment incentives considerably; as illustrated above, these values are an obvious precondition to short cut DCF present value and rate of return calculations.

PRECALCULATING PRESENT VALUES OF INVESTMENT INCENTIVES

If, as we have stated above, the precise life of an investment project has little effect upon the present value of investment incentives for which it may qualify, then for general purposes, where the duration of investment projects may show considerable variation from one project to the next, it is unnecessary to calculate such present values for a number of different lives; one life period suffices—it is merely necessary to repeat the calculation for a range of discount-rates taking all calculations up to infinity. Moreover, it is unnecessary, even if it were possible, to work out the series of capital allowances on a principle of unity up to infinity and then discount each value in the series individually. That is to say, *we do not compute* a series of annual inducements and discount as below. For example, a principle of unity eligible for a 25% cash grant and 25% annual allowance would, with two time-lags of 12 months (between receipt of cash grant and incurring of expenditure, and between earning of income and payment of tax thereon), give rise to the following present value, S,†

$$S = \frac{0 \cdot 325}{1+r} + \frac{0 \cdot 056}{(1+r)^2} + \frac{0 \cdot 042}{(1+r)^3} + \frac{0 \cdot 0315}{(1+r)^4} + \frac{0 \cdot 024}{(1+r)^5} \quad \text{etc.}$$

This tedious calculation is obviated by formulating the present value of investment incentives algebraically as explained under the following sub-headings. The advantages of this elementary algebraic process need no emphasising; it gives rise to a formula for the present value of investment incentives from which numerical values for an extensive range of discount rates can quickly be calculated with the aid of a desk

---

* This assertion is illustrated numerically on pp. 89–91.
† The series in Illustration 11(b), line 3 divided by £2000.

calculator. As explained it is, of course, necessary to calculate *
such present values for each category of investment incentives defined
in the recent White Paper.†

PRESENT VALUE OF INVESTMENT INCENTIVES

INVESTMENT IN PLANT AND EQUIPMENT FOR MANUFACTURING AND
EXTRACTIVE INDUSTRIES QUALIFYING FOR A 25% CASH GRANT AND
ANNUAL ALLOWANCES ON THE 75% BALANCE OF EXPENDITURE

assumptions and notation

C = capital cost incurred at the end of year 0 qualifying for investment
incentives;

P = cash grant as a percentage of C;

D = annual allowance (which may be at 15, 20 or 25%) on a reducing
balance basis as a percentage of the eligible capital expenditure
minus the cash grant, i.e., on $C(1-P)$;

T = corporation tax rate expressed as a percentage;

k = time-lag (in years) between the incurring of the eligible expenditure and the receipt of the cash grant;

z = time-lag (in years) between the incurring of the eligible expenditure and the tax payments reduced by the first annual allowance
(z clearly depends upon the time-lag between the company's
financial year-end and the income tax year-end).

The present value of the cash grant is given by

$$\frac{PC}{(1+r)^k}.$$

The present value of the first annual allowance is thus

$$\frac{C(1-P)DT}{(1+r)^z},$$

i.e., present value of eligible expenditure *minus* cash grant multiplied
by the annual allowance, multiplied by the tax rate. After taking the
first annual allowance the written down balance is thus $C(1-P)(1-D)$;
hence the present value of the second annual allowance is

$$\frac{C(1-P)(1-D)DT}{(1+r)^{1+z}}.$$

---

* All the tables presented in this book have, in fact, been obtained from a com-
puter.   † Op. cit.

7

Likewise the written down balance after taking the second annual allowance is $C(1-P)(1-D)(1-D)$, i.e., $C(1-P)(1-D)^2$ and the present value of the third annual allowance is

$$\frac{C(1-P)(1-D)^2 DT}{(1+r)^{2+z}}.$$

Thus, the complete series of investment incentives continuing to infinity has a present value S given by

$$S = \frac{PC}{(1+r)^k} + \frac{C(1-P)DT}{(1+r)^z} + \frac{C(1-P)(1-D)DT}{(1+r)^{1+z}} + \frac{C(1-P)(1-D)^2 DT}{(1+r)^{2+z}} +$$

$$\frac{C(1-P)(1-D)^3 DT}{(1+r)^{3+z}} + \cdots$$

$$= \frac{PC}{(1+r)^k} + \frac{C(1-P)DT}{(1+r)^z}\left[1 + \frac{1-D}{1+r} + \frac{(1-D)^2}{(1+r)^2} + \frac{(1-D)^3}{(1+r)^3} + \cdots\right]. \qquad (1)$$

Whence, denoting the infinite sum in the square brackets by S_∞, i.e.,

$$S_\infty = 1 + \frac{1-D}{1+r} + \frac{(1-D)^2}{(1+r)^2} + \frac{(1-D)^3}{(1+r)^3} + \cdots \qquad (2)$$

and, using the result (5) of Appendix 1, Chapter 4, p. 141,

$$S_\infty = \frac{1}{1 - \dfrac{1-D}{1+r}}$$

$$= \frac{1}{\dfrac{r+D}{1+r}}$$

$$= \frac{1+r}{r+D}.$$

Substituting for S_∞ in equation (1) we obtain,

$$S = \frac{PC}{(1+r)^k} + \frac{C(1-P)DT(1+r)}{(1+r)^z(r+D)}.$$

If the present values are calculated on a principle of unity then in the above formula the symbol C may be omitted and the resulting tabular values can thereafter be multiplied by any given capital cost to determine the required present value of investment incentives. Hence the tables of present values of investment incentives on plant qualifying for cash grants included in Appendix E are labelled

$$S = \frac{P}{(1+r)^k} + \frac{(1-P)DT(1+r)}{(1+r)^z(r+D)}. \tag{3}$$

Substituting in this formula the numerical values used in Illustration 11 to calculate the present value of the investment incentives at a 10% discount rate [i.e., $P = 0.25$, $k = 1$ (year), $D = 0.25$, $T = 0.40$ and $z = 1$ (year)] we obtain

$$S = \frac{0.25}{(1+0.1)^1} + \frac{(1-0.25) \times 0.25 \times 0.4 \times (1+0.1)}{(1+0.1)^1(0.1+0.25)}$$

$$= 0.4416.$$

This value of 0·4416 compares with the present value of 0·4498 calculated on p. 84 from Illustration 11 in which, rather than continuing to infinity, the investment incentives cease at the end of year 5 when a balancing allowance is claimed. The deviation of $0.4498 - 0.4416 = 0.0082$ thus gives provisional indication of the significance of the substitution of a life estimate of 5 years at a *10% discount rate* so far as the present value of the investment incentives is concerned; the error is 0·82 of 1%. Put another way, this short cut calculation *understates* the present value (discounting at 10%) of a whole project with £1000 of eligible expenditure by £8·2.* Obviously, such minor computational deviations as this are not critical to decision-taking in practice. Furthermore, as we have already emphasised, this small deviation is essentially relative to a project with a five year life with discounting at 10%. The deviation will be smaller the longer is the project life and the higher the rate of discount chosen. For example, if we now calculate the rate of return promised by the project in Illustration 11 using the formula for the present value of investment incentives (in effect this is to raise the discount rate whilst holding the life constant at 5 years), the present value of the investment incentives S at 21% is given by

$$S = \frac{0.25}{(1+0.21)^1} + \frac{(1-0.25) \times 0.25 \times 0.4 \times (1+0.21)}{(1+0.21)^1 \times (0.21+0.25)}$$

$$= 0.3697.$$

* Where there is working capital in addition, as was the case in Illustration 11, the understatement in relation to total capital costs is evidently proportionately smaller.

The present value of the taxed cash-flows, Q, at 21% is given by

$$Q = £1000\left[1-\frac{0\cdot4}{(1+0\cdot21)^1}\right]\left[\frac{1-(1+0\cdot21)^{-5}}{0\cdot21}\right]$$

$$= £1000 \times 0\cdot6694^* \times 2\cdot9260$$

$$= £1958\cdot7.$$

Thus, discounting at 21%

capital cost		present value of investment incentives, S, at 21%		present value of taxed cash-flows, Q, at 21%
£2689	$\simeq$	£2000 × 0·3697	+	£1958·7
	$\simeq$	£739·4 + £1958·7		
	$\simeq$	£2698.		

Discounting at 22%

£2689	$\simeq$ (£2000 × 0·3645) + (£1000 × 0·6721 × 2·8636)
	$\simeq$ £729·0 + £1924·6
	$\simeq$ £2654.

Using linear interpolation:

$$£$$

present value at 21% = 2698
present value at 22% = 2654

difference   44

present value at 21% = 2698
cost of project   = 2689

difference   9

$$\therefore\quad r = 21\% + \frac{9}{44} \times 1$$

$$= 21\cdot2\% \text{ to one decimal place.}$$

Thus using the long hand computation form of Illustration 11 the rate of return is 21·5%; using the short cut form the answer is understated by 0·3%, i.e., by little more than $\frac{1}{4}$%. For practical purposes this

* Appendix E, column (5), $r = 21\%$, $z = 1$ year.

short cut method of calculation is therefore a very powerful time-saving tool.*

* It should not, of course, be inferred that we are suggesting that the above calculations constitute a rigorous mathematical test of accuracy. Such an exercise would clearly require more extensive numerical analysis. The above calculations however permit the non-mathematical practical inferences which we have drawn.

A rigorous test of the accuracy of the short-cut method is a comparison of the present value of investment incentives based upon a *finite* life with the present value of investment incentives over an *infinite* time-period. For example, as shown above, the present value, S, of a cash grant and infinite series of annual allowances is given by:

$$S = \frac{PC}{(1+r)^k} + \frac{C(1-P)DT(1+r)}{(1+r)^z(r+D)}$$

whereas, assuming zero salvage value and a consequent balancing allowance, the present value, S_f, of investment incentives over a finite period of n years is given by:

$$S_f = \frac{PC}{(1+r)^k} + \frac{C(1-P)DT}{(1+r)^z}\left[1 + \frac{1-D}{1+r} + \frac{(1-D)^2}{(1+r)^2} + \cdots + \frac{(1-D)^{n-1}}{(1+r)^{n-1}}\right]$$
$$+ \frac{C(1-P)(1-D)^nT}{(1+r)^{n+z}}$$

The expression, S_f-S, given by

$$S_f-S = \frac{C(1-P)T}{(1+r)^z}\left[\frac{r(1-D)^{n+1}}{(r+D)(1+r)^n}\right]$$

represents the extent to which the net present value of an investment proposal is understated when the computation of the present value of investment incentives is based upon an infinite life assumption (assuming zero salvage value).

The significance of this difference can, for any given magnitude of capital expenditure, C, be ascertained by substituting in the expression, S_f-S, ranges of values for P, T, r, D, z, and n, covering all values of the latter of practical relevance.

Substituting the ranges:

$$P = 0 \cdot 25 \text{ and } 0 \cdot 45;$$
$$T = 0 \cdot 4;$$
$$r = 0 \cdot 05, 0 \cdot 10, 0 \cdot 15, 0 \cdot 20 \text{ and } 0 \cdot 25;$$
$$D = 0 \cdot 15, 0 \cdot 20 \text{ and } 0 \cdot 25;$$
$$z = 0 \cdot 75 \text{ and } 1 \cdot 75 \text{ (9 months and 21 months);}$$
$$n = 5, 10, 15, 20, 25 \text{ and } 30;$$

in the expression S_f-S, the maximum value (on a capital cost of unity) is found to be $0 \cdot 0262$ (i.e., the net present value of a project costing £100 would be understated by £2 12/-) for the values $P = 0 \cdot 25$, $T = 0 \cdot 4$, $r = 0 \cdot 1$, $D = 0 \cdot 15$, $z = 0 \cdot 75$, $n = 5$. In practice these values would constitute typical minima in which case the understatement of net present value is negligible for, as each of the latter (excluding T, the tax rate, which is constant) increases the value of S_f-S decreases.

Thus, where

$$P = 0 \cdot 25, T = 0 \cdot 4, r = 0 \cdot 10, D = 0 \cdot 25, z = 1 \cdot 75 \text{ and } n = 10$$
$$S_f = 0 \cdot 001\ 2$$
$$= £0 \cdot 12, \text{ i.e., 2/5d. on £100 of expenditure.}$$

The last formula will clearly also apply in the case of plant, etc., *qualifying* for a cash grant in a development area. It is only in the numerical computation of the present value of investment incentives where differences arise in which, in the case of a development area, the value of P would be taken at 45% rather than 25% in the case of a plant qualifying outside a development area.

PLANT AND MACHINERY NOT QUALIFYING FOR CASH GRANTS

Under the White Paper published on 17th January,* 1966, plant and machinery which does not qualify for a cash grant is eligible for an initial allowance R at the rate of 30% and annual allowances D, on a reducing balance basis at either 15%, 20% or 25%. The present value S_1 of this series of capital allowances is given by

$$S_1 = \frac{(R+D)CT}{(1+r)^z} + \frac{C[1-(R+D)]DT}{(1+r)^{1+z}} + \frac{C[1-(R+D)](1-D)DT}{(1+r)^{2+z}} + \frac{C[1-(R+D)](1-D)^2DT}{(1+r)^{3+z}} + \cdots$$

which reduces to

$$S_1 = \frac{T}{(1+r)^z}\left[\frac{Rr+D(1+r)}{r+D}\right]$$

where z is the time-lag between the incurring of the eligible expenditure and the tax payments reduced by the first annual allowances; and the present values are calculated on a principal of unity.

INDUSTRIAL BUILDINGS ALLOWANCES

National. The initial allowance R is at the rate of 15% and annual allowances are at the rate of 4% on *a straight-line basis.* The present value S_2 of the initial allowance and the subsequent 21 annual allowances is thus given by:

$$S_2 = \frac{RCT}{(1+r)^z} + \frac{DCT}{(1+r)^z} + \cdots + \frac{DCT}{(1+r)^{z+20}}$$

$$= \frac{RCT}{(1+r)^z} + \frac{DCT}{(1+r)^z}\left[1 + \frac{1-(1+r)^{-20}}{r}\right].$$

* *Investment Incentives*, op. cit.

On unit investment, after further factorising, the above reduces to

$$S_2 = \frac{T}{(1+r)^z}\left\{(R+D)+D\left[\frac{1-(1+r)^{-20}}{r}\right]\right\}$$

where z is again defined as in the two previous formulations.

Development area—new industrial buildings and structures. Subject to the satisfaction of certain conditions new industrial buildings and structures in a development area qualify for a cash grant of either 25% * or 35%,† an initial allowance of 15% and an annual allowance of 4% on a fixed instalment basis. The present value formula for these incentives is

$$S_3 = \frac{P}{(1+r)^k} + \frac{T(1-P)}{(1+r)^z}\left\{(R+D)+D\left[\frac{1-(1+r)^{-20}}{r}\right]\right\}$$

where k and z are again defined as above.

USE OF THE TABLES

The appendix to this chapter contains a series of examples illustrating the use of the tables of present values of investment incentives given in Appendix E.

LOOKING AT THE PRESENT VALUE OF INVESTMENT INCENTIVES IN ISOLATION

Hitherto we have examined the impact of investment incentives on investment projects in conjunction with the impact of taxation on cash-flows. It is often useful to look at the present value of investment incentives in isolation on the grounds that the eligible capital cost of a project may be much more certain and therefore more accurately quantifiable than the stream of future cash-flows. Furthermore the effect of discounting conjoined with the reducing balance method of calculating annual allowances (reinforced by the eligibility of a project for a cash grant or 30% initial allowance as the case may be) is to concentrate the benefits of investment incentives into the early years of a project's life. Consequently, if a company confidently expects to be in a tax-paying position over the three or four years succeeding

* The 25% grant is conditional upon an adequate provision of employment (see *Investment Incentives*, op. cit., p. 19, footnote (2)).

† "The 35% rate of building grant, which is also conditional on employment being provided, will be given to certain new undertakings where the Board of Trade consider that the problems involved justify additional assistance." (*Investment Incentives*, loc. cit., footnote (3)).

the inception of a project, the value of investment incentives is known with some certainty.

The point we are leading up to is that in examining *per se* the capital costs of investment projects, the capital cost to a company in a tax paying position is acquisition cost *less* the present value of investment incentives on the eligible proportion of expenditure. For example a project costing £100 000 all of which is eligible for a 25% cash grant and annual allowances at the rate of 25% would, at a 10% rate of discount and 40% corporation tax rate, qualify for investment incentives having a present value of £100 000 × 0·4210 = £42 100. In other words assuming that a company's weighted average cost of finance is 10%, the net capital cost of such a project is not £100 000 but £57 900. (Here we have taken both k and z as 18 months.)

There can be small doubt that rational decision-makers will always place more emphasis on capital costs, which may be certain irreversible commitments, than the emphasis they attach to a contingent stream of cash-flows. Irreversible commitments are very serious phenomena and the very seriousness (of an investment decision), which multiplies as the size of the commitment increases in absolute terms, is a reason which strongly militates against the decision itself. However, as we have attempted to show, the seriousness of an irreversible commitment is considerably ameliorated once investment incentives have been correctly allowed for; a clear statement of the value of investment incentives *per se* must therefore be regarded as a precondition to the setting of a decision-making climate in which views of the future do not begin out of focus and constitutes a strong psychological reason for examining capital costs net of the present value of investment incentives.*

Having emphasised certain advantages of viewing the present value of investment incentives either in isolation or as a deduction from the gross capital costs of a project, we would stress that this procedure is a separate way of adding to the information available about an investment decision. Lest there be any confusion about the nature of this separate procedure, we would point out that having arrived at capital costs net of investment incentives, the latter should be presented as a separate statement and *not* incorporated into rate of return or present

---

* A further interesting way of viewing the impact of investment incentives is as follows: in the above example the Inland Revenue in effect underwrites 42·1% of a virtually certain capital cost in return for 34·67% of a much-less certain cash-flow, i.e., at a 10% discount rate the effective net of tax factor is 0·6533, giving the Inland Revenue a tax rate of $1 - 0·6533 = 0·3467$.

value calculations which are an additional computation. The matter we are at pains to stress is that to deduct the present value of investment incentives from capital costs and then to calculate a rate of return on such expenditure using the short cut tables would, of course, constitute the double-counting of investment incentives.

APPENDIX TO CHAPTER 3: ILLUSTRATIONS OF THE USES OF APPENDICES A, B AND E FOR SHORT-CUT NET OF CORPORATION TAX DCF PRESENT VALUE AND RATE OF RETURN CALCULATIONS

1. BASIC CALCULATION WHEN (UNTAXED) CASH-FLOWS ARE CONSTANT

(a) *DCF rate of return*

$$C = CWx + ya\left[\frac{1-(1+r)^{-n}}{r}\right]$$

(b) *Net present value (NPV)*

$$NPV = CWx + ya\left[\frac{1-(1+i)^{-n}}{i}\right] - C$$

where: C = total cost of investment project (including working capital) incurred at the end of year 0.

W = proportion of capital expenditure eligible for investment incentives.

x = present value of investment incentives on a principle of unity (tabular value from Appendix E, column 2, 3 or 4).

y = effective net of tax factor (Appendix E, column 5).

a = constant end-year cash-flow.

$\left[\frac{1-(1+r)^{-n}}{r}\right]$ and $\left[\frac{1-(1+i)^{-n}}{i}\right]$ = constant cash-flow discount factors. (Appendix B; r = rate of return, i = cost of finance).

Example

Find the net of corporation tax rate of return *and* net present value at 10% p.a. of the following project.

Capital cost (all qualifying for investment incentives) = £5288; life of project = 6 years; uniform annual (end-year) cash-flow = £1600; cash grant is 25%, annual allowances 15% on a reducing balance basis; cash grant time-lag = 18 months, time-lag between company's year-end and date of tax payments = 9 months; rate of corporation tax = 40%.

Solution

(*a*) The net of corporation tax DCF rate of return can be initially approximated by calculating the gross DCF rate of return, i.e., solve for *r* in the equation

$$£5288 = £1600\left[\frac{1-(1+r)^{-6}}{r}\right]$$

whence

$$3\cdot305 = \frac{1-(1+r)^{-6}}{r}.$$

As the value 3·305 lies between the 20% tabular value of 3·3255 in the year 6 line of Appendix B and the year 6 21% tabular value of 3·2446, the *gross* of corporation tax DCF rate of return is between 20% and 21%.

Trying 20% in seeking the *net* of corporation tax DCF rate of return the calculation is:

$$C \quad\quad C \quad W^* \quad\quad x \quad\quad\quad y \quad\quad\quad\quad a \quad \frac{1-(1+0\cdot2)^{-6}}{0\cdot2}$$

$$£5288 \simeq (£5288 \times 1 \times 0\cdot3247) + (0\cdot6511 \times £1600 \times 3\cdot3255)$$
$$\simeq £5181.$$

The DCF net of corporation tax rate of return is clearly less than 20%. Repeating the calculation at 17% we obtain

$$£5288 \simeq (£5288 \times 1 \times 0\cdot3438) + (0\cdot6444 \times £1600 \times 3\cdot5892)$$
$$\simeq £5519$$

whence the net of corporation tax rate of return can be linearly interpolated thus:

$$\begin{array}{lr} & £ \\ \text{present value at } 17\% &= 5519 \\ \text{present value at } 20\% &= 5181 \\ \hline \text{difference} &= 338 \\ \hline \text{present value at } 17\% &= 5519 \\ \text{capital cost} &= 5288 \\ \hline \text{difference} &= 231 \\ \hline \end{array}$$

$$\therefore \quad r = 17\% + \frac{231}{338} \times 3 = 19\cdot1\% \text{ to one decimal place.}$$

* $W = 1$ in this case because all the capital cost is eligible for investment incentives.

(b) *Net present value at 10%*

$$C \quad W \quad x \quad y \quad a\left[\frac{1-(1+0\cdot1)^{-6}}{0\cdot1}\right] \quad C$$

$$\text{NPV} = (\pounds5288 \times 1 \times 0\cdot4010) + (0\cdot6276 \times \pounds1600 \times 4\cdot3553) - \pounds5288$$
$$= \pounds1206$$

2. BASIC CALCULATION WHEN (UNTAXED) CASH-FLOWS ARE IRREGULAR

(a) *DCF rate of return*

$$C = CWx + y\left[\frac{a_1}{1+r} + \frac{a_2}{(1+r)^2} + \cdots + \frac{a_n}{(1+r)^n}\right]$$

(b) *Net present value (NPV)*

$$\text{NPV} = CWx + y\left[\frac{a_1}{1+i} + \frac{a_2}{(1+i)^2} + \cdots + \frac{a_n}{(1+i)^n}\right] - C$$

where $a_1, a_2, \ldots, a_n$ is the stream of irregular cash-flows; C, W, x, y, r and i are defined as previously.

Example

Find the net of corporation tax net present value at 12% p.a. of the following project and its net of tax rate of return.

Capital cost (70% qualifying for capital allowances) = £3248; life of project = 4 years; cash-flows: end-year 1 = £1000, end-year 2 = £1200, end-year 3 = £1300, end-year 4 = £1600; cash grant of 25%; annual allowances of 20%; corporation tax at 40%; cash grant time-lag = 18 months; annual allowances time-lag = 12 months.

Solution

(a) *Net present value at 12%*

	cash-flows £	discount factors at 12% (Appendix A)	£
	$1000 \times 0\cdot892\ 857 =$		$892\cdot857$
	$1200 \times 0\cdot797\ 194 =$		$956\cdot633$
	$1300 \times 0\cdot711\ 780 =$		$925\cdot314$
	$1600 \times 0\cdot635\ 518 =$		$1016\cdot829$

$$\begin{array}{cccc} C & W & x & y \end{array}$$
$$\text{NPV} = (\pounds3248 \times 0\cdot7 \times 0\cdot3984) + (0\cdot6429 \times$$

$$\pounds3791\cdot633)$$

Minus

C

−£3248

i.e.,

NPV $= (£3248 \times 0.7 \times 0.3984) + (0.6429 \times £3791.63) - £3248.$
$= £3343 - £3248$
$= £95.$

(*b*) *Rate of return*

As the project gives a NPV of £95 when discounted at 12%, the net of corporation tax rate of return is therefore higher.

Trying 14% we obtain:

<table>
<tr><td></td><td>discount
factors</td><td></td></tr>
<tr><td>£</td><td>at 14%</td><td>£</td></tr>
</table>

£3248 ≏ (£3248 × 0·7 × 0·3819) + (0·6491 ×

$1000 \times 0.877\ 193 = 877.193$
$1200 \times 0.769\ 467 = 923.360$
$1300 \times 0.674\ 971 = 877.462$
$1600 \times 0.592\ 080 = 947.328$

£3625·343)

i.e.,

£3248 ≏ (£3248 × 0·7 × 0·3819) + (0·6491 × £3625·34)
≏ £3221.

Using linear interpolation

£

present value at 12% = 3343
present value at 14% = 3221

difference   122

present value at 12% = 3343
capital cost   = 3248

difference   95

∴ $r = 12\% + \dfrac{95}{122} \times 2 = 13.6\%$ to one decimal place.

3. BASIC CALCULATION WHEN THE CAPITAL COST IS A MIXTURE OF EX-
PENDITURE QUALIFYING FOR INVESTMENT INCENTIVES AT DIFFERENT
RATES (CONSTANT CASH-FLOWS)

(a) *DCF rate of return*

$$C = CWx + C(1-W)x_1 + ay\left[\frac{1-(1+r)^{-n}}{r}\right]$$

(b) *Net present value (NPV)*

$$\text{NPV} = CWx + C(1-W)x_1 + ay\left[\frac{1-(1+i)^{-n}}{i}\right] - C$$

where x and x_1 are present values of investment incentives at different
rates.

Example

Find the net of corporation tax net present value at 8% p.a. of the
following project and also its net of tax rate of return.

Capital cost = £12 000; life of project 10 years; uniform end-year
cash-flow = £2000; 60% of capital cost attracts a 25% cash grant
and annual allowances at 25%; 40% of capital cost attracts an
initial allowance of 30% and annual allowances at 15% p.a. on
a reducing balance basis; rate of corporation tax is 40%; the time-
lag between the incurring of capital expenditure and receipt of the
cash grant is 18 months and also between the company's year-end
and date of corporation tax payments.

Solution

(a) *NPV at 8%*

$$
\begin{array}{ccccc}
C & W & x & C & (1-W) & x_1
\end{array}
$$

$$\text{NPV} = (£12\,000 \times 0{\cdot}6 \times 0{\cdot}4414) + (£12\,000 \times 0{\cdot}4 \times 0{\cdot}2882) +$$

$$
\begin{array}{ccc}
 & & \frac{1-(1+0{\cdot}08)^{-10}}{0{\cdot}08} \\
y & a & C
\end{array}
$$

$$(0{\cdot}6436 \times £2000 \times 6{\cdot}7101) - £12\,000$$

$$= £13\,199 - £12\,000$$
$$= £1199.$$

(b) Rate of return

As the project gives a positive net present value when discounted at
8% its rate of return is clearly higher.

Trying 12% * we obtain

$$£12\ 000 \simeq (£12\ 000 \times 0\cdot6 \times 0\cdot4025) + (£12\ 000 \times 0\cdot4 \times 0\cdot2550) +$$
$$(0\cdot6625 \times £2000 \times 5\cdot6502)$$
$$\simeq £11\ 609.$$

Using linear interpolation

$$£$$

present value at $8\% = 13\ 199$
present value at $12\% = 11\ 609$

difference $\qquad 1\ 590$

present value at $8\% = 13\ 199$
capital cost $\qquad = 12\ 000$

difference $\qquad 1\ 199$

$$\therefore \quad r = 8\% + \frac{1199}{1590} \times 4 = 11\cdot0\% \text{ to one decimal place.}$$

4. BASIC CALCULATION WHEN CAPITAL COST IS PHASED OVER A PERIOD
OF YEARS

(In this case constant cash-flows, arising at the end of each of n years
are assumed to commence one year after the completion of the capital
expenditure.)

(a) DCF rate of return

$$C_0 + \frac{C_1}{1+r} + \frac{C_2}{(1+r)^2} + \ldots + \frac{C_g}{(1+r)^g} = C_0 Wx + \frac{C_1 Wx}{1+r} + \frac{C_2 Wx}{(1+r)^2} + \ldots +$$
$$\frac{C_g Wx}{(1+r)^g} + ya \left[\frac{1 - (1+r)^{-n}}{r} \right] \frac{1}{(1+r)^g}.$$

---

* 12% is chosen as the next trial discount factor for the reason that 4% is about
the maximum interest interval which should be used for linear interpolation.

(b) *Net present value (NPV)*

$$\text{NPV} = C_0 Wx + \frac{C_1 Wx}{1+i} + \frac{C_2 Wx}{(1+i)^2} + \ldots + \frac{C_g Wx}{(1+i)^g} +$$

$$ya\left[\frac{1-(1+i)^{-n}}{i}\right]\frac{1}{(1+i)^g} - \left[C_0 + \frac{C_1}{1+i} + \frac{C_2}{(1+i)^2} + \ldots + \frac{C_g}{(1+i)^g}\right]$$

where $C_0, C_1, C_2, \ldots, C_g$ is the succession of capital expenditures phased over g years.

Example

Find the net of corporation tax net present value (at 12%) and rate of return of the following project:

Capital cost phased over three years: end-year 0 £800, end-year 1 £700, end-year 2 £900; all capital costs are eligible for 25% cash grant and 15% annual allowances. The constant annual cash-flow of the project arising end-year 3 to end-year 9 (inclusive) is £953. The time-lag between the incurring of expenditure and the receipt of the cash grant is 18 months, and 21 months between the company's financial year-end and the date of corporation tax payments.

Solution

(a) *Net present value at 12%*

$$
\begin{array}{lllll}
 & C & W & (1+i)^{-n} & £ & x \\
\text{NPV} = & £800 \times 1 & & = 800\cdot00 \\
 & 700 \times 1 \times 0\cdot892\ 857 & = 625\cdot00 \\
 & 900 \times 1 \times 0\cdot797\ 194 & = 717\cdot47 \\
\end{array}
$$

$$2142\cdot47 \times 0\cdot3640 = \quad £780$$

Plus

$$\underset{y}{}\quad\underset{a}{}\quad\frac{1-(1+0\cdot12)^{-7}}{0\cdot12}\quad(1+i)^{-2}$$

$$0\cdot6720 \times £953 \times 4\cdot5638 \times 0\cdot797\ 194 \qquad = £2330$$

$$£3110$$

Minus

$$
\begin{array}{ll}
& £ \\
£800 & = 800{\cdot}00 \\
700 \times 0{\cdot}892\ 857 & = 625{\cdot}00 \\
900 \times 0{\cdot}797\ 194 & = 717{\cdot}47 \qquad\qquad £2142 \\
\end{array}
$$

Net present value at 12% £968

(b) DCF rate of return

This project gives a net of corporation tax DCF rate of return of 25% calculated as below:

capital costs

$$£800 + (£700 \times 0{\cdot}800\ 000) + (£900 \times 0{\cdot}640\ 000) = £1936$$

cash-(in)flows

$$
\begin{array}{llll}
C & W & (1+r)^{-n} & £ \qquad x \\
£800 \times 1 & & & = 800 \\
700 \times 1 & \times 0{\cdot}800\ 000 & = 560 \\
900 \times 1 & \times 0{\cdot}640\ 000 & = 576 \\
\end{array}
$$

$$1936 \times 0{\cdot}2740 = £530$$

Plus

$$
\begin{array}{cccc}
 & & \dfrac{1-(1+r)^{-7}}{r} & \\
y & a & & (1+r)^{-2} \\
0{\cdot}7293 \times £953 & \times 3{\cdot}1611 & \times 0{\cdot}6400 & = £1406 \\
\end{array}
$$

£1936

5. THE EFFECT OF A CHANGE IN THE RATE OF TAX ON THE PROFITABILITY OF INVESTMENT

We complete this appendix by illustrating the fallacious nature of the often heard argument that the ever-present possibility of changes in tax rates makes it impossible for businessmen to plan investment programmes with any degree of confidence. (For this exercise it is obviously necessary to have present values of investment incentives and effective net of tax factors at some tax rate other than 40%. In this appendix and to avoid confusion with Appendix E are therefore included such values for a corporation tax rate of 42·5%.)

The following projects all qualify for a 25% cash grant and 15% annual allowances on total capital expenditure. The time-lag between the incurring of the expenditure and receipt of the cash grant is 18 months; between the company's financial year-end and the date of corporation tax payments there is a time-lag of 9 months.

project	capital cost	life (years)	constant end-year cash-flow
X	£2978	7	£1000
Y	£4147	7	£1000
Z	£6585	7	£1000

With corporation tax at 40%, the rates of return of X, Y and Z are respectively 25%, 15% and 5%, i.e.,

Project X (25%)

$$\begin{matrix} C & C & W & x & y & a & \dfrac{1-(1+0{\cdot}25)^{-7}}{0{\cdot}25} \end{matrix}$$
$$£2978 = (£2978 \times 1 \times 0{\cdot}2978) + (0{\cdot}6616 \times £1000 \times 3{\cdot}1611)$$
$$= £2978.$$

Project Y (15%)

$$\dfrac{1-(1+0{\cdot}15)^{-7}}{0{\cdot}15}$$
$$£4147 = (£4147 \times 1 \times 0{\cdot}3581) + (0{\cdot}6398 \times £1000 \times 4{\cdot}1604)$$
$$= £4147.$$

Project Z (5%)

$$\dfrac{1-(1+0{\cdot}05)^{-7}}{0{\cdot}05}$$
$$£6585 = (£6585 \times 1 \times 0{\cdot}4601) + (0{\cdot}6144 \times £1000 \times 5{\cdot}7864)$$
$$= £6585.$$

With corporation tax at 42·5%, the DCF rates of return are shown to be:

Project X
Try 23%
$$£2978 \simeq (£2978 \times 0{\cdot}3158) + (0{\cdot}6361 \times £1000 \times 3{\cdot}3270)$$
$$\simeq £3057.$$

8

Try 25%

$$£2978 \eqsim (£2978 \times 0 \cdot 3053) + (0 \cdot 6405 \times £1000 \times 3 \cdot 1611)$$
$$\eqsim £2934.$$

Linear interpolation

$$\begin{array}{rl} & £ \\ \text{present value at } 23\% = & 3057 \\ \text{present value at } 25\% = & 2934 \\ \hline \text{difference} & 123 \\ \hline \end{array}$$

$$\begin{array}{rl} \text{present value at } 23\% = & 3057 \\ \text{capital cost} \quad\quad = & 2978 \\ \hline \text{difference} & 79 \\ \hline \end{array}$$

$$\therefore \quad r = 23\% + \frac{79}{123} \times 2 = 24 \cdot 3\% \text{ to one decimal place.}$$

Project Y

Try 15%

$$£4147 \eqsim (£4147 \times 0 \cdot 3678) + (0 \cdot 6173 \times £1000 \times 4 \cdot 1604)$$
$$\eqsim £4093.$$

Try 14%

$$£4147 \eqsim (£4147 \times 0 \cdot 3758) + (0 \cdot 6148 \times £1000 \times 4 \cdot 2883)$$
$$\eqsim £4195.$$

Linear interpolation

$$\begin{array}{rl} & £ \\ \text{present value at } 14\% = & 4195 \\ \text{present value at } 15\% = & 4093 \\ \hline \text{difference} & 102 \\ \hline \end{array}$$

$$\begin{array}{rl} \text{present value at } 14\% = & 4195 \\ \text{capital cost} \quad\quad = & 4147 \\ \hline \text{difference} & 48 \\ \hline \end{array}$$

$$\therefore \quad r = 14\% + \frac{48}{102} \times 1 = 14 \cdot 5\% \text{ to one decimal place.}$$

Project Z

Try 5%

$$£6585 \simeq (£6585 \times 0.4744) + (0.5903 \times £1000 \times 5.7864)$$
$$\simeq £6540.$$

Try 4%

$$£6585 \simeq (£6585 \times 0.4898) + (0.5873 \times £1000 \times 6.0021)$$
$$\simeq £6750$$

Linear interpolation

	£
present value at 4% =	6750
present value at 5% =	6540
difference	210

present value at 4% =	6750
capital cost =	6585
difference	165

$$\therefore \quad r = 4\% + \frac{165}{210} \times 1 = 4.8\% \text{ to one decimal place.}$$

From the foregoing calculations, two main inferences can be drawn:

1. The higher the net of corporation tax rate of return promised by a proposal *before* a change in the rate of corporation tax, the more the net of corporation tax rate of return will be affected by a change in the tax rate and vice versa.

2. A change in the tax rate, to an extent to which we have become accustomed in recent years (e.g., at most 6d in £) when changes in tax rates have been made, will in general have only an insignificant effect upon the profitability of investment. That is to say, projects which are relatively highly profitable will remain so and those which are only marginally profitable before a tax change will be virtually unaffected by it.

One is thus left with the conclusion that the argument that possible changes in tax rates have serious effects upon investment plans is symptomatic of investment appraisal based either upon inaccurate arithmetic or upon computations which ignore taxation and investment incentives or, of an appraisal which merely guesses at the impact of these two determinants without any serious attempt to calculate it.

In all cases where it is felt that changes in tax rates are imminent, the obvious prescription which can be given is that investment computations should be repeated for, at most, two further tax rates which are (say) 6d ($2\frac{1}{2}$%) and 1/- (5%) in the £ higher than the existing rate. As stated, it will generally be found that the effect upon the respective rates of return of an array of investment proposals is such that it cannot be sensibly argued that changes in tax rates substantially disrupt investment plans. Thus, to repeat the point made above, the argument that the possibility of tax changes upsets investment plans is really the argument that inadequate tax analysis disrupts investment plans.

Plant Qualifying for Cash Grants—National

1. Present value, S, of investment incentives on a principal of unity (columns 2, 3 and 4)

$$S = \frac{P}{(1+r)^k} + \frac{(1-P)DT(1+r)}{(1+r)^z(r+D)}.$$

2. Effective net of tax factor, y, (column 5)

$$y = 1 - \frac{T}{(1+r)^z}, \quad \text{i.e., } 1 - T(1+r)^{-z}.$$

P = cash grant; D = annual allowance on a reducing balance basis; T = corporation tax at 42·5%; k = 18 months time-lag between incurring of capital expenditure and receipt of cash grant; z = time-lag between company's financial year-end and date of corporation tax payment; r = rate of discount.

$z = 9$ months, $T = 42.5\%$

(1)	(2)	(3)	(4)	(5)
r	$P = 25\%$ $D = 15\%$	$P = 25\%$ $D = 20\%$	$P = 25\%$ $D = 25\%$	$1 - T(1+r)^{-z}$
1	0·5459	0·5506˙	0·5536	0·5782
2	0·5253	0·5339	0·5393	0·5813
3	0·5068	0·5184	0·5259	0·5843
4	0·4898	0·5040	0·5132	0·5873
5	0·4744	0·4905	0·5012	0·5903
6	0·4601	0·4779	0·4899	0·5932
7	0·4469	0·4660	0·4791	0·5960
8	0·4347	0·4548	0·4689	0·5988
9	0·4232	0·4443	0·4592	0·6016
10	0·4120	0·4343	0·4499	0·6043
11	0·4025	0·4249	0·4410	0·6070
12	0·3931	0·4159	0·4325	0·6096
13	0·3842	0·4073	0·4243	0·6122
14	0·3758	0·3991	0·4165	0·6148
15	0·3678	0·3913	0·4090	0·6173
16	0·3602	0·3839	0·4018	0·6198
17	0·3529	0·3767	0·3949	0·6222
18	0·3460	0·3699	0·3882	0·6246
19	0·3395	0·3633	0·3817	0·6270
20	0·3332	0·3570	0·3755	0·6293
21	0·3271	0·3509	0·3695	0·6316
22	0·3213	0·3450	0·3637	0·6339
23	0·3158	0·3394	0·3581	0·6361
24	0·3104	0·3339	0·3527	0·6383
25	0·3053	0·3287	0·3474	0·6405
26	0·3003	0·3236	0·3423	0·6426
27	0·2955	0·3187	0·3374	0·6447
28	0·2909	0·3139	0·3326	0·6468
29	0·2864	0·3093	0·3279	0·6489
30	0·2821	0·3048	0·3234	0·6509
31	0·2779	0·3005	0·3190	0·6529
32	0·2739	0·2963	0·3147	0·6549
33	0·2700	0·2922	0·3105	0·6568
34	0·2662	0·2882	0·3065	0·6588
35	0·2625	0·2843	0·3025	0·6607
36	0·2589	0·2806	0·2987	0·6625
37	0·2554	0·2769	0·2950	0·6644
38	0·2520	0·2733	0·2913	0·6662
39	0·2487	0·2699	0·2877	0·6680
40	0·2455	0·2665	0·2843	0·6698
41	0·2424	0·2632	0·2809	0·6715
42	0·2393	0·2600	0·2776	0·6733
43	0·2363	0·2569	0·2743	0·6750
44	0·2334	0·2538	0·2712	0·6767
45	0·2306	0·2508	0·2681	0·6784
46	0·2279	0·2479	0·2651	0·6800
47	0·2252	0·2450	0·2621	0·6817
48	0·2226	0·2423	0·2593	0·6833
49	0·2200	0·2395	0·2564	0·6849
50	0·2175	0·2369	0·2537	0·6864

Chapter 4

THE CALCULATION OF CUT-OFF RATES IN CAPITAL BUDGETING

EXTERNAL EQUITY FINANCE

In the previous chapter we illustrated the use of short-cut methods of calculating the DCF rates of return on, or DCF net present value of, investment. As already stated such rates of return or net present values are net of corporation tax relieved as appropriate by investment incentives. The corporation tax does not of itself constitute the whole burden of taxation on investment in the company sector of the economy; on the payment of a dividend a company must now deduct and remit standard rate income tax to the tax collectors. Furthermore, capital gains realised on the selling of shares result in a capital gains tax assessment on the seller.

These three taxes on private investment have a direct impact on the prospective net returns which companies should seek on equity financed capital investment projects. The purpose of this chapter is to outline the factors which determine the cut-off rate with which a company's net of corporation tax return on investment should be compared.

From a computational standpoint it is convenient to calculate net of corporation tax returns to a company, as we have done in Chapter 3, because under the new system of taxation, the investment inducements (other than cash grants to which this point has no relevance) can be set against corporation tax *only*. Hence an equity cut-off rate needs to embody an allowance for income tax and capital gains tax.

THE COST OF FINANCE

Before we can formulate a model for the calculation of equity cut-off rates it is first necessary to return to the definition of the cost of finance in general. It is convenient to begin by considering the cost of fixed interest finance say, preference shares and debentures. Furthermore, it is only when fixed interest finance is introduced into the general

schema that the objects of capital budgeting in a tax environment begin
to emerge with some degree of clarity.

FIXED INTEREST FINANCE

The cost of an issue of redeemable debentures *to a company* is given
by the value of i_c in the equation

$$A(1-b) = a(1-T)\left[\frac{1-(1+i_c)^{-n}}{i_c}\right] + \frac{R}{(1+i_c)^n}$$

where A = the market price of the issue which may be at a discount,
        at par or a premium.

a = annual interest payment to debenture holders (assumed
      in this case to be made end-year).

T = rate of corporation tax: the annual interest payment is
      thus reduced because the latter is (corporation) tax
      deductible.

n = number of years the debenture is in issue.

b = issue expenses.

R = the redemption price which may be at a discount, at par
      or at a premium.

The rate of return to an individual investor on the above debenture
is the value of i_s which satisfies the equation

$$A = a(1-d)\left[\frac{1-(1+i_s)^{-n}}{i_s}\right] + \frac{R}{(1+i_s)^n}$$

where d = debentureholder's tax rate on investment income.

If A is a par price and R is a redemption price at a premium there
would however be a tax on the premium at the investor's capital gains
tax rate, t.   Hence the terminal receipt of the debentureholder would be

$$\frac{R-t(R-A)}{(1+i_s)^n} \quad \text{and not} \quad \frac{R}{(1+i_s)^n}$$

Individual members of the investing public must be assumed to be
primarily interested in net of tax returns on fixed interest investment
because such returns constitute the increase, or potential increase, in
the purchasing power from which consumption or personal investment
may be increased.   Thus, although the cost of debenture finance to
a *company* is i_c (as above), the values of A, a and R need to be set by

a company in relation to i_s which, however, in terms of the market structure of interest rates, e.g., quoted redemption yields, may be stated *gross* of personal taxes, i.e., as $i_s/(1-d)$.

Illustration

On a particular class of fixed interest (corporation tax deductible) stock the market *gross* redemption yield is 7·25%. To give such a rate of return to investors a company floats a debenture issued at par and redeemable at par (20 years later) bearing a nominal rate of 7·25%.

Assume

       1. issue costs amounting to say 5%,
       2. corporation tax at 40%,
       3. personal taxes at 41·25%.

The net of tax cost to the company is the value of i_c in the equation:

$$100(1-0\cdot05) = 7\cdot25(1-0\cdot4)\left[\frac{1-(1+i_c)^{-20}}{i_c}\right]+\frac{100}{(1+i_c)^{20}}$$

whence $i_c = 4\cdot75\%$.

The net of tax rate of return to investors (assuming they pay standard rate income tax) is the value of i_s satisfying the equation:

$$100 = 7\cdot25(1-0\cdot4125)\left[\frac{1-(1+i_s)^{-20}}{i_s}\right]+\frac{100}{(1+i_s)^{20}}$$

whence $i_s = 4\cdot26\%$.

The substance of the foregoing paragraph is that a company should work back from i_s in setting the values of A, a and R; in practice this is unnecessary because of the convention of quoting redemption yields gross of personal taxes.   Hence a company can in practice begin with gross yields in fixing issue price, annual (gross) interest and redemption price.   Once these values are fixed at a level assumed to be the minimum inducement to the investing public, the net cost of finance to the company is then the value of i_c as defined previously.

It follows from the foregoing discussion that the rate of return to an investor is obtained from a stream of receipts which, in the case of fixed interest securities, include a succession of interest payments and a terminal receipt if and when the security is redeemed, or when the security holder sells out.   The higher is the terminal receipt in relation to any given stream of receipts, the higher will be the rate of return and vice versa.

PREFERENCE SHARES

It is perhaps unnecessary to discuss preference shares separately in depth; the general principles outlined above applicable in the analysis of the cost of debenture finance to a company are of similar relevance to the preference share. One fact should, however, be strongly emphasised: whilst the gross yield on preference stock necessary to induce investment by the market may be only marginally higher than the gross yield which would induce investment in debentures, the new system of corporation tax discriminates heavily against preference share finance from the standpoint of a company (and hence its equity shareholders).

Unlike debenture interest, preference dividends are *not* tax deductible for corporation tax purposes. Consequently if a company determines that gross yields of (say) 7% and 8% would induce investment in debentures and preference shares respectively, the net of tax costs to the company would, ignoring issue costs, be

$$\text{debentures } 7\% \, (1 - 0.40) = 4.2\%,$$
$$\text{preference shares} \qquad = 8.0\%.$$

Hence a company which chooses 8% preference share finance to undertake a project promising a net of corporation tax (and investment incentives) return of (say) 14% when it could have used 7% debentures explicitly elects to leave a net margin of $14\% - 8\% = 6\%$ for its *equity* shareholders when in fact it could have given $14\% - 4.2\% = 9.8\%$.

From a capital budgeting standpoint the inference to be drawn is that, providing the other conditions attaching to a debenture *vis-à-vis* preference shares are not severely restrictive in the sense that they expose a company to risks which, when quantified and loaded on to the net of corporation tax cost of debentures, would equate the latter with the gross yield on preference shares, a company should now always prefer debentures (or some equivalent long term debt form) to preference share finance. Because of this tax discrimination against preference shares it is reasonable to speculate that, in the absence of appropriate amendments to the 1965 Finance Act, the future will see the demise of the preference share as an instrument of finance.

This impression seems to be supported by events succeeding the Chancellor's statement on 8th December, 1964. Relatively speaking debenture issues have flooded the capital market since that date whilst preference shares have been conspicuous by their absence.* This situation is not entirely explained by the tax discrimination against preference shares. Excluding issue costs, the cost of a 7% debenture to a company has risen from

$$7\% (1 - 0.5375) = 3.24\% \text{ (old regime)}$$
to $\quad 7\% (1 - 0.4) \quad = 4.20\% \text{ (new regime)}.$

As we argue later the cost of equity finance has risen from something like 9% to typically about 12·5%. A rise of about 3·5% (equity) compared with a rise of about 1% (debt), must clearly increase the relative attractiveness of debentures *vis-à-vis* further equity finance. Hence we may not only be witnessing the demise of the preference share but, as hinted in Chapter 1, also the adjustment of capital gear ratios to levels more closely approximating optima.

Tax discrimination causing the disappearance of preference shares is cause for alarm for a number of reasons of which we mention one in the present context. Given parity of tax treatment, preference share finance must necessarily be more attractive to a company than a debenture issue simply because the latter is debt, a word which frequently breeds an illogical aversion notwithstanding that a company may have an almost impregnable financial structure. Typically such an aversion would not characterise a company's view of the expediency of preference share financing in which case such shares would provide a means of introducing leverage with a resultant fall in the weighted average cost of finance and hence a potentially higher profitable level of investment within a company. The discriminatory tax treatment of preference dividends thus conflicts with one of the major objectives of economic policy in the U.K.: the encouragement of a higher level of investment.

THE COST OF EXTERNAL EQUITY FINANCE

Whereas the measurement of the cost of fixed interest finance to a company is largely a question of contractual agreement resulting in

---

* Tax discrimination in the manner described above has led to the virtual disappearance of the preference share in the U.S.A.

a succession of interest payments and (possible) redemption on pre-determined conditions, the case of equity capital is much less straight-forward. Before an attempt to measure the cost of equity finance can be made it must first be defined. Here an analogy with the cost of fixed interest finance can be drawn. We made the point earlier that the cost of fixed interest finance is the minimum net of (personal) taxes return i_s, which will induce investment. Such a return a company in effect " grosses up " to arrive at the " gross yield " which must be paid and which is tax deductible for corporation tax purposes. We then stated that the return to an investor is obtained through the stream of interest receipts and a terminal receipt obtained on redemp-tion or on realisation.

Similarly, the cost of external equity finance can be defined as the minimum rate of return (net of all taxes) to shareholders which will induce equity investment. Furthermore, just as the owner of a fixed interest security obtains his net of tax return from a stream of future interest payments and terminal receipt on sale or redemption, an equity shareholder obtains his net of taxes return from a stream of future dividends and terminal receipt on ultimate sale. Hence the cost of external equity finance is exactly analogous to the cost of fixed interest finance; the former may be defined in symbolic terms as the value of r_e which satisfies the following equation

$$B = \frac{a_1}{1+r_e} + \frac{a_2}{(1+r_e)^2} + \ldots + \frac{a_n}{(1+r_e)^n} + \frac{D}{(1+r_e)^n}$$

where B is the purchase price of the share, $a_1, a_2, \ldots, a_n$ is the antici-pated stream of dividends net of personal taxes and D is the antici-pated selling price obtainable on realisation n years hence, net of capital gains taxes. As just stated and worth emphasising, the anticipated rate of return to the shareholder resides in two basic com-ponents: the anticipated stream of dividends; and the anticipated terminal receipt obtained on realisation. Any share value appreciation (or depreciation) will clearly be embodied in D and thus enters the rate of return accordingly.

In that the cost of external equity finance resides in the stream of dividends and share value appreciation (depreciation), the former could clearly be defined as the prospective stream of future dividends or share value appreciation (depreciation) which a company needs to hold out in order to induce equity investment. Such a statement perhaps elucidates the concept of the cost of external equity finance but of itself offers little guide as to its measurement for the purposes of decision-taking in capital budgeting. In seeking to quantify the cost of external equity finance it is necessary to relate concept to numerical values obtained elsewhere; before attempting this exercise it is however convenient to introduce the impact of the new system of taxation upon the cost of external equity finance.

THE IMPACT OF THE NEW SYSTEM OF TAXATION

Assume that under the new system of taxation a company is earning constant annual assessable profits (net of deductions for capital allowances) of £1000 and that such a sum corresponds to its accounting profits after allowing for depreciation sufficient to maintain capital intact.* Assuming corporation tax at the rate of 40% and a *full* distribution of profit, the net of tax dividend in the hands of shareholders amounts to £352·5 as shown:

	£	
assessable profits	1000·0	
corporation tax (40%)	400·0	
	600·0	i_e
income tax (41·25%)	247·5	
dividend (net)	£352·5	r_e.

Assume further that the company's dividend policy amounting to a 100% pay-out stabilises the value of its shares, i.e., results in a constant dividend yield.† Thus, if the annual net dividend to shareholders amounting to £352·5 represents a return of r_e then, to give shareholders such a return, the company clearly requires to earn a return of i_e given by:

$$i_e = \frac{r_e}{1 - 0\cdot4125}.$$

* This assumption will generally not hold but is not basic to the argument about to be adduced.

† This is also an assumption which will generally not hold in reality but again it is not vital in the present context in which we are primarily concerned to present the important factors in the problem in a manner conducive to systematic analysis. We deal with the behaviour of share values as a separate issue later, see pp. 135–38.

For example, if a company can earn 10% net of corporation tax under these assumptions, shareholders receive $10(1-0.4125) = 5.875\%$. This calculation can in fact be presented in DCF form as follows: assume that a shareholder buys for £1000, that the company earns 10% net of corporation tax all of which is distributed, and that share values remain constant. A shareholder investing for 5 years would obtain a return equal to the value of r_e in the equation

$$1000 = 100(1-0.4125)\left[\frac{1-(1+r_e)^{-5}}{r_e}\right] + \frac{1000}{(1+r_e)^5}$$

whence $r_e = 5.875\%$.

Whatever the holding period it can be shown that if the dividend and the share value remain constant, then r_e must also be constant.* In presenting the net of tax return r_e to the shareholder as a DCF calculation we obtain a useful starting point in determining the net of corporation tax rate of return, i_e, which a company needs to earn in order to give shareholders a given net of all taxes rate of return r_e, in the case of companies distributing less than 100% of profits and when share values *do not* remain constant. In introducing a company's pay-out ratio into the analysis we have however imported a further factor which requires some preliminary discussion.

The assumption that a company ploughs back some proportion of its profits raises the presumption that these reinvested earnings will

* For example, if the holding period is 10 years the calculation is

$$1000 = 100(1-0.4125)\left[\frac{1-(1+r_e)^{-10}}{r_e}\right] + \frac{1000}{(1+r_e)^{10}}$$

whence $r_e = 5.875\%$.

A rigorous proof that the above rate of return r_e is independent of the holding period, n years, is as follows:

$$P = a\left[\frac{1-(1+r_e)^{-n}}{r_e}\right] + \frac{P}{(1+r_e)^n}$$

$$= a\left[\frac{1}{r_e} - \frac{(1+r_e)^{-n}}{r_e}\right] + \frac{P}{(1+r_e)^n}$$

$$= \frac{a}{r_e}\left[1 - \frac{1}{(1+r_e)^n}\right] + \frac{P}{(1+r_e)^n}$$

$$P\left[1 - \frac{1}{(1+r_e)^n}\right] = \frac{a}{r_e}\left[1 - \frac{1}{(1+r_e)^n}\right]$$

$$\therefore \quad P = \frac{a}{r_e} \quad \text{whence} \quad r_e = \frac{a}{P}$$

themselves cause a growth in future company earnings. Indeed we have already argued in Chapter 1 that a company should not retain shareholders' profits to finance investment unless the latter promises at least the return which shareholders could themselves obtain by reinvesting elsewhere. As we have said, this is the economist's so-called opportunity cost rule applied in the context of company finance. Another way of looking at this is to state that retained earnings have a market price to the extent that they can be invested elsewhere at *some* rate of return. In that retained earnings are the ultimate property of equity shareholders the appropriate rate of return for measuring the opportunity cost is the return on similar equity investment.

Under the corporation tax regime a company can escape taxation on inter-company investment if the returns on such investments are distributed to its own shareholders. Hence company X which reinvests its profits in another can obtain a higher rate of return on such (external) reinvestment than could company X's shareholders because a distribution to X's shareholders to provide the latter with the opportunity to reinvest elsewhere would immediately give rise to a leakage of income tax leaving a reduced sum available for reinvestment. These points are best illustrated numerically (see Illustration 12).

Illustration 12

Company X and its shareholders both have the opportunity to invest funds in other companies elsewhere which are earning 15% p.a. net of corporation tax. (Like the company in the previous example these companies are assumed to have constant share values and distribute all profits.) Company X has £1000 of retained earnings and wishes to determine whether external reinvestment by itself is more advantageous than a distribution to shareholders followed by reinvestment by the latter. It is assumed that the ultimate 15% return on investment would be paid to company X's shareholders in full via a dividend distribution.

(i) If company X reinvests externally, a return of £150 p.a. will be received by company X. This return would suffer income tax at source which can however be offset by company X to the extent that the return is passed on to X's shareholders, i.e., income tax is only deducted once. The shareholders of company X therefore receive a net return of $15(1 - 0.4125) = 8.8125\%$ p.a.

(ii) If company X initially distributes £1000 to its shareholders there is an immediate tax leakage at the rate of 41·25% leaving £587·5 for reinvestment on which, on a full distribution of profit in companies elsewhere, shareholders would receive a net return of £587·5 × 0·15 $(1 - 0·4125) = £51·773$ i.e., a net return on the original £1000 of 5·177% p.a.

The inference which should be drawn from the foregoing illustration is that because a company can always obtain a higher net of all taxes rate of return for its shareholders by investing elsewhere than can the shareholders themselves, the opportunity cost of profits which are retained should be measured accordingly.* Thus, if a company

---

* (Readers may find it useful to omit this footnote until they have first read the remainder of Chapter 4.)   Support for the view expressed below is to be found in Ezra Solomon, *The Theory of Financial Management* (Columbia University Press, 1963), p. 54.

The assertion in the context amounts to our endorsement of the second of the two schools of thought outlined in Chapter 1, pp. 6 to 8.   Although we now anticipate some of the later argument of Chapter 4 it is probably useful at this juncture to state and attempt to justify in unambiguous terms our prescription for measuring the cost of retained earnings.

Our view is that the opportunity cost of retained earnings ought to be measured by the equity return obtainable *by a company* which, in turn, reflects the net of corporation tax equity cut-off rates fixed by other companies.   Our justification for this viewpoint resides in two simple arguments; the one relates to the interests of the shareholders of a particular company whilst the other is concerned with the wider interests of the community at large of which the shareholders of a particular company are a part.

First, we would argue that a company ought to use its corporate status to obtain the best available returns for its equity shareholders; we argued in Chapter 1 that this objective must be regarded as the *raison d'être* of a limited company.   Hence, if a company has exhausted all internal investment projects promising " external " equity returns but still possesses retained earnings over and above the requirements of " established dividend policy " and, at the same time, other companies are seeking external equity finance, the first company can always find external uses of funds at a prospective external equity return.

The second argument is that if other companies are continuously seeking external equity funds the presumption is raised that the economy is confronted with a continuous array of projects promising at least external equity returns.   The mobilisation and direction of " surplus " retained earnings into other companies with such (higher) investment opportunities is therefore justifiable on national economic grounds and should be looked upon as part of the process of optimal resource allocation.

A counter-argument which can be raised is that *as a matter of policy* the directorate of a company may have no wish to invest externally in which case the alternative uses of retained earnings are either internal reinvestment or a distribution to shareholders in which event a management could justify the measurement of the opportunity cost of retentions in terms of the returns *available to shareholders themselves*

desires to give its shareholders 8% net of all taxes on *external* equity finance and needs, at a plough-back ratio of 50% and rate of share turnover of 1/7, to set a cut-off rate (net of corporation tax) of 11·25% in order to provide 8% then, on earnings reinvested by the company (either internally or externally), the company should set a cut-off rate, net of corporation tax, also of 11·25%.*

Having set forth the above rule for the measurement of the cost of retained earnings we can now return to the formulation of the cut-off rate i_e (net of corporation tax) which a company distributing less than 100% of its profits needs to set. As stated: a company ploughing back and reinvesting some proportion of its profits at an opportunity cost rate of return will effect a continuous growth in its earnings.†

Following the argument adduced above, we now define the cut-off rate i_e which a company needs to set to give its equity shareholders some net of all taxes rate of return r_e, also as the return which the

---

(after allowing for the tax leakage on a dividend distribution as explained on pp. 116–17).

The first observation which can be made on this argument is that it is obviously invalidated by companies which are accustomed to investing surplus funds in low-yielding fixed interest securities. But even if this is not the case our view is that generally speaking, company directorates do not have a mandate to pursue policies which result in sub-optimal returns for shareholders, and if such is the policy they feel justified in pursuing they should first inform shareholders of the likely consequences to the latter in financial terms. Similarly, if a directorate feels that it is exceeding the power of its mandate in undertaking external equity investment shareholders can again be consulted.

Having argued the principles underlying the measurement of the opportunity cost of retentions and reached the conclusion that directorates should, as a matter of policy, undertake external equity investment where necessary, one further observation concerning the probable magnitude and frequency of this (external investment) problem is perhaps pertinent lest it be viewed in entirely the wrong perspective.

It should by no means be inferred that some companies are continuously confronted with chronic or persistent " surplus retentions " situations, or that even if they were, the only solution would reside in continuous external equity investment. If a company does find itself with a persistent surplus of retentions the obvious corrective would be to lift " established dividend policy " to a new level. Surplus retentions must therefore be regarded only as a temporary phenomenon, the external investment of which, in compliance with the correct opportunity cost rule, can by no means be regarded as a policy leading to the transformation of manufacturing and trading companies into investment trusts.   * See Appendix F.

† This assertion is ostensibly not borne out by the available empirical evidence. See, for example, I. D. M. Little, " Higgledy Piggledy Growth ", *Oxford Bulletin of Statistics*, November 1962, who finds no correlation between retained earnings and earnings growth. The result may, of course, only be symptomatic of the fact that companies depart from the opportunity cost rule (with respect to investment), the satisfaction of which is one of the basic conditions of the model formulated here.

company must seek either internally or externally on retained earnings. Consequently if a company ploughs back profits in the proportion p and is satisfying the opportunity cost rule outlined above, the profits ploughed back must thereafter earn a rate of return (net of corporation tax) of $i_e\%$ p.a. Furthermore, if the proportion of profits ploughed back is assumed to be held constant at p, then the company's pay-out ratio is by definition held constant at $(1-p)$. Hence if we postulate a situation in which a company commences with equity finance of unity on which, and on profits ploughed back, it earns an opportunity cost rate of return (net of corporation tax) i_e then with a constant plough back ratio p, and a dividend tax at the rate d the following results emerge (Illustration 13):

Illustration 13

	finance deployed (1)	earnings (net of corpn. tax) (2)	plough-back (3)	dividends (4)
end-year 0	1	—	—	—
end-year 1	$1+pi_e$	i_e	pi_e	$i_e(1-p)(1-d)$
end-year 2	$(1+pi_e)^2$	$i_e(1+pi_e)$	$pi_e(1+pi_e)$	$i_e(1+pi_e)(1-p)(1-d)$
end-year 3	$(1+pi_e)^3$	$i_e(1+pi_e)^2$	$pi_e(1+pi_e)^2$	$i_e(1+pi_e)^2(1-p)(1-d)$
....				
end-year n	$(1+pi_e)^n$	$i_e(1+pi_e)^{n-1}$	$pi_e(1+pi_e)^{n-1}$	$i_e(1+pi_e)^{n-1}(1-p)(1-d)$
....				

Note to Illustration 13

An example of the manner in which these results have been derived is as follows: At the end of year 1, the finance deployed in the company is as shown, $1+pi_e$, by the end of year 2, this finance will have generated earnings of $i(1+pi_e)$. The constant proportion p of earnings is ploughed back; hence, at the end of year 2 the company ploughs back $pi_e(1+pi_e)$.

Thus, by the end of year 2 the finance deployed in the company is end-year 1 finance plus end-year 2 plough-back, i.e., $(1+pi_e)+pi_e(1+pi_e) = (1+pi_e)(1+pi_e)$, i.e., $(1+pi_e)^2$. Similarly, end-year 3 finance deployed is $(1+pi_e)^2+pi_e(1+pi_e)^2 = (1+pi_e)^2(1+pi_e)$, i.e., $(1+pi_e)^3$, etc.

In any given year the dividend net of the dividend tax is determined simply by multiplying that year's earnings by the pay-out ratio $(1-p)$ and then the net of tax factor $(1-d)$, e.g., in year 3.

$$\text{earnings} \times \text{pay-out ratio} \times \text{net of tax factor}$$
$$i_e(1+pi_e)^2 \quad (1-p) \quad (1-d)$$

Excluding the terminal receipt to shareholders when holdings are realised, the net of taxes return to a shareholder realising after n years

9

is the value of r_e in the equation:

$$1 = \frac{i_e(1-p)(1-d)}{1+r_e} + \frac{i_e(1+pi_e)(1-p)(1-d)}{(1+r_e)^2} +$$

$$\frac{i_e(1+pi_e)^2(1-p)(1-d)}{(1+r_e)^3} + \cdots + \frac{i_e(1+pi_e)^{n-1}(1-p)(1-d)}{(1+r_e)^n}. \quad (1)$$

However, as implied, on realisation after n years a shareholder will obtain a terminal receipt which must now be brought into account. A further assumption about the behaviour of share values is thus required. Assuming that the stream of dividends results in a constant dividend yield, i.e., maintains a constant ratio between dividends and share values, the value of the company's shares if they originally stood at par must, after n years, have a value of $(1+pi_e)^n$.* (We discuss the implications of this assumption under the separate sub-heading " The Share Value Appreciation Assumption ".†)

On realisation after n years a capital gains tax on a realised capital gain of $[(1+pi_e)^n-1]$ will be assessed; if such tax is at the rate t the net terminal receipt to the shareholder is thus $(1+pi_e)^n-t[(1+pi_e)^n-1]$ and his net of all taxes rate of return is the value of r_e in the equation:

$$1 = \frac{i_e(1-p)(1-d)}{1+r_e} + \frac{i_e(1+pi_e)(1-p)(1-d)}{(1+r_e)^2} + \frac{i_e(1+pi_e)^2(1-p)(1-d)}{(1+r_e)^3} +$$

$$\cdots + \frac{i_e(1+pi_e)^{n-1}(1-p)(1-d)}{(1+r_e)^n} + \frac{(1+pi_e)^n-t[(1+pi_e)^n-1]}{(1+r_e)^n}. \quad (2)$$

The return r_e defined by equation (2) is the return obtained by a *single* shareholder over a holding period of n years. Equation (2) is not however a complete formulation for the reasons explained below, although, incidentally, it gives numerical results almost identical with those derived from equation (3) which we now formulate as a complete cut-off rate model.

The life of a company does not terminate after n years but must be regarded as continuing in perpetuity; the equity proprietorship thus

* End-year 1 dividend yield is given by $\dfrac{i_e(1-p)(1-d)}{1}$; end year n dividend is given by $i_e(1+pi_e)^{n-1}(1-p)(1-d)$ which is end-year 1 dividend multiplied by $(1+pi_e)^{n-1}$. If the dividend yields of end-year 1 and end-year n are equal, the denominator of the yield-calculation at end-year n must also be multiplied by $(1+pi_e)^{n-1}$. Hence the value of the shares under the constant dividend yield assumption is $(1+pi_e)^{n-1}$ at end-year $n-1$ and $(1+pi_e)^n$ at end-year n.

† See pp. 135–38.

constitutes a succession of shareholdings each for a period of n years. But when a shareholder sells out and is replaced by another the value of the company's shares enters the perpetual receipt stream twice; once as a receipt and again as an outlay by the buyer. The terminal receipt to the seller is:

$$+(1+pi_e)^n - t[(1+pi_e)^n - 1]$$

whilst the buyer pays:

$$-(1+pi_e)^n.$$

Consequently on a sale after n years the value of the shares cancels out leaving only the capital gains tax leakage of:

$$-t[(1+pi_e)^n - 1].$$

For greater realism it can be assumed that whilst on average shares are turned over every n years the proportion $1/n$ is sold every year, i.e., if 7 years is the average rate of share turnover it is more realistic to assume that $1/7$ of the shares is sold every year. Under this second assumption there will be a capital gains tax leakage every year when the proportion $1/n$ is realised. (This series of capital gains taxes taken up to infinity is derived in Illustration 14.) Accordingly, the equity cut-off rate i_e which a company needs to set in order to give r_e to a succession of shareholders in perpetuity is calculated from a perpetual stream of dividends *minus* a perpetual series of capital gains taxes.

Illustration 14

	(1) value of shares realised	(2) capital gains taxes *
end-year 1	$\dfrac{1(1+pi_e)}{n}$	$\dfrac{-t[(1+pi_e)-1]}{n}$
end-year 2	$\dfrac{1(1+pi_e)^2}{n}$	$\dfrac{-t[(1+pi_e)^2-1]}{n}$
end-year 3	$\dfrac{1(1+pi_e)^3}{n}$	$\dfrac{-t[(1+pi_e)^3-1]}{n}$
end-year n	$\dfrac{1(1+pi_e)^n}{n}$	$\dfrac{-t[(1+pi_e)^n-1]}{n}$
end-year $n+1$	$\dfrac{1(1+pi_e)^{n+1}}{n}$	$\dfrac{-t[(1+pi_e)^{n+1}-(1+pi_e)]}{n}$
end-year $n+2$	$\dfrac{1(1+pi_e)^{n+2}}{n}$	$\dfrac{-t[(1+pi_e)^{n+2}-(1+pi_e)^2]}{n}$

* It might be objected that the rate of capital gains tax in the first year would be paid at the standard rate of income tax and therefore exceed the rate ruling in subsequent years. Shareholders desiring to realise after one year would simply

If we now collate the perpetual stream of dividends in Illustration 13, column 4, with the perpetual stream of capital gains taxes in Illustration 14, column 2, factorising the former by $i_e(1-p)(1-d)$ and the latter by t/n, the net of all taxes rate of return, r_e, to shareholders in perpetuity is defined in equation (3).

$$
\begin{aligned}
1 = {} & i_e(1-p)(1-d)\left[\frac{1}{1+r_e}+\frac{1+pi_e}{(1+r_e)^2}+\frac{(1+pi_e)^2}{(1+r_e)^3}+\frac{(1+pi_e)^3}{(1+r_e)^4}+\cdots\right]- \\
& \frac{t}{n}\left[\frac{(1+pi_e)-1}{1+r_e}+\frac{(1+pi_e)^2-1}{(1+r_e)^2}+\frac{(1+pi_e)^3-1}{(1+r_e)^3}+\cdots+\frac{(1+pi_e)^n-1}{(1+r_e)^n}+\right. \\
& \frac{(1+pi_e)^{n+1}-(1+pi_e)}{(1+r_e)^{n+1}}+\frac{(1+pi_e)^{n+2}-(1+pi_e)^2}{(1+r_e)^{n+2}}+ \\
& \left.\frac{(1+pi_e)^{n+3}-(1+pi_e)^3}{(1+r_e)^{n+3}}+\cdots\right]
\end{aligned}
\tag{3}
$$

which simplifies to :*

$$
1 = \frac{i_e(1-p)(1-d)}{r_e-pi_e}-\frac{t}{n}\left\{\frac{[(1+r_e)^n-1]pi_e}{r_e(1+r_e)^{n-1}(r_e-pi_e)}\right\}^{\dagger}
\tag{4}
$$

Example

To give numerical illustration of the use of equation (4) assume for the moment that:

(*a*) a company wishes to give its equity shareholders a rate of return, r_e of 10% p.a. net of all taxes;
(*b*) the plough-back ratio is $p = 50\%$;
(*c*) on average shareholders turn over 1/7 of their shares every year;
(*d*) on average shareholders pay a dividend tax, d, of 41·25% and that in consequence they suffer tax at the rate $t = 20\cdot625\%$ on realised capital gains.

---

need to hold their shares one day longer to avoid capital gains taxes at income tax rates. Thus for analytical purpose the first year's capital gains tax can be taken at 0·206 25 as in later years.

  * The full derivation of equation (4) is shown in the appendix to this chapter.

  † A comprehensive series of numerical values derived from equation (4) is given in Appendix F covering the range $n = 2$ to $n = 12$ (inclusive); tabular values for $n = 20$ and $n = 30$ are also included to illustrate the small degree to which the cut-off rate i_e is sensitive to changes in the value of n.

  Figs. 12–16 included in Appendix F are a diagrammatic method of presenting equity cut-off rates which may facilitate quicker interpretation and usage.

The dependent variable in the calculation is therefore the net of corporation tax equity cut-off rate for capital budgeting purposes which has a value of 13·99% as is confirmed by solving for i_e in

$$1 = \frac{i_e(1-0·5)(1-0·4125)}{0·10-0·5i_e} - \frac{0·20625}{7}\left\{\frac{[(1+0·1)^7-1]0·5i_e}{0·1(1+0·1)^6(0·1-0·5i_e)}\right\}.$$

Although it can be put to other restrictive uses, equation (4) should be regarded primarily as the formula from which a company derives its net of corporation tax equity cut-off rate i_e for capital budgeting.

DETERMINING NUMERICAL VALUES FOR THE CUT-OFF RATE FORMULATION

Before equation (4) can be put to work as a practical bench-mark for equity cut-off rates numerical values need to be ascribed to the variables p, r_e and n as shown in the previous example; for most practical purposes the respective tax rates d and t can be regarded as constants. The purpose of the ensuing sections is therefore to consider r_e, p and n in some detail and to examine the implications of the share value appreciation assumption. As elaborated later, we lay particular emphasis on the fact that a company's pay-out ratio should be treated as a variable determined externally to our formulation by a separate managerial decision.

THE NET OF ALL TAXES RETURN r_e TO EQUITY SHAREHOLDERS

Whilst the above formulation leads to the determination of the gross cut-off rates, i_e, for some given net of all taxes rate of return to shareholders r_e, it does not of course indicate the value of r_e with which the calculation should begin. The following observations on the net of taxes return which will induce equity investment are perhaps pertinent.

First, it seems intuitively obvious that the structure of equity returns (where return is defined in the sense used hitherto and not in terms of dividend and earnings yields commonly quoted in the financial press) must, assuming rational investor behaviour, always attain a long-run equilibrium level above the general level of fixed interest rates. This assertion rests largely upon arguments adduced in Chapter 1; thus companies which split their total income, into an amount paid preferentially to service fixed interest finance and an amount paid residually to equity shareholders, produce two income streams of inherently different risk. The degree of risk inherent in a stream of income is clearly the main determinant of the rate of return such an income needs to provide. Hence, in the same company, and in general, residual (equity) finance will earn a higher return.

The general level of fixed interest rates clearly sets the absolute lower limit to the cost of equity finance. That is to say, if a company finds it necessary to offer a gross rate of return on fixed interest finance of 7·5% in monetary terms, i.e., a net of tax return of $7·5(1-0·4125) = 4·406\%$ to fixed interest security holders, it is reasonable to suppose that *in the same company* equity shareholders would expect a net of all taxes return of at least 6·5 to 7·5% in monetary terms.

A second approach which might be tried in initially approximating the net of all taxes rate of return anticipated to induce investment in equity finance is an appeal to the available evidence on the historical rate of return on equity investment. The relevant major U.K. study * reveals that investors would have received a return in *real terms* of 5·8% p.a. net of taxes over the 44 years ended 1963. [The elements embodied in this return are net of tax dividends and capital appreciation, i.e., a rate of return calculated on a DCF basis and therefore comparable with the returns discussed in this context.]

Allowing for price inflation at the rate of about 3% p.a. the investigators cited above conclude that until further evidence is forthcoming on the impact of the new system of taxation on equity returns, it should be assumed that equity shareholders can in future expect to earn about 10% p.a. net of all taxes in monetary terms.† (As we have already seen, if the required net of taxes equity return is taken as 10% then with values of $p = 0·5$, $d = 0·4125$, $t = 0·206\ 25$ and $n = 7$ the gross cut-off rate implied is 13·99%.)

We would summarise our remarks under this sub-heading as follows:

Aside from the individual risk premium which a company may require from individual capital projects, it is clearly necessary that a cut-off rate on equity finance should be unambiguously defined in numerical terms to avoid internal inconsistencies in investment programming.

---

* Merrett and Sykes, " Return on Equities and Fixed Interest Securities, 1919–1963 ", *District Bank Review*, December 1963; also " Return on Equities and Fixed Interest Securities, 1919–1966 ", ibid., June 1966.

† The general question of inflation is discussed in the second appendix to this chapter.

In fixing such a rate a company may find reasonable general guidance in drawing comparisons with fixed interest rates and in referring to historical data showing as it does the resilience of the return on equity investment over a long period of time.*   Whatever the gross cut-off rate finally fixed for equity finance the formulation presented here will at least enable the executive of a company to appreciate the implications of its financial policy for its equity shareholders.   To take a hypothetical case; a company which argued that a 7·25% gross redemption yield on fixed interest finance implied that the company should aim for a gross equity return of say 11% would, on the assumption of a 50% pay-out ratio and share turnover period of 7 years be aiming to give its equity shareholders a net of all taxes return approximating to 7·85% in monetary terms (see Appendix F).

THE PLOUGH-BACK RATIO, p

The Assumption of a Constant Plough-back Ratio

In the above formulation it is assumed that once decided the company's pay-out ratio remains constant.   Whether this is a tolerable simulation of reality is of course a question of fact; the leading empirical evidence on this point is for U.S. Corporations and is provided by Lintner † one of whose conclusions is " . . . our evidence indicates that dividends represent the primary and active decision variable in most situations ".‡

In the sample studied by Lintner two thirds of the companies had rather definite policy regarding the ideal or target ratio of dividends to current earnings.   " In all but two of these companies, however, . . . this normal pay-out ratio was considered to be a target or an ideal towards which the company would move, but not a restrictive requirement dictating a specific percentage payment within each year . . . most of the companies had . . . reasonably well-defined standards regarding the speed with which they would try to move towards a full adjustment of dividends to current earnings." §   " The corresponding standards in the other companies with fixed pay-out targets were expressed more in terms of having and maintaining a reasonably consistent pattern of action which would both meet the company's particular needs most of the time and also reasonably balance the

---

* Merrett and Sykes, *District Bank Review*, op. cit.
    † " Distribution of incomes of corporations among dividends, retained earnings, and taxes ", *American Economic Review*, **44**, 97–113, 1956.
    ‡ Op. cit.   § Lintner, op. cit., p. 102.

longer term interests of the stockholders of the company and their shorter term interests in current income." *

Although applicable to U.S. Corporations the findings of Lintner at least suggest that the constant pay ratio assumption used in our cut-off rate formulation is not lacking reality, although in practice there may be some delay in the adjustment of pay-out to the level of achieved earnings.

As regards company dividend policies in the U.K., an impressionistic opinion is that they generally conform to the Lintner finding that they constitute an active decision variable. In practice dividend policies are usually well established and a deviation from a previous pay-out ratio representing more than say 5% of taxed profits would amount to a significant change. As can be seen by inspecting Appendix F, even a variation in a pay-out ratio of the order of 10% is not numerically significant, i.e., if $r_e = 10\%$ and $n = 7$, then

for $p = 0.4,$ $i_e = 14.51;$

for $p = 0.5,$ $i_e = 13.99;$ and

for $p = 0.6,$ $i_e = 13.51.$

That is to say a change of 10% *over the complete period of* $n = 7$ *years* has an effect of about $\frac{1}{2}\%$ on the gross cut-off rate. If however one is concerned with a pay-out ratio which *fluctuates* between say 0.4 and 0.5 the effect on gross cut-off rate would obviously be negligible. Our conclusion is therefore that the assumption of a constant pay-out ratio in the cut-off rate formulation presented here will generally be satisfactory for the purposes of capital budgeting.

The precise numerical value of p which an individual company itself uses is naturally a question of the dividend policy which that company pursues.

The Relationship Between the Plough-back Ratio, p, and the Gross Cut-off Rate, i_e

Inspection of Fig. 13 shows that at a cut-off rate $i_e = 13\%$ the net of tax returns r_e to shareholders at plough-back ratios between $p = 0.3$ and $p = 0.7$ are approximately as follows:

p	0.0	0.3	0.5	0.7
r_e	7.65	8.60	9.30	9.95

* Loc. cit.

This cut-off rate of 13% *could be interpreted as a company's level of earnings net of corporation tax*; the direct relationship between the net of all taxes rate of return, r_e, and the level of plough-back, p, implies that shareholders will be better off the higher is the level of plough-back. This result necessarily follows as a matter of arithmetic from a formulation in which, whilst dividend and share value appreciation are both at the rate pi_e% p.a., dividends are taxed at a higher rate than realised capital gains.* Given these assumptions the numerical results are merely a reflection of the intuitively obvious fact that shareholders will obtain a higher net of all taxes return the greater the rate of return component residing in share value appreciation.

These numerical results apparently support one of the claims which has been made for the new system of corporation tax: that the latter will induce companies to retain a higher proportion of profits than hitherto. In fact these results ostensibly suggest the inference that for any given level of earnings (net of corporation tax), i_e, a company will maximise shareholder net returns with 100% plough-back. In practice this outcome would not follow; as we again argue later, the retention of a very high proportion of profits would almost certainly cause a serious undervaluation of a company's shares in relation to its earning capacity.

This " external " market effect raises two separate but related issues. The one is whether this cut-off rate model should persuade companies to retain a greater proportion of profits than hitherto; the other is whether the cut-off rate formulation is valid for companies which already retain a substantial proportion of profits. The second issue is taken up later,† here we are concerned with the first, which revolves upon the central question of the importance of established dividend policy.

In the previous section we concluded that the assumption of a constant pay-out ratio was a tolerable simulation of dividend policy in reality in which dividends are " an active decision variable ". The appeal of an established dividend policy to the investing public lies in the fact that it results in a stream of future dividends which can be predicted with reasonable accuracy and which in turn gives rise to a desirable stability in share values.

---

* Even if the capital gains tax were at the same rate as the dividend tax, the rate of return to shareholders would still vary directly with the level of ploughback, except in the case of realisation after one year when the net of all taxes rate of return, r_e, would be independent of the level of ploughback, p. † See pp. 135–38.

Whether an investing public aware of a major change in the system of taxation, one of the advantages of which is claimed to be its built-in inducement to higher plough-back, would react unfavourably to a substantial change in dividend policy, is clearly a matter for speculation. The possibility of unfavourable reaction and a consequent fall in the value of a company's shares, hence a rise in the marginal cost of external equity finance,* should not be gainsaid. The point we are at pains to stress is that our cut-off rate formulation clearly takes no cognisance of market reaction to *changes* in, and should not therefore be regarded as a model suggesting for, dividend policy. That is to say, the dividend decision should be treated as being determined in another area of financial management; once decided the numerical size of the plough-back ratio can then be fed into the cut-off rate formulation.

THE TRANSITIONARY PERIOD

The period of adjustment of dividend policies from the old tax regime to the system of corporation tax is a necessary consideration from a capital budgeting standpoint for the reason that such notions as pay-out ratio take on a new meaning in the new tax regime.

An important factor which needs to be held clearly in view in examining a company's pay-out ratio is that its taxable profit does not generally coincide with its reported accounting profits. It has been roughly estimated † that for the 3000 largest quoted companies taxable profit amounts to about 65% of reported profit. Whilst aggregates of this nature should be treated with some caution in analysis at the level of the individual company they do however provide a useful basis on which to equate pay-out ratios under the old regime with pay-out ratios under the new.‡

---

* To say nothing of such other dangers as exposure to take-over bidders for reasons which, if a company has consistently managed internal investment programmes and financing efficiently from an economic standpoint, are by definition not justified in the interests of efficient resource allocation.

† See Merrett and Sykes, " Taxation, Investment and Equities under a Labour Government ". *The Investment Analyst*, May 1964, pp. 4 and 5.

‡ One further pertinent fact is that the change in the structure of investment incentives has somewhat altered the concept of assessable profit. The precise relationship between taxable and reported accounting profits in the future is an issue left on one side in this chapter. The discussion presented here is nevertheless relevant in considering the transition to corporation tax and the lack of equivalence between pay out ratios in the respective tax regimes.

One other leading consideration which must be squared up in comparing ratios in two systems of taxation is what in fact the pay-out ratio is designed to achieve in terms of the absolute sizes of dividends and retentions respectively. Hitherto we have argued that dividends are the active decision variable and have explicitly recognised the possibility of lagged adjustment of a target pay-out ratio with changes in earnings. The essence of such a rationale of dividend policy is that a substantial constituent of the total is largely fixed and that the lagged adjustment effects only marginal changes to the total. If such is the case and characteristic of U.K. company attitudes, the switch-over to the new tax regime might be expected to bring about an *initial* situation in which companies attempt to leave their shareholders as well off in terms of net dividends as they were hitherto.* (In the longer term companies may be persuaded of the apparent tax advantages of a higher level of plough-back and begin to plough-back an *increasing* proportion of *increases* in earnings.)

Whether companies do or do not initially attempt to place the same net dividend in the hands of shareholders the fact of the matter is that a pay-out ratio of $X\%$ under the old regime is not $X\%$ under the new; a precondition to the fixing of cut-off rates in capital budgeting in the new tax system is therefore the knowledge of a company's dividend and/or plough-back proposals. This statement must again be qualified with the caveat issued earlier: thus, if a company's dividend policy has hitherto been a dependent residual † resulting from a primary decision on the level of plough-back, and in the future the company intends to maintain plough-back, the consequent adverse effect upon dividends in the new tax regime could cause the serious consequences mentioned before. Furthermore although the effect would be a " once and for all " change in dividends (shifting them to a new lower level) such a change may well result in a (high) level of plough-back which would cast serious doubts upon the share value appreciation assumption (in the cut-off rate formulation) which we discuss in the next section.

The effect on net dividends of an attempt to maintain plough-back is shown in Illustration 15(b). In Illustration 15(a) a comparison is

* Typical support for this view is contained in a speech by Mr. Kenneth Keith, deputy chairman of Hill Samuel Ltd., reported in the *Financial Times*, March 6th, 1966, p. 10.

† Even as a dependent residual the pay-out ratio may well have resulted in stability or only small variation in dividends in the past.

made of pay-out ratios under the old and new regimes on the assumption that *net* dividends are maintained.

The data shown in Illustration 15 can readily be translated into Figs. 10 and 11 which thus give a more complete picture of equivalent

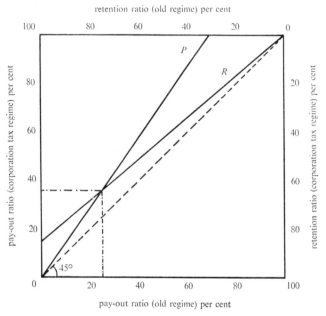

Fig. 10   Comparison of pay-out and retention ratios under the corporation tax and previous system of taxation (assumed ratio of taxable to reported profits is 67%).

Notes: (a) P = corresponding pay-out ratios;
R = corresponding retention ratios.

(b) Intersection of P and R indicates that a company distributing 24·8% of its taxed profits under the old regime would maintain its previous level of net dividends and retentions if it distributed 35·9% of its corporation taxed profits in the new regime.

pay-out ratios under the two tax regimes.   Fig. 10 (the box diagram) shows that all pay-out ratios defined for the new regime are numerically larger than under the old and, consequently, that equivalent plough-back ratios under the new regime are numerically lower.   The intersection of the pay-out and plough-back curves indicates that for the taxable and reported profit ratio, 0·67, which we have postulated, a company which, under the old regime, had a pay-out ratio of about 25% would, if it adopted a pay-out ratio of about 36% under the new regime, maintain net dividends and plough-back at exactly the same levels.

The intersection of the two curves in Fig. 11 gives the same information. As indicated, the co-ordinates are calibrated in levels of dividends

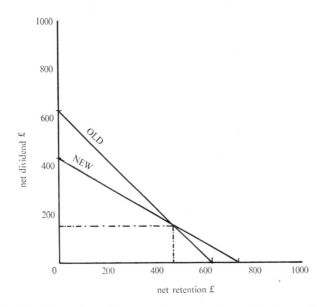

Fig. 11 Comparison of corporation tax regime with the previous system. Allocation of £1000 of reported profit (less tax) between dividends and retentions (assumed ratio of taxable to reported profit is 67%).

Note: The intersection of the two curves indicates the net dividend-retention policy which could be sustained under both regimes.

and retentions respectively for £1000 reported profits (£667 of taxable profit). Two kinds of information can be derived from Fig. 11: first, the extent to which retentions would need to be cut to maintain the same net dividend under the new regime as previously. Likewise the necessary cut in net dividends to maintain the previous level of plough-back can also be read off Fig. 11. (The manner in which the charts are interpreted is indicated in the appended notes.)

Illustration 15(a)

COMPARISON OF PAY-OUT RATIOS UNDER OLD AND NEW TAX SYSTEMS

OLD TAX REGIME

	£	£	£
(1) accounting profit	1000·00	1000·00	1000·00
(2) taxation	375·00	375·00	375·00
(3) taxed profits	625·00	625·00	625·00
(4) dividend (net)	187·50	312·50	437·50
(5) retentions	437·50	312·50	187·50
(6) pay-out ratio (4) ÷ (3)	0·3	0·5	0·7

15·00% profits tax	taxable profit	666·7
41·25% income tax	profits tax	100·0
	income tax	275·00
		375·0

CORPORATION TAX REGIME

	£	£	£
(1) accounting profit	1000·00	1000·00	1000·00
(2) corporation tax	266·68	266·68	266·68
(3) taxed profits	733·32	733·32	733·32
(4) dividend (net)	187·50	312·50	437·50
(5) income tax	131·64	219·41	307·18
(6) gross dividend	319·14	531·91	744·68
(7) retentions	414·18	201·41	−11·36
(8) pay-out ratio (6) ÷ (3)	0·4352	0·7253	1·015

40·00 % corporation tax	taxable profit	666·70
	corporation tax	266·68

Illustration 15(b)

CORPORATION TAX REGIME

Effect on net dividends of an attempt to maintain the same level of retentions as under the previous system of taxation

	£	£	£	£
taxable profit	666·70			
40·00 % corporation tax	266·68			
(1) accounting profit		1000·00	1000·00	1000·00
(2) corporation tax		266·68	266·68	266·68
		733·32	733·32	733·32
(3) retentions in old regime (12(*a*) line 5)		437·50	312·50	187·50
GROSS DIVIDEND		295·82	420·82	545·82
(4) income tax (41·25%)		122·03	173·59	225·15
(5) net dividend		173·79	247·23	320·67
(6) net dividend under old regime (12(*a*), line 4)		187·50	312·50	437·50
(7) fall in dividend		13·71	65·27	116·83
(8) percentage decline in net dividend (7) ÷ (6)		7·3%	20·9%	26·7%

The Assumption that a Company can Reinvest a Constant Proportion p of its Profits at an Opportunity Cost Rate of Return i_e

Whilst a constant pay-out ratio may be an acceptable simulation of reality, it is not unreasonable to question whether a company will always be able to *reinvest* a constant proportion of the profits generated by new investment (the initial investment of unity in our formulation) at an opportunity cost rate of return. Bearing in mind that a growing stream of earnings emerges from this formulation, the assumption of continuous reinvestment at opportunity cost ostensibly implies that a company is confronted with an array of investment projects growing at a rate which is large enough to absorb the growing stream of retentions plus, in optimal financing conditions, a growing stream of debt finance.

A leading question which should therefore be asked is whether the supposition that companies in general face such internal growth situations is tolerable. The answer to this problem is much less involved than may first appear and evidently depends upon the values of p and i_e. If p is relatively low (say 0·3) and i_e is about 13% which, after allowing for inflation at the rate of $3\frac{1}{2}$% p.a., is approximately $9\frac{1}{2}$% in real terms, then the implied rate of increase of internally financed net capital formation in the company is $0·3 \times 9·5 = 2·85$% p.a. in real terms. In optimal financing conditions where debt and equity are utilised in the proportions (say) $\frac{1}{3}$ and $\frac{2}{3}$, the implied rate of real capital formation would be $1·5 \times 2·85 = 4·28$% p.a. On the other hand if p is taken at 0·7 the implied rate of increase real capital formation would be $0·7 (13·0 - 3·5) \times 1·5 = 9·98$%.

Whether these particular rates of net capital formation should be regarded as being high or low clearly depends upon the facts of the case but, in relation to the rates of growth of net investment implied in the National Plan in which there is of course considerable variation between one industry and the next, they are by no means extravagant. There is, however, no need to pursue this line further for, if companies are unable to sustain the rates of increase of net capital formation implied in this formulation, such a situation will readily be revealed in the process of capital budgeting and " surplus " retained earnings will result. Thus we return to the problem raised earlier; if the surplus is of a temporary nature (persisting for say one or two years) and arises largely out of the fact that investment projects are forthcoming in a lumpy fashion rather than the smooth rate apparently, but not in any real sense, necessary to satisfy the cut-off rate formulation, the " surplus " can be deployed in external equity investment until such time as it is required as internal equity finance.

A company which is confronted with a persistent cash surplus situation is one whose dividend policy is in the fundamental disequilibrium which ought to be corrected by a larger pay-out ratio. Such an adjustment would then by definition reduce the proportion of profits ploughed back and the consequent implied rate of net capital formation; thereafter the company would adopt the cut-off rate applicable to its new plough-back ratio. The cut-off rate formulation is thus valid for any internal growth conditions provided that in a " low " growth situation a company's dividend policy is a long run reflection of the company's equity financing requirements.

THE SHARE VALUE APPRECIATION ASSUMPTION

The value $(1+pi_e)^n$ to which, in this formulation, the price of shares is assumed to appreciate after n years is not only one which follows axiomatically from the constant dividend yield assumption but, as is seen by reference to Illustration 13, also represents the value of finance deployed in the company by the end of year n. Now if finance deployed in a company is assumed to produce $i_e\%$ p.a. (implicitly in perpetuity) such a return is by definition net of depreciation adequate to maintain capital intact. Thus, the value $(1+pi_e)^n$ represents net capital formation within the company by the end of year n or, to retreat from the jargon of the economist into the jargon of the accountant, the value of assets (minus depreciation) at acquisition cost. This assumption is therefore that the value of the company's shares reflects asset acquisition cost (minus depreciation realistically calculated). Furthermore this is to define the value of the company's shares as their initial value plus the aggregate value of plough-back (excluding depreciation); that is to say, a pound of retained earnings adds an equivalent amount to the value of a company's shares. This so-called " neutralist view " has been widely challenged * on the grounds that in reality a pound of retained earnings generally adds much less to the value of the shares.†
As yet no definitive analysis of the determinants of share values exists, but partial explanation may reside in statistical results of the kind

* See, for example, Rubner, *The Ensnared Shareholder*, Chapter VI.
† Precisely how much less is, as yet, unagreed.

10

obtained by I. D. M. Little* who concludes *inter alia* that "those [firms] which retain a relatively high proportion of profits select relatively unprofitable investments ". It seems reasonable to suppose that in the absence of a correlation between retained earnings and growth of earnings there is small likelihood that there will be significant, or indeed any, correlation between retained earnings and share values. The apparent selection and financing of unprofitable investments with retained earnings may in fact be due to a combination of two factors. Either firms may have initially selected investments with *prospective* profitability exceeding the opportunity cost of retained earnings which did not materialise or, there may have been a departure from the opportunity cost rule in measuring the cost of retained earnings † and the subsequent adoption of investment *projects promising less than an opportunity cost rate of return*. Whilst the evidence cited here possibly explains lack of correlation between retained earnings and growth in earnings (and hence between retained earnings and growth in share values) in terms of poor quality investment and financing decisions, such evidence clearly does not render inadmissible the earnings, dividends and plough-back streams which emerge from our formulation—given the assumption of the achievement of an opportunity cost rate of return on retained earnings, these results must follow simply because arithmetic imposes its own logic. Indeed an alternative way of viewing our model would be to regard it as a collection of rules designed to achieve the very correlation between earnings and growth of earnings which appears to be absent in reality.

But even if in reality a perfect positive correlation between retained earnings and growth of earnings could be expected there may still remain grounds for supposing that an additional pound of retained earnings would in many cases add less than an equivalent amount to the value of a company's shares. That is to say, as we have hinted earlier, a company's pay-out ratio may of itself constitute an important determinant of share values; consequently a company which maintains a consistently meagre dividend policy distributing say less than 25% of its profits runs the risk of causing a serious undervaluation in its shares (in relation to the earning power of its assets) and exposes itself to the danger of a take-over bid for no other reason than the

---

* Op. cit.

† Possible evidence of such a departure is found in Lawson, " The cost of ploughed-back profits ", *The Banker's Magazine*, February 1966.

investing public's apparent preference for a rate of return residing pre-eminently in the dividend stream component.

Thus it becomes necessary to ask whether the cut-off rate formulation presented in this chapter is relevant for companies which intend to continue a meagre dividend policy in the future. This question presents an almost intractable problem because of the interstice in the evidence. If, as is concluded by I. D. M. Little,* companies with high plough-back ratios are apparently inefficient in internal investment allocation, the impact of pay-out ratios on share values becomes very difficult to isolate.

The relevance of the foregoing remarks to the share value assumption adopted in our formulation can now be crystallised as follows:

None of the empirical evidence cited here would apparently add up to a negation of the " neutralist view "; empirical evidence approaching support for a conclusive refutation would need to be drawn from a well stratified sample of companies of varying pay-out ratios all of whom showed strong positive correlation between plough-back and growth of earnings. We do not conclude that the cut-off rate model can be applied with indifference to pay-out ratios and emphasise that it should be regarded as a means of calculating sensible † cut-off rates in a clearly defined situation satisfying two important conditions. The one, discussed in previous sections, is in effect that the cut-off rate formulation should be primarily restricted in its application to situations in which future (net) dividend policy will continue largely as a projection of the past. The other condition should be added to meet the problem of share undervaluation arising out of a low pay-out ratio *per se* but can only be attached as a matter of opinion (or recommendation) which is difficult to challenge or support with currently existing evidence: it is suggested that this formulation will provide a fairly accurate guide

---

* Op. cit.

† By " sensible " in this context we mean a cut-off rate which results from an analysis and quantification of the important factors impinging on the problem, rather than a rate which is determined by such rules of thumb as, " We never invest in anything unless it promises a 20% rate of return ". Such approaches not only militate against the adoption of a substantial volume of profitable investment but overlook the fact that projects with high profit-making potential are frequently only available because they are unexploited and hence highly risky. In short the arbitrary fixing of a high cut-off rate tends in its attempt to play safe to introduce a bias in favour of projects which should be loaded with a high risk premium and discriminates against those which appear less profitable but which are frequently characterised by small inherent risk, i.e., introduces the very danger it is designed to exclude.

to cut-off rates at pay-out ratios exceeding say 25 to 30% under the old tax regime (i.e., approximately 36 to 44% under the new regime assuming a ratio of taxable to reported profits of about 65%).* If companies pay out substantially less than the proportions mentioned here some addition clearly needs to be made to the cut-off rate set to give shareholders the required net of all taxes rate of return r_e, that is to say, the lower rate of share value appreciation at a low pay-out ratio reduces the rate of return component embodied in share value appreciation and consequently suggests that at low pay-out ratios companies must seek higher profit levels to countervail the adverse effects of meagre dividends.

The Rate of Share Turnover $1/n$

As explained earlier the capital gains tax on investment makes its impact when shareholders realise capital gains by selling shares; because this tax is assessed on *realised* rather than *accrued* gains its incidence is determined by the rate of share turnover. There is of course no reason to suppose that the turnover of shares will follow a regular pattern or that, in the case of a quoted company whose shares may change hands continuously without such transfers being recorded in the company's share register, an average rate of share turnover can be readily calculated.

Happily this is not an insurmountable difficulty for the reason that the cut-off rates emerging from the formulation are not highly sensitive to substantial variations in the assumed average rate of share turnover. Thus we have assumed that on average the proportion $1/n$ is realised by shareholders every year which is equivalent to the assumption that *all* shares are turned over *every n* years. Hence, whilst a company may

---

* One further reason for suggesting that the cut-off rate formulation developed in this chapter cannot be applied with indifference to pay-out ratios is imposed by the underlying mathematics. It will be noted that we have stated on p. 143:

" For the applications considered here this condition (12) effectively reduces to:

$$r_e > pi_e$$ "

In other words the formulation holds so long as the net of all taxes rate of return, r_e, required by equity shareholders exceeds the growth rate of earnings, dividends and capital formation. As will be seen by reference to Appendix F, in which the asterisks denote cases in which the condition $r_e > pi_e$ is not satisfied, this condition means that the model is generally satisfactory for a plough-back ratio not exceeding approximately 70% which is an interesting correspondence with the recommendation in the context.

not be prepared to hazard that its rate of share turnover averages 7 years (i.e., 1/7 turned over every year), it may be prepared to estimate that the rate could be 7 ± 5. If so, a choice of a 7 year turnover period when p (proportion of profits ploughed back) $= 0.5$ and r_e (net of all taxes return to equity shareholders in monetary terms) $= 0.10$, would cause a cut-off rate error of $13.99 - 13.71 = 0.28\%$ (where 13·99 is a cut-off rate for $n = 7$ and 13·71 is the equivalent rate for $n = 12$) if the actual rate of turnover were 1/12 of the company's shares per annum. Similarly, if the actual rate of share turnover were $n = 2$, the cut-off rate error resulting from the choice of $n = 7$ would be $13.99 - 14.38$ (cut-off rate for $n = 2$) $= 0.39\%$. In short, the deviation in cut-off rates over a difference of 10 years (when $r_e = 0.10$, and $p = 0.5$) is only $0.28 + 0.39 = 0.67\%$.

For two reasons this degree of deviation can be regarded as being trivial. First, in practice, the individual risk premium sought from a specific project will typically not lead to an investment decision being taken on the basis of a return which exceeds the cost of finance by as little as $\frac{1}{4}$ or $\frac{1}{2}\%$. Second, in adherence to the principles of financing, a company should attempt to minimise the cost of finance. Hence if the next programme of capital expenditure is to be financed in the proportions 1/3 and 2/3 with fixed interest and equity funds respectively costing (say) $7.5(1 - 0.4) = 4.5\%$, and 13.99%, a deviation to $13.99 + 0.39$ or $13.99 - 0.28$ would have the following effect upon the weighted average cost of finance:

	%
$n = 12$	
1/3 fixed interest finance at 4·5%	= 1·50
2/3 equity at 13·71%	= 9·14
weighted average	10·64
$n = 7$	
1/3 fixed interest finance at 4·5%	= 1·50
2/3 equity at 13·99%	= 9·33
weighted average	10·83
difference between $n = 12$ and $n = 7 = 0.19$	

$$n = 2$$

	%
1/3 fixed interest finance at 4·5%	= 1·50
2/3 equity at 14·38%	= 9·59
weighted average	11·09
difference between $n = 2$ and $n = 7$	= 0·26

The inference which can be drawn is therefore that the higher the degree of gearing a company introduces into its financial structure, the less significant of the estimating error in the rate of share turnover; but in any case the equity cut-off rate i_e is so highly insensitive to the rate of share turnover that the numerical value of the latter is largely a matter of indifference.

APPENDIX I—CHAPTER 4

GEOMETRIC SERIES

A series of terms each of which is formed by multiplying the term which precedes it by a constant factor is called a *geometric series* and the factor is called the *common ratio* of the series. Let the first term of such a series be denoted by a and the common ratio by r. Then the sum S_n of the first n terms is

$$S_n = a + ar + ar^2 + \ldots + ar^{n-1}. \tag{1}$$

Multiplying both sides of (1) by r gives

$$rS_n = ar + ar^2 + \ldots + ar^{n-1} + ar^n, \tag{2}$$

and subtracting the second series from the first

$$S_n - rS_n = a - ar^n.$$

Hence

$$(1-r)S_n = a(1-r^n)$$

and so

$$S_n = \frac{a(1-r^n)}{1-r}. \tag{3}$$

THE SUM TO INFINITY

Formula (3) may be re-written

$$S_n = \frac{a}{1-r} - a \cdot \frac{r^n}{1-r}. \tag{4}$$

Considering the second term of the right-hand side of (4), if r lies between -1 and $+1$, then r^n diminishes to zero as n increases *or* in mathematical terms $r^n \to 0$ as $n \to \infty$ (r^n tends to zero as n tends to infinity). Consequently, as $n \to \infty$ (i.e., the *number* of terms of the geometric series tends to infinity) the term

$$a \cdot \frac{r^n}{1-r} \to 0.$$

Thus the right-hand side of (4) approaches $\frac{a}{1-r}$ as a limit; this is called the *sum to infinity* of the series and is represented by S_∞, i.e.,

$$S_\infty = \frac{a}{1-r} \quad \text{provided} \quad -1 < r < 1. \tag{5}$$

In deriving equation (4) of Chapter 4 it is required to formulate the sum to infinity of the geometric progression

$$1 + \frac{1+pi_e}{1+r_e} + \frac{(1+pi_e)^2}{(1+r_e)^2} + \cdots \tag{6}$$

where, in the notation of (5),

$$a = 1$$

and

$$r = \frac{1+pi_e}{1+r_e}.$$

Hence, for (6),

$$S_\infty = \frac{1}{1 - \dfrac{1+pi_e}{1+r_e}} = \frac{1+r_e}{r_e - pi_e}. \tag{7}$$

It is also required to formulate the sum (finite)

$$1 + \frac{1}{1+r_e} + \frac{1}{(1+r_e)^2} + \cdots + \frac{1}{(1+r_e)^{n-1}} \tag{8}$$

where, in the notation of (3),

$$a = 1$$

and

$$r = \frac{1}{1+r_e}.$$

Hence, for (8),

$$S_n = \frac{1\left[1-\left(\dfrac{1}{1+r_e}\right)^n\right]}{1-\dfrac{1}{1+r_e}} = \frac{[(1+r_e)^n-1]}{(1+r_e)^n}\frac{(1+r_e)}{r_e}. \tag{9}$$

Equation (3) of Chapter 4 is

$$1 = i_e(1-p)(1-d)\left[\frac{1}{1+r_e}+\frac{1+pi_e}{(1+r_e)^2}+\frac{(1+pi_e)^2}{(1+r_e)^3}+\frac{(1+pi_e)^3}{(1+r_e)^4}+\cdots\right]$$

$$-\frac{t}{n}\left[\frac{(1+pi_e)-1}{1+r_e}+\frac{(1+pi_e)^2-1}{(1+r_e)^2}+\frac{(1+pi_e)^3-1}{(1+r_e)^3}+\right.$$

$$\cdots+\frac{(1+pi_e)^n-1}{(1+r_e)^n}+\frac{(1+pi_e)^{n+1}-(1+pi_e)}{(1+r_e)^{n+1}}+$$

$$\left.\frac{(1+pi_e)^{n+2}-(1+pi_e)^2}{(1+r_e)^{n+2}}+\frac{(1+pi_e)^{n+3}-(1+pi_e)^3}{(1+r_e)^{n+3}}+\cdots\right].$$

This equation may be rewritten as:

$$1 = \frac{i_e(1-p)(1-d)}{(1+r_e)}\left[1+\frac{1+pi_e}{1+r_e}+\frac{(1+pi_e)^2}{(1+r_e)^2}+\frac{(1+pi_e)^3}{(1+r_e)^3}+\cdots\right]-$$

$$\frac{t}{n}\left[\frac{1+pi_e}{1+r_e}\left\{1+\frac{1+pi_e}{1+r_e}+\frac{(1+pi_e)^2}{(1+r_e)^2}+\cdots+\frac{(1+pi_e)^n}{(1+r_e)^n}+\right.\right.$$

$$\frac{(1+pi_e)^{n+1}}{(1+r_e)^{n+1}}+\cdots\Bigg\}-\frac{1}{1+r_e}\left\{1+\frac{1}{1+r_e}+\frac{1}{(1+r_e)^2}+\right.$$

$$\left.\cdots+\frac{1}{(1+r_e)^{n-1}}\right\}-\frac{(1+pi_e)}{(1+r_e)^{n+1}}\left\{1+\frac{1+pi_e}{1+r_e}+\frac{(1+pi_e)^2}{(1+r_e)^2}+\cdots\right\}\Bigg], \tag{10}$$

and using (7) and (9), equation (10) simplifies to

$$1 = \frac{i_e(1-p)(1-d)}{(1+r_e)}\cdot\frac{(1+r_e)}{r_e-pi_e}-\frac{t}{n}\left[\frac{1+pi_e}{1+r_e}\cdot\frac{(1+r_e)}{r_e-pi_e}-\right.$$

$$\left.\frac{1}{1+r_e}\cdot\frac{[(1+r_e)^n-1](1+r_e)}{(1+r_e)^n r_e}-\frac{(1+pi_e)}{(1+r_e)^{n+1}}\frac{(1+r_e)}{(r_e-pi_e)}\right],$$

i.e.,

$$1 = \frac{i_e(1-p)(1-d)}{r_e-pi_e}-\frac{t}{n}\left[\frac{1+pi_e}{r_e-pi_e}-\frac{[(1+r_e)^n-1]}{r_e(1+r_e)^n}-\frac{(1+pi_e)}{(1+r_e)^n(r_e-pi_e)}\right]. \tag{11}$$

Equation (11) may be rewritten as

$$1 = \frac{i_e(1-p)(1-d)}{r_e - pi_e} -$$

$$\frac{t}{n}\left[\frac{r_e(1+pi_e)(1+r_e)^n - (r_e - pi_e)[(1+r_e)^n - 1] - r_e(1+pi_e)}{r_e(1+r_e)^n(r_e - pi_e)}\right]$$

$$= \frac{i_e(1-p)(1-d)}{r_e - pi_e} - \frac{t}{n}\left[\frac{(1+r_e)pi_e[(1+r_e)^n - 1]}{r_e(1+r_e)^n(r_e - pi_e)}\right], \text{ i.e.,}$$

$$1 = \frac{i_e(1-p)(1-d)}{r_e - pi_e} - \frac{t}{n}\left\{\frac{[(1+r_e)^n - 1]pi_e}{r_e(1+r_e)^{n-1}(r_e - pi_e)}\right\}$$

which is the required form of equation (4) of Chapter 4.

Note: The expression (7) applies to the infinite series (6) only for those values of p, i_e and r_e which satisfy the relation

$$-1 < \frac{1+pi_e}{1+r_e} < 1. \tag{12}$$

For the applications considered here this condition (12) effectively reduces to

$$r_e > pi_e.$$

Appendix II—Chapter 4

A NOTE ON THE IMPACT OF INFLATION UPON INVESTMENT COMPUTATIONS

1. Under the sub-heading " The net of all taxes return r_e to equity shareholders " (pp. 123–25) we cited the opinion that in allowing for inflation at the rate of about 3% p.a. companies should attempt to give equity shareholders a net of all taxes rate of return of about 10% p.a. in monetary terms.

This 3% assumed rate of annual inflation should of course reflect the extent to which shareholders as recipients of income are affected by a rising cost of living and, in attempting to provide say 9 or 10% p.a. net of all taxes in monetary terms, it is clearly necessary for a company to forecast each constituent of a stream of future cash-flows in monetary

terms * and thereafter, assuming a project is entirely equity financed,†
to discount at a cut-off rate i_e which would provide 9 or 10% p.a. net
of all taxes in monetary terms. (If the DCF rate of return variant is
used it should be calculated on the same series of cash-flows projected
in monetary terms.)

2. The point requiring emphasis is that the cost and revenue constituents
of future cash-flows may however be subject to rates of inflation which
not only differ in themselves but also from the rate of inflation reflected
in the (shareholder's) cost of living index. For example, assume that
a businessman is about to lay down extra plant to provide a constant
annual increase in saleable output and that in terms of *current prices*
the anticipated (constant) cash-flow is a arising at the end of each of
n years; assume also that the cash-flow a is given by $(b-d)$ where b
is the annual turnover (cash-(in)flow) anticipated from the new project,
and d is the annual operating cash-(out)flow (b and d are by definition
both expressed in terms of current prices). If the turnover is expected
to remain constant in physical terms but increase by 3% p.a. in monetary terms whilst the operating outflows increase by 4% p.a. in monetary
terms the project's stream of cash-flows is thus:

$$\text{end-year}$$

$$\overset{1}{b(1+0\cdot03)-d(1+0\cdot04)}, \qquad \overset{2}{b(1+0\cdot03)^2-d(1+0\cdot04)^2}, \ldots,$$

$$\overset{n}{b(1+0\cdot03)^n-d(1+0\cdot04)^n}$$

which, depending upon the mode of financing, should be discounted
at the company's cut-off rate expressed in monetary terms; or, if the
DCF rate of return criterion is applied, a net of corporation tax rate
of return should be calculated on the above series and compared with
the cut-off rate expressed in monetary terms.

---

* The most convincing reason for forecasting future cash-flows in monetary
terms lies in the fact that corporation tax is charged on monetary profits and that
cash grants, initial and annual allowances are all based on historical costs. Consequently considerable computational difficulties are obviated if all anticipations
are expressed in future monetary as opposed to future real terms.

† If the next project is to be financed with a mixture of $\frac{1}{3}$ debt costing (say) 7%
$(1-0\cdot4) = 4\cdot2\%$ net of corporation tax and $\frac{2}{3}$ equity costing 13·99% which is the
cut-off rate i_e for a net of all taxes rate of return $r_e = 10\%$ (when $p = 0\cdot5$ and
$n = 7$), the monetary cut-off rate should be:

$$(\tfrac{1}{3}\times4\cdot2)+(\tfrac{2}{3}\times13\cdot99) = 10\cdot73\%.$$

3. If, in the previous case, b and d were assumed to inflate at the same rate (say) 3% p.a. the series of cash-flows would have been:

end-year

$$\begin{array}{ccc} 1 & 2 & n \\ (b-d)(1+0{\cdot}03), & (b-d)(1+0{\cdot}03)^2, \ldots, & (b-d)(1-0{\cdot}03)^n. \end{array}$$

The assumption of a constant turnover b in monetary terms but operating cash-(out)flows inflating at $h\%$ p.a. would give a series of cash-flows of:

end-year

$$\begin{array}{ccc} 1 & 2 & n \\ b-d(1+h), & b-d(1+h)^2, \ldots, & b-d(1+h)^n. \end{array}$$

4. *Labour-saving investments*

In the case of labour-saving investments an anticipated saving of a p.a. in terms of current prices will generally inflate at a much higher rate than an assumed increase of 3 to 4% p.a. in the general level of prices. An increase of 6 to 7% would be much more realistic hence the DCF rate of return expressed in monetary terms (taking 6% p.a. for illustrative purposes) would be given by the value of r satisfying the equation:

$$C = \frac{a(1+0{\cdot}06)}{1+r} + \frac{a(1+0{\cdot}06)^2}{(1+r)^2} + \cdots + \frac{a(1+0{\cdot}06)^n}{(1+r)^n} \qquad (x)$$

which reduces to:

$$C = \frac{a(1+0{\cdot}06)}{r-0{\cdot}06}\left[1 - \frac{(1+0{\cdot}06)^n}{(1+r)^n}\right] \qquad (y)$$

Again it is worth emphasising that the value of r in equation (y) should be compared with a cut-off rate expressed in monetary terms.

5. If the cash-flow of a project is fixed (perhaps by contractual agreement) in monetary terms at a p.a. the latter clearly should not be inflated but must of course be discounted at a cut-off rate expressed in monetary terms and therefore embodying an allowance for price inflation for the self-evident reason that a sum of money which is constant in monetary terms is declining in real terms.

CAPITAL BUDGETING

6. *The joint impact of taxation, investment incentives and inflation*

We can now introduce a rather more complicated example in which the components of the operating cash-(out)flow d are inflating at different rates. Assume that the turnover b and the operating cash-(out)flow d are constant *in terms of current prices*. Suppose d is made up of three components: materials d_1, labour d_2 and some other incremental cost d_3, which are estimated to inflate at the respective rates h_1, h_2 and h_3, whilst turnover inflates at the rate h_4. The series of cash-flows can thus be set out as in Table 9.

TABLE 9

	cash-flows (end-year)			
	1	2		n
turnover	$b(1+h_4)$	$b(1+h_4)^2$	...	$b(1+h_4)^n$
MINUS				
outflows	$d_1(1+h_1)$	$d_1(1+h_1)^2$	...	$d_1(1+h_1)^n$
	$d_2(1+h_2)$	$d_2(1+h_2)^2$	...	$d_2(1+h_2)^n$
	$d_3(1+h_3)$	$d_3(1+h_3)^2$	...	$d_3(1+h_3)^n$

Either (*a*) Each one of the separate cash-flow components in Table 9 could first be evaluated to convert them into expected monetary values using reciprocals of Appendix A, e.g., $(1+h_1)^n = \dfrac{1}{(1+h_1)^{-n}}$, then, the sum of each vertical cash-(out)flow column could be deducted from its associated turnover similarly evaluated. This procedure would leave a series of net cash-flows expressed in monetary terms to which an appropriate net of tax factor could be applied. Finally, Appendix E could then be used in the normal way to give the present value of investment incentives on the eligible proportion of capital expenditure.

Or (*b*) Because the various cash-flow components are assumed to accumulate at compound rates of inflation a short-cut formula for the present value of a series increasing at a compound rate could be applied to each of the cash-flow components. Thus, the present value V of the whole series in Table 9 net of corporation tax, discounted at a cut-off rate i (expressed in monetary terms) is given by:

$$V = y\left\{\frac{b(1+h_4)}{i-h_4}\left[1-\frac{(1+h_4)^n}{(1+i)^n}\right] - \frac{d_1(1+h_1)}{i-h_1}\left[1-\frac{(1+h_1)^n}{(1+i)^n}\right] - \frac{d_2(1+h_2)}{i-h_2}\left[1-\frac{(1+h_2)^n}{(1+i)^n}\right] - \frac{d_3(1+h_3)}{i-h_3}\left[1-\frac{(1+h_3)^n}{(1+i)^n}\right]\right\} + CWx$$

where C = capital cost of the project,

        y = effective net of tax factor,

       W = proportion of capital expenditure eligible for investment incentives, and

       x = present value of investment incentives on a principal of unity.

If $V > C$ profitability is indicated. Clearly the DCF net of corporation tax rate of return would be calculated in a like manner.

Chapter 5

Summary and Conclusions

In this chapter we attempt to summarise and crystallise some of the previous discussion and, at the same time, underline some of the wider implications of the cut-off rate formulation developed in Chapter 4.

GENERAL

The position outlined earlier was that the quantitative aspect of capital budgeting resolves itself on the one hand into the evaluation of investment proposals *per se* net of a corporation tax partially countervailed by investment incentives. On the other hand having evaluated investment *per se* it is necessary to compare investment returns with some standard which reflects the minimum return inducing investment by the public in various classes of company securities in issue.

In principle this is the case whether investment projects are evaluated with either the rate of return or present value variants of the DCF formula.* Risk premiums aside, the use of the former amounts to a comparison of a net of corporation tax (net of investment incentives) rate or return with a cut-off rate which not only reflects the proportions in which a company raises finance from a variety of sources but, as appropriate, takes personal taxes (including the capital gains tax) into account.

Aside again from allowances for the degree of uncertainty inherent in individual projects, the application of the present value approach amounts to the discounting of a stream of corporation taxed (net of investment incentives) cash-flows at a discount rate equal to the cut-off rate used for rate of return comparisons.

---

* Here we are implicitly referring to *independent* projects and not of course to the mutually exclusive complication which requires the special treatment described in Chapter 2.

At the practical level it is clearly of administrative advantage to adopt accurate time-saving computational procedures. One of the basic aims of this book has been to explain the use of these short-cut methods and at the same time demonstrate their simple correctness for the reason that the use of methods which are clearly understood is both more satisfying and appealing to the people who adopt them.

In discussing the computational aspect of capital budgeting one crucial fact should be emphasised, this is that the purpose of DCF criteria is pre-eminently to facilitate comparisons between sums of money arising at various points in time and thence to evaluate investment proposals accordingly. That such an exercise *ought* to be attempted follows quite sensibly from the fact that money has a time-value. In a world characterised by risk and uncertainty the accuracy of estimates is inevitably in doubt. Thus, impressive-looking though mathematically correct DCF investment criteria may be, they cannot of themselves improve the quality of estimates. Hence the use of DCF methods can only be regarded as a way of making correct comparisons, or of undertaking correct analysis, of assumptions in the form of estimates. As indicated earlier, there are systematic ways of allowing for the tolerance in estimates but this exercise should be carefully separated from the use of correct criteria themselves. Even where there is considerable tolerance the argument for using correct criteria still remains for then the problem becomes one of making correct comparisons at and within the limits of tolerance.

This kind of analytical approach provides an effective rebuttal to two popular fallacies. The one is that because the future is so uncertain (and estimates therefore unreliable) there is little point in applying mathematically correct criteria to them. The answer to this objection is that there is surely less point in compounding estimating error by using crude investment criteria. (The other fallacy to which reference has already been made is that DCF methods improve the quality of estimates.) The basic weakness inherent in both these rather popular notions is that they are symptomatic of a lack of analytical approach and appreciation. Apart from their mathematical correctness the great advantage which ought to be seen in DCF criteria is that they clearly suggest considerations which need to be taken into account, a systematic way of stating them (and hence the entire problem) and, finally, the extent to which the profitability of an investment is sensitive to variations in each separate potential determinant. It is a truism to suggest that an *approach* to the statement and resolution of a typically difficult problem will generally be assisted by systematic analysis on terms which are set by the problem itself.

THE CUT-OFF RATE MODEL

The basic feature of the cut-off rate model formulated in Chapter 4 is that a company ploughs back a constant proportion of its profits and therefore pays out a constant proportion of profits as dividends. Whilst a constant pay-out ratio may be a tolerable simulation of reality, the logical implication of constant plough-back at an opportunity cost rate of return is, as argued previously, that some companies may find it necessary to reinvest externally.

The recognition of this possibility, coupled with action where appropriate, is clearly of importance to shareholders and the economy in general for it will introduce a degree of mobility of capital which is held to be generally desirable in a capitalistic system on the grounds that mobility is a precondition to the direction of resources to the points at which the economy is growing at the highest rate of return. The substance of this argument is not negated by the correction of a cash surplus situation through higher dividend distributions for then investors are given freedom to reinvest elsewhere at the best available rates. In the latter event there would, as recognised earlier, be the consideration of the tax leakages which would be obviated if investment were undertaken directly by companies themselves.

One is thus led to the conclusion that companies actively seeking to correct a persistent cash surplus situation should, taking cognisance of the tax affairs of their shareholders, obtain some clear directive from their proprietors in the manner of external reinvestment.

AN ILLUSTRATION OF CAPITAL BUDGETING PROCEDURE

As it transpires the hypothetical case built up in this section is concerned with a cash surplus situation ;* this is not meant to imply that cash

---

* Our apparent preoccupation with cash surplus situations is not intended to give the impression that this is a problem of huge dimensions pervading a substantial proportion of the private sector of the economy and which therefore manifests itself in large cash balances. The point is rather that the heavy dependence of U.K. companies on retained earnings is associated with the danger that the opportunity cost of the latter may not be correctly measured and that if a plough-back ratio is high substantial amounts of profit-financed investment may promise less than the

surplus situations necessitate fundamental changes in the *approach* to project and financial analysis. Indeed, a surplus of retentions to internal investment requirements will only emerge from the general application of the capital budgeting rules enumerated in the previous chapters. That is to say, the procedure outlined below should be regarded as the basic decision-making approach applicable to all capital budgeting situations.

PROCEDURE

1. A company should evaluate the return * on all investment proposals sponsored in the preliminary stages of budgeting whence it is possible to arrive at the potential internal investment demand for finance as shown in Illustration 16 (in which the 26 proposals are assumed to be independent of each other).

Illustration 16

Investment proposals sponsored in Company X

	DCF rate of return net of corporation tax and investment incentives	capital costs (including working capital)
	%	£000s
a	16	90
b	15	100
c	14	110
d	13	40
e	10	70
f	14	35
g	13	200
h	7	105
i	21	100
j	20	90
k	19	110
l	6	45

level of returns necessary to justify the use of equity finance. It is possible that even when the cost of retentions is correctly measured a cash surplus situation (defined in the sense in which the expression has been used in this book) is a rare occurrence in reality notwithstanding the fact that companies are making full use of gearing potential. But even if this were so there would still remain good reason for developing rules for dealing with the (possibly) occasional appearance of cash surplus conditions.

* Here the word return is used rather loosely and includes evaluation with both DCF variants.

11

	DCF rate of return net of corporation tax and investment incentives %	capital costs (including working capital) £000s
m	15	95
n	17	130
o	14	30
p	12	65
q	4	80
r	4	50
s	5	20
t	12	70
u	9	40
v	12	110
w	18	70
x	13	100
y	18	20
z	16	60

At this juncture reference should be made to the question of the risk or, more precisely, uncertainty premia required from individual proposals. Ultimately the acceptance or rejection of individual proposals should depend upon whether the margin by which the prospective return on investment exceeds the cost of finance, is enough to allow for the decision-maker's subjective evaluation of uncertainty. For example, a decision-maker looking at Illustration 16 can, assisted by sensitivity diagrams, readily decide whether in relation to the cost of finance individual projects are acceptable in which case the aggregate level of investment is automatically determined. These remarks will assume a clearer perspective when read in conjunction with the suggestions which follow.

2. An exercise which should be undertaken concurrently with the evaluation of the potential investment demand curve is an analysis of the sources, costs and proportions in which the next increment of finance can be raised. Here considerations of gearing, which are not only beset with such problems of adherence to conventional ratios, but also with the further difficulty posed by the fact that an external issue is relatively costly unless fairly substantial in absolute terms, are important. Hence it may not always be expedient or even possible to raise long-term fixed interest finance to take up small gearing potential. We return to this problem in the appendix to this chapter; at this stage (with reference to Illustrations 16 and 17) we assume for argument's sake that £250 000 is the minimum economic size of an external issue which could be raised and that, in any case, in the next increment of finance

the maximum proportion of fixed interest finance which ought to be attempted, in the light of accepted conventions of gearing *and* the company's current financial position (revealed in the following balance sheet), is 30%.

balance sheet as at:

	£000s		£000s
equity capital and reserves	2650	fixed assets	2000
proposed dividend	350		
long term debt finance	600	liquid assets (see note)	1100
		other net working capital	500
	£3600		£3600

Note The liquid assets are assumed to be net of the company's liquidity requirements (predicted possibly with the aid of a formal system of budgetary control) in the forthcoming operating period which, in turn, are assumed to be included in the £500 000 " other net working capital " shown in the balance sheet.

If fixed interest finance costs (say), 7% p.a. gross and hence $7(1-0\cdot4) = 4\cdot2\%$ net of corporation tax, and equity finance has an imputed cost of $12\cdot62\%$,* the company's weighted average cost of finance is:

$$(0\cdot3 \times 4\cdot2) + (0\cdot7 \times 12\cdot62) = 10\cdot1\% \text{ p.a.}$$

3. We now return to Illustration 16; aware that the cost of finance has been calculated at $10\cdot1\%$, a decision-taker(s) can now appraise the projects listed and eliminate those which are not considered to offer a return sufficiently in excess of the cost of finance when individual uncertainty premia are taken into account. It is assumed that the process of elimination leaves only the projects listed in Illustration 17; the company has thus decided upon £920 000 of capital expenditure (including working capital) and must revert to the financing problem once again.

* $12\cdot62\%$ is taken from Appendix F, page 220 and is based upon the assumptions that the company's average rate of share turnover is 7 years (i.e., $n = 7$), that the plough-back ratio, p is $0\cdot5$ and that the company aims to give its equity shareholders a net of all taxes rate of return, r_e, of 9% in monetary terms.

Illustration 17

Investment proposals adopted by Company X

	DCF rate of return, etc.	capital costs (including working capital)
	%	£000s
a	16	90
b	15	100
c	14	110
d	13	40
i	21	100
j	20	90
k	19	110
n	17	130
w	18	70
y	18	20
z	16	60
	Aggregate capital cost	£920

4. If 30 % of the next increment of finance represents the agreed maximum *additional* quantity of long term debt, the company should seek to raise:

$$0 \cdot 3 \times \text{£}920\,000 = \text{£}276\,000 \text{ (long term debt)}$$

with the balance of £644 000 to be drawn from retained earnings.

However, if £276 000 is raised externally as fixed interest finance then, after the payment of the proposed dividend, a surplus of £106 000 will result, i.e.,

liquid assets	*plus*	further debt	*minus*
£1 100 000	+	£276 000	—

dividends and capital expenditure	*equals*	surplus
(£350 000 + £920 000)	=	£106 000.

A more comprehensive picture of the company's prospective financial position after the implementation of its financial and investment plans is shown in the following balance sheet:

projected balance sheet as at:

	£000s			£000s
equity capital and reserves	2650	fixed assets		2000
		plus capital expenditure		
		(including working capital)		920
				2920
long term debt finance 600				
plus further issue 276	876	liquid assets	1100	
	——	*plus* debt issue	276	
			1376	
		less capital		
		expenditure 920		
		dividend 350		
			1270	
		surplus		106
		other net working capital		500
	£3526			£3526

This surplus of £106 000 should, if the company's dividend policy is held to be inviolate, be deployed externally in equity investment in other companies for then, and only then, is the basic condition justifying retentions satisfied.*

* It might be objected at this juncture that having decided to invest £106 000 externally in equity investments the company's aggregate capital expenditure becomes £920 000 + £106 000 = £1 026 000 to be financed as to

		£000s
debt		276
equity	644	
equity	106	750
		£1026

and that, in consequence, the cost of finance rises to:

$$\frac{276}{1026} \times 4\cdot2 + \frac{750}{1026} \times 12\cdot62 = 10\cdot4\%.$$

As we argued in Chapter 1 (equity) financial investments should be excluded from gearing calculations and, in effect, should therefore be equity-based. Hence

The objection that there is little point in raising £276 000 of long term *debt* in the capital market if the company then proposes to deploy £106 000 externally in equity investments in order to extricate itself from a cash surplus situation does not stand up to analysis. Had it been a viable proposition, from a flotation standpoint, to restrict the externally-raised debt finance to £170 000 the following consequences would have ensued:

(*a*) The cost of finance would have risen to:

$$\frac{170\ 000}{920\ 000} \times 4 \cdot 2 + \frac{750\ 000}{920\ 000} \times 12 \cdot 62 = 11 \cdot 1 \%$$

(*b*) This rise in the cost of finance may well have rendered unprofitable some projects which, after allowing for risk, were judged profitable at a cost of finance of 10·1%.* But even if this were not the case a 1% rise in the cost of financing £920 000 of expenditure is in principle tantamount to a reduction in equity profits (gross of income tax) of about £9000 p.a.

By raising additional debt of £276 000 and investing the £106 000 surplus in equities promising a return approximating the cost of equity finance, i.e., 12·62% the company in effect provides its equity share-holders with a net return of 12·62% *minus* 4·2% (net cost of debt) *equals* 8·42% on an additional project costing £106 000 in return for no additional injection of equity finance.

One further objection which might be raised, but which also does not hold, is that in raising £276 000 in debt a company does not have a mandate from its long term creditors to invest some of it, i.e., £106 000, externally in equity which generates an income of lower quality then the preferential stream for which the providers of debt have bargained.

---

although in the above case, the internal and external investments are adopted con-currently, they are subject to separate modes of financing. That is to say, the cost of finance for internal investment is, as stated above:

$$\frac{276}{920} \times 4 \cdot 2 + \frac{644}{920} \times 12 \cdot 62 = 10 \cdot 1 \%,$$

and, for external investments:

$$\frac{106}{106} \times 12 \cdot 62 = 12 \cdot 62 \%.$$

* This result would clearly be the most probable outcome of rational decision-taking.

In fact, this situation does not come about in the foregoing case. The interest of the long-term creditors resides in a preferential income stream in the company itself which is provided from internal investment policy. Furthermore, in so far as it is true that conventional standards of gearing do not have an adverse effect upon the quality of equity income, the interests of the company's equity shareholders have, as first explained, also improved.

The rationale of the prescription suggested above is merely the logic of the dual aims of minimising the cost of finance and ascribing the correct opportunity cost to retained earnings.

So much for the destination of surplus retentions in the above illustration; for completeness it is useful to consider what the strategy of the company should have been if the level of profitable investment (after due allowance for risk) had amounted to (say) £1 300 000 with liquid reserves (net of forthcoming operating requirements) of £800 000 and the same proposed dividend of £350 000. Thus:

capital expenditure	*plus*	dividends	*minus*
£1 300 000	+	£350 000	—

liquid reserves	*equals*	external requirements
£800 000	=	£850 000

Assuming again that debt and equity can be employed in the proportions 0·3 and 0·7, respectively, in financing the forthcoming programme of capital expenditure, the implied financial plan of the company is:

		£
total equity: 0·7 × £1 300 000		910 000
retentions	800 000	
less dividends	350 000	450 000
external equity		460 000
debt: 0·3 × £1 300 000		390 000
total external requirements		£850 000

THE CAPITAL GEARING PARADOX

We conclude this chapter with a brief examination of the capital gearing paradox (referred to on p. 8) which bears some, albeit only superficial, resemblance to the line of argument adduced with respect to the surplus retentions problem.

The reasoning leading to this apparent paradox runs: a company will minimise its cost of finance by attaining an optimal capital gear ratio. Thus if 0·3 and 0·7 are the optimal proportions for debt and equity respectively, costing respectively (say) 6% and 12%, the cost of finance is $(0·3 \times 6\%) + (0·7 \times 12\%) = 10·2\%$. It is then argued that having obtained finance at 10·2% this rate should never be regarded as a cut-off rate in capital budgeting for the reason that 12% can always be obtained by investing in equity elsewhere.

It is not to be denied that equity returns may be available elsewhere but it should be noted that in the process of obtaining them a company which has itself already attained an optimal capital gear ratio would, if it were to invest in other companies geared in any degree, become overgeared.

For example, assume that the balance sheets of X Ltd. which is optimally financed, and Y Ltd. which is undergeared, are respectively:

balance sheet of X Limited, as at:

	£		£
debt	300	cash	1000
equity	700		
	£1000		

balance sheet of Y Limited, as at:

	£		£
debt	100	assets	1100
equity at par	1000		
	£1100		

If X Ltd. now buys up the equity of Y Ltd., the equity of X Ltd. is automatically levered above 0·3.

aggregate balance sheet of X and Y, as at:

	£		£
debt	400	assets	1100
equity	700		
	£1100		

Now if the equity of *X* Ltd. is levered above the optimal ratio, then, as a matter of definition, it must be assumed that the respective qualities of both the debt and equity income streams in *X* Ltd. have been lowered in which case both shareholders and long term creditors will require higher returns to compensate for lower quality income. In other words, the higher gearing resulting from external investment in (geared) companies brings about a rise in the weighted average cost of finance to *X* Ltd.; if, as stated, company *X* is optimally financed then the higher the gear ratio(s) of the investee company(ies), the more nearly will the weighted average cost of finance approach the rate of return on equity investment.

In short, a widespread existence of gearing would effectively remove the conditions in which the paradox could exist. Thus the rise in the cost of finance to company *X* would clearly only be avoided in the following circumstances:

(i) *X* Ltd. can succeed in investing in other *purely equity-financed* companies;

(ii) *X* Ltd. is itself undergeared and, though unable to invest in companies which are purely equity financed, can invest in other companies which are sufficiently undergeared to avoid joint overgearing. For example, if 0·3 is regarded as an optimal gear-ratio then, in the following example, if *X* Ltd. were to buy up the equity of *Y* Ltd., the resultant gear-ratio would, in fact, be 0·3.

balance sheet of X Ltd. as at:

	£		£
debt	200	cash	1000
equity	800		
	£1000		

balance sheet of Y Ltd. as at:

	£		£
debt	143	assets	1143
equity at par	1000		
	£1143		

(iii) X Ltd. invests its finance in other companies in debt and equity in the proportions in which such finance was initially raised.

As regards circumstance (iii), the weighted average cost of finance and the return on the composite investment coincide—the capital gearing paradox does not therefore obtain in this case.

At the present time circumstances (i) and (ii) cannot be ruled out for there is a widespread tendency for companies to be lightly geared ;* hence even in the event of a departure from the principle that financial (equity) investments should be equity-based, it may still, *in present conditions*, be possible for a company to reinvest a composite increment of debt and equity in the equity of other companies without violating optimal gearing proportions. The potential dangers of such an operation should however be clearly recognised; investee companies which are ungeared or undergeared now may not remain so in the future. That is to say, in so far as the general attainment of optimal capital gear ratios is defined as a situation of financial equilibrium in the company sector of the economy, the capital gearing paradox can only be widely sustained in a general condition of disequilibrium and, because of the incentive to gearing built in to the new system of taxation, allied to the fact that in the recent past the advantages of gearing have been variously publicised and recommended, can now only be regarded as a transitory phenomenon. Such being the case the capital gearing paradox is, in our view, not admissible as the basis of an operational rule for determining a company's cost of finance.

Our conclusion is therefore an affirmation of the position taken in Chapter 1 namely that in applying a fundamental principle of financing a company should, through gearing, minimise the cost of finance; having done so it should then, after allowing for risk premia, take its investment to the level promising a marginal rate of return equal to the weighted average cost of finance. We would argue that the general application of this rule will promote a universal optimum use of resources.

The foregoing discussion of the capital gearing paradox, in which we use concrete examples to illustrate hypothetical situations to help

* But reference should be made to the fact that the new system of corporation tax is itself a powerful factor contributing to the removal of the conditions in which the capital gearing paradox could exist. As has been mentioned previously, the new system of taxation has brought about a higher absolute rise in the cost of equity finance than in the cost of long term debt, consequently companies now have a much greater incentive to take up gearing than has ever been the case hitherto.

derive the opportunity cost of a composite increment of debt and equity, should not be confused with the prescription for dealing with a cash surplus situation: such a surplus should, if not to be distributed as dividends, be invested in equity elsewhere. As explained earlier, provided the capital gear ratio of a company is based pre-eminently upon the value and profitability of its trading and productive assets the external investment of a cash surplus has a neutral effect upon gearing.

APPENDIX TO CHAPTER 5

In the illustration in Chapter 5 it was assumed that an external issue of less than £250 000 would be too costly in terms of issue costs, etc. In the later part of the example it was seen that a desire on the part of the company to utilise retained earnings of £750 000 (and thus not take up its gearing potential to the full) would suggest that £170 000 of fixed interest finance should be raised. If it is necessary to rule out a long term issue of such a size a further possibility might be temporary bank overdraft or bank loan * accommodation until such time as the aggregate of current and future needs of fixed interest financing is large enough to make an approach to the capital market worthwhile, thereafter bank borrowings could be repaid.

A similar problem may confront companies which are determined to exploit gearing to the full but who may find that this objective is seemingly frustrated by capital budgeting on a year-to-year basis since the implied levels of fixed interest financing may not be large enough to justify a sequence of external issues. Projections two or three years into the future may however result in an entirely different picture; two observations are perhaps pertinent. First, as stated, the tapping of the capital market is expensive in terms of time and money; hence there is a need for adequate forward financial planning, unconstrained by such notions as annual capital budgeting, and a resultant policy decision to tap the capital market at relatively infrequent intervals when market conditions and the size of a fixed interest external issue are suitable. It should not however be inferred that the adoption of projects should generally be deferred because of short-term inability to take up gearing to the full; many projects will remain viable despite

---

* It is worth mentioning that bank loan (as opposed to overdraft) financing by companies is so uncommon that it is of little practical relevance.

the mode of financing and, so far as possible, a company should bridge the time-lag which may preface an external issue on terms which are not prohibitive by substituting short-term fixed interest financing. If for various institutional reasons or reasons of national economic policy, etc., temporary bank financing is either impossible or only a partial expedient, a company may unavoidably be forced into the use of retained earnings. The cost of such financial policy should then be clearly recognised for the proportion of retained earnings in a sub-optimal capital gear-ratio will raise the weighted average cost of finance until further gearing lowers it.

A multi-period financing problem in which a company in effect switches from retentions to debt may remain reasonably manageable if the sequence of future investment decisions results from a phasing of expenditure for purely technological reasons. In other, perhaps exceptional cases, sequential planning may lead to extremely involved analytical problems and fundamental questions of logic. Thus sequential financial planning is inextricably bound up with sequential investment policy, a complication which not only raises the issue of why projects which are deemed acceptable in future periods are not worthy of inclusion in the current budget, but which also highlights the fact that the predictive power of human beings is by nature limited. The naturally limited perspicacity of individuals who sponsor investment proposals today is compounded when they are called upon to declare the proposals which will prove viable tomorrow. The structure of this kind of sequential investment problem is essentially one which must embody allowances for the development and rate of technological progress and the randomness of major break-throughs in research.

Such factors, sensibly recognised, should not however be allowed to dominate financial planning and it must be emphasised that in reality the economy is replete with examples of four- or five-year investment planning. In general such policy is implicitly based upon the assumption that investment plans for (say) the next four or five years are unlikely to be significantly affected by technological change or discovery; nevertheless, a company which seriously adheres to the logical implications of its future investment plans is in a position to formulate future financing policy and, subject to market conditions, to determine when a debt issue of the right size ought to be raised. Even if technological break-through or discovery should render a four- or five-year plan obsolete, ultimately the outcome will often be the substitution

of a new set of projects for those which were previously adopted *
and a financing problem which itself remains fundamentally the same
though perhaps of adjusted dimensions. The fact of the matter is
that the scope for error on the financing side is much smaller because
here the problem is basically quantitative; on the investment side the
problem is both quantitative and qualitative. We conclude this
appendix by affirming the principle that a company should always
strive to attain an optimal capital gear ratio and that the unavoidable
lumpiness which characterises the supply of long term debt introduces
the need for forward financial planning which, though occasionally
beset with extreme complications, will generally remain within manageable proportions.

Explanation of footnote in Appendices A, C and D.

Using Appendix A ascertain $(1+0.25)^{-42}$

$$\text{Tabular value for } (1+0.25)^{-42} = 8.51, \ -5$$
$$= 8.51 \times 10^{-5}$$
$$= 8.51 \times \frac{1}{10^5}$$
$$= 0.000\ 085\ 1.$$

Using Appendix C ascertain $(1-0.25)^{-19}$

$$\text{Tabular value for } (1-0.25)^{-19} = 2.3650,2$$
$$= 2.3650 \times 10^2$$
$$= 236.50.$$

Using Appendix D ascertain $\dfrac{(1-0.04)^{-8}-1}{0.04}$

$$\text{Tabular value for } \frac{(1-0.04)^{-8}-1}{0.04} = 9.6553,0$$
$$= 9.6553 \times 10^0$$
$$= 9.6553.$$

---

* A recent example of this is the change of the electricity industry's investment
plans to accommodate the massive discoveries of North Sea gas.

APPENDIX A

Present value of 1 due n years hence $v_{\overline{n}/r} = (1+r)^{-n}$

PERCENTAGE

	1	2	3	4	5
1	0·990 099	0·980 392	0·970 874	0·961 538	0·952 381
2	0·980 296	0·961 169	0·942 596	0·924 556	0·907 029
3	0·970 590	0·942 322	0·915 142	0·888 996	0·863 838
4	0·960 980	0·923 845	0·888 487	0·854 804	0·822 702
5	0·951 466	0·905 731	0·862 609	0·821 927	0·783 526
6	0·942 045	0·887 971	0·837 484	0·790 314	0·746 215
7	0·932 718	0·870 560	0·813 091	0·759 918	0·710 681
8	0·923 483	0·853 490	0·789 409	0·730 690	0·676 839
9	0·914 340	0·836 755	0·766 417	0·702 587	0·644 609
10	0·905 287	0·820 348	0·744 094	0·675 564	0·613 913
11	0·896 324	0·804 263	0·722 421	0·649 581	0·584 679
12	0·887 449	0·788 493	0·701 380	0·624 597	0·556 837
13	0·878 663	0·773 032	0·680 951	0·600 574	0·530 321
14	0·869 963	0·757 875	0·661 118	0·577 475	0·505 068
15	0·861 349	0·743 015	0·641 862	0·555 264	0·481 017
16	0·852 821	0·728 446	0·623 167	0·533 908	0·458 111
17	0·844 377	0·714 162	0·605 016	0·513 373	0·436 296
18	0·836 017	0·700 159	0·587 394	0·493 628	0·415 520
19	0·827 740	0·686 431	0·570 286	0·474 642	0·395 734
20	0·819 544	0·672 971	0·553 676	0·456 387	0·376 889
21	0·811 430	0·659 776	0·537 549	0·438 833	0·358 942
22	0·803 396	0·646 839	0·521 892	0·421 955	0·341 850
23	0·795 442	0·634 156	0·506 692	0·405 726	0·325 571
24	0·787 566	0·621 721	0·491 934	0·390 121	0·310 068
25	0·779 768	0·609 531	0·477 605	0·375 117	0·295 303
26	0·772 048	0·597 579	0·463 695	0·360 689	0·281 240
27	0·764 404	0·585 862	0·450 189	0·346 816	0·267 848
28	0·756 836	0·574 374	0·437 077	0·333 477	0·255 093
29	0·749 342	0·563 112	0·424 346	0·320 651	0·242 946
30	0·741 923	0·552 071	0·411 987	0·308 318	0·231 377
31	0·734 577	0·541 246	0·399 987	0·296 460	0·220 359
32	0·727 304	0·530 633	0·388 337	0·285 058	0·209 866
33	0·720 103	0·520 229	0·377 026	0·274 094	0·199 872
34	0·712 973	0·510 028	0·366 045	0·263 552	0·190 355
35	0·705 914	0·500 028	0·355 383	0·253 415	0·181 290
36	0·698 925	0·490 223	0·345 032	0·243 668	0·172 657
37	0·692 005	0·480 611	0·334 983	0·234 297	0·164 435
38	0·685 153	0·471 187	0·325 226	0·225 285	0·156 605
39	0·678 370	0·461 948	0·315 753	0·216 620	0·149 148
40	0·671 653	0·452 890	0·306 557	0·208 289	0·142 045
41	0·665 003	0·444 010	0·297 628	0·200 278	0·135 281
42	0·658 419	0·435 304	0·288 959	0·192 575	0·128 839
43	0·651 900	0·426 769	0·280 543	0·185 168	0·122 704
44	0·645 445	0·418 401	0·272 372	0·178 046	0·116 861
45	0·639 055	0·410 197	0·264 438	0·171 198	0·111 296
46	0·632 728	0·402 154	0·256 736	0·164 614	0·105 997
47	0·626 463	0·394 268	0·249 259	0·158 282	0·100 949
48	0·620 260	0·386 538	0·241 999	0·152 195	0·096 142
49	0·614 119	0·378 958	0·234 950	0·146 341	0·091 564
50	0·608 039	0·371 528	0·228 107	0·140 712	0·087 204

YEAR

APPENDIX A

Present value of 1 due n years hence $v_{\overline{n}|r} = (1+r)^{-n}$

PERCENTAGE

YEAR	6	7	8	9	10
1	0·943 396	0·934 579	0·925 926	0·917 431	0·909 091
2	0·889 996	0·873 439	0·857 339	0·841 680	0·826 446
3	0·839 619	0·816 298	0·793 832	0·772 183	0·751 315
4	0·792 094	0·762 895	0·735 030	0·708 425	0·683 013
5	0·747 258	0·712 986	0·680 583	0·649 931	0·620 921
6	0·704 960	0·666 342	0·630 169	0·596 267	0·564 474
7	0·665 057	0·622 750	0·583 490	0·547 034	0·513 158
8	0·627 412	0·582 009	0·540 269	0·501 866	0·466 507
9	0·591 898	0·543 934	0·500 249	0·460 427	0·424 097
10	0·558 395	0·508 349	0·463 193	0·422 411	0·385 543
11	0·526 787	0·475 093	0·428 883	0·387 533	0·350 494
12	0·496 969	0·444 012	0·397 114	0·355 534	0·318 631
13	0·468 839	0·414 964	0·367 698	0·326 178	0·289 664
14	0·442 301	0·387 817	0·340 461	0·299 246	0·263 331
15	0·417 265	0·362 446	0·315 241	0·274 538	0·239 392
16	0·393 646	0·338 734	0·291 890	0·251 869	0·217 629
17	0·371 364	0·316 574	0·270 269	0·231 073	0·197 844
18	0·350 344	0·295 864	0·250 249	0·211 993	0·179 859
19	0·330 513	0·276 508	0·231 712	0·194 489	0·163 508
20	0·311 804	0·258 419	0·214 548	0·178 431	0·148 643
21	0·294 155	0·241 513	0·198 655	0·163 698	0·135 130
22	0·277 505	0·225 713	0·183 940	0·150 181	0·122 846
23	0·261 797	0·210 947	0·170 315	0·137 781	0·111 678
24	0·246 978	0·197 146	0·157 699	0·126 405	0·101 525
25	0·232 998	0·184 249	0·146 018	0·115 968	0·092 296
26	0·219 810	0·172 195	0·135 202	0·106 392	0·083 905
27	0·207 368	0·160 930	0·125 187	0·097 608	0·076 278
28	0·195 630	0·150 402	0·115 914	0·089 548	0·069 343
29	0·184 557	0·140 563	0·107 327	0·082 154	0·063 039
30	0·174 110	0·131 367	0·099 377	0·075 371	0·057 308
31	0·164 255	0·122 773	0·092 016	0·069 148	0·052 099
32	0·154 957	0·114 741	0·085 200	0·063 438	0·047 362
33	0·146 186	0·107 235	0·078 889	0·058 200	0·043 057
34	0·137 911	0·100 219	0·073 045	0·053 395	0·039 142
35	0·130 105	0·093 663	0·067 634	0·048 986	0·035 584
36	0·122 741	0·087 535	0·062 624	0·044 941	0·032 349
37	0·115 793	0·081 809	0·057 986	0·041 230	0·029 408
38	0·109 239	0·076 457	0·053 690	0·037 826	0·026 735
39	0·103 055	0·071 455	0·049 713	0·034 703	0·024 304
40	0·097 222	0·066 780	0·046 031	0·031 837	0·022 095
41	0·091 719	0·062 411	0·042 621	0·029 209	0·020 086
42	0·086 527	0·058 328	0·039 464	0·026 797	0·018 260
43	0·081 629	0·054 513	0·036 541	0·024 584	0·016 600
44	0·077 009	0·050 946	0·033 834	0·022 554	0·015 091
45	0·072 650	0·047 613	0·031 328	0·020 692	0·013 719
46	0·068 538	0·044 498	0·029 007	0·018 984	0·012 472
47	0·064 658	0·041 587	0·026 859	0·017 416	0·011 338
48	0·060 998	0·038 867	0·024 869	0·015 978	0·010 307
49	0·057 546	0·036 324	0·023 027	0·014 659	0·009 370
50	0·054 288	0·033 948	0·021 321	0·013 448	0·008 519

APPENDIX A

Present value of 1 due n years hence $v\frac{}{n/r} = (1+r)^{-n}$

PERCENTAGE

	11	12	13	14	15
1	0·900 901	0·892 857	0·884 956	0·877 193	0·869 565
2	0·811 622	0·797 194	0·783 147	0·769 467	0·756 143
3	0·731 191	0·711 780	0·693 050	0·674 971	0·657 516
4	0·658 731	0·635 518	0·613 318	0·592 080	0·571 753
5	0·593 451	0·567 427	0·542 760	0·519 368	0·497 176
6	0·534 641	0·506 631	0·480 318	0·455 586	0·432 327
7	0·481 658	0·452 349	0·425 060	0·399 637	0·375 937
8	0·433 926	0·403 883	0·376 160	0·350 559	0·326 901
9	0·390 924	0·360 610	0·332 885	0·307 508	0·284 262
10	0·352 184	0·321 973	0·294 588	0·269 744	0·247 184
11	0·317 283	0·287 476	0·260 697	0·236 617	0·214 943
12	0·285 841	0·256 675	0·230 706	0·207 559	0·186 907
13	0·257 514	0·229 174	0·204 164	0·182 069	0·162 528
14	0·231 995	0·204 620	0·180 676	0·159 710	0·141 328
15	0·209 004	0·182 696	0·159 891	0·140 096	0·122 894
16	0·188 292	0·163 121	0·141 496	0·122 891	0·106 865
17	0·169 632	0·145 644	0·125 218	0·107 800	0·092 926
18	0·152 822	0·130 039	0·110 812	0·094 561	0·080 805
19	0·137 677	0·116 107	0·098 064	0·082 948	0·070 265
20	0·124 034	0·103 667	0·086 782	0·072 762	0·061 100
21	0·111 742	0·092 559	0·076 798	0·063 826	0·053 131
22	0·100 669	0·082 642	0·067 963	0·055 988	0·046 200
23	0·090 692	0·073 788	0·060 144	0·049 112	0·040 174
24	0·081 705	0·065 882	0·053 225	0·043 081	0·034 934
25	0·073 608	0·058 823	0·047 102	0·037 790	0·030 378
26	0·066 313	0·052 521	0·041 683	0·033 149	0·026 415
27	0·059 742	0·046 893	0·036 888	0·029 078	0·022 970
28	0·053 821	0·041 869	0·032 644	0·025 507	0·019 974
29	0·048 488	0·037 383	0·028 888	0·022 375	0·017 368
30	0·043 683	0·033 378	0·025 565	0·019 627	0·015 103
31	0·039 354	0·029 802	0·022 624	0·017 217	0·013 133
32	0·035 454	0·026 609	0·020 021	0·015 102	0·011 420
33	0·031 940	0·023 758	0·017 718	0·013 248	0·009 930
34	0·028 775	0·021 212	0·015 679	0·011 621	0·008 635
35	0·025 924	0·018 939	0·013 876	0·010 194	0·007 509
36	0·023 355	0·016 910	0·012 279	0·008 942	0·006 529
37	0·021 040	0·015 098	0·010 867	0·007 844	0·005 678
38	0·018 955	0·013 481	0·009 617	0·006 880	0·004 937
39	0·017 077	0·012 036	0·008 510	0·006 035	0·004 293
40	0·015 384	0·010 747	0·007 531	0·005 294	0·003 733
41	0·013 860	0·009 595	0·006 665	0·004 644	0·003 246
42	0·012 486	0·008 567	0·005 898	0·004 074	0·002 823
43	0·011 249	0·007 649	0·005 219	0·003 573	0·002 455
44	0·010 134	0·006 830	0·004 619	0·003 135	0·002 134
45	0·009 130	0·006 098	0·004 088	0·002 750	0·001 856
46	0·008 225	0·005 445	0·003 617	0·002 412	0·001 614
47	0·007 410	0·004 861	0·003 201	0·002 116	0·001 403
48	0·006 676	0·004 340	0·002 833	0·001 856	0·001 220
49	0·006 014	0·003 875	0·002 507	0·001 628	0·001 061
50	0·005 418	0·003 460	0·002 219	0·001 428	0·000 923

Y E A R

APPENDIX · A

Present value of 1 due n years hence $v_{\overline{n}|r} = (1+r)^{-n}$

PERCENTAGE

	16	17	18	19	20
1	0·862 069	0·854 701	0·847 458	0·840 336	0·833 333
2	0·743 163	0·730 513	0·718 184	0·706 165	0·694 444
3	0·640 657	0·624 370	0·608 631	0·593 416	0·578 703
4	0·552 291	0·533 650	0·515 789	0·498 668	0·482 253
5	0·476 113	0·456 111	0·437 109	0·419 049	0·401 877
6	0·410 442	0·389 838	0·370 431	0·352 142	0·334 898
7	0·353 829	0·333 195	0·313 925	0·295 918	0·279 081
8	0·305 025	0·284 782	0·266 038	0·248 670	0·232 568
9	0·262 953	0·243 403	0·225 456	0·208 967	0·193 806
10	0·226 683	0·208 037	0·191 064	0·175 602	0·161 505
11	0·195 417	0·177 809	0·161 919	0·147 565	0·134 588
12	0·168 463	0·151 974	0·137 219	0·124 004	0·112 156
13	0·145 226	0·129 892	0·116 288	0·104 205	0·093 464
14	0·125 195	0·111 019	0·098 549	0·087 567	0·077 886
15	0·107 927	0·094 888	0·083 516	0·073 586	0·064 905
16	0·093 040	0·081 101	0·070 776	0·061 837	0·054 088
17	0·080 207	0·069 317	0·059 980	0·051 964	0·045 073
18	0·069 144	0·059 245	0·050 830	0·043 667	0·037 561
19	0·059 607	0·050 637	0·043 077	0·036 695	0·031 301
20	0·051 385	0·043 279	0·036 506	0·030 836	0·026 084
21	0·044 298	0·036 991	0·030 937	0·025 913	0·021 737
22	0·038 188	0·031 616	0·026 218	0·021 775	0·018 114
23	0·032 920	0·027 022	0·022 218	0·018 299	0·015 095
24	0·028 380	0·023 096	0·018 829	0·015 377	0·012 579
25	0·024 465	0·019 740	0·015 957	0·012 922	0·010 483
26	0·021 091	0·016 872	0·013 523	0·010 859	0·008 735
27	0·018 182	0·014 420	0·011 460	0·009 125	0·007 280
28	0·015 674	0·012 325	0·009 712	0·007 668	0·006 066
29	0·013 512	0·010 534	0·008 230	0·006 444	0·005 055
30	0·011 648	0·009 004	0·006 975	0·005 415	0·004 213
31	0·010 042	0·007 695	0·005 911	0·004 550	0·003 511
32	0·008 657	0·006 577	0·005 009	0·003 824	0·002 925
33	0·007 463	0·005 622	0·004 245	0·003 213	0·002 438
34	0·006 433	0·004 805	0·003 598	0·002 700	0·002 032
35	0·005 546	0·004 107	0·003 049	0·002 269	0·001 693
36	0·004 781	0·003 510	0·002 584	0·001 907	0·001 411
37	0·004 121	0·003 000	0·002 190	0·001 602	0·001 176
38	0·003 553	0·002 564	0·001 856	0·001 347	0·000 980
39	0·003 063	0·002 192	0·001 573	0·001 132	0·000 816
40	0·002 640	0·001 873	0·001 333	0·000 951	0·000 680
41	0·002 276	0·001 601	0·001 129	0·000 799	0·000 567
42	0·001 962	0·001 368	0·000 957	0·000 671	0·000 472
43	0·001 692	0·001 170	0·000 811	0·000 564	0·000 394
44	0·001 458	0·001 000	0·000 687	0·000 474	0·000 328
45	0·001 257	0·000 854	0·000 583	0·000 398	0·000 273
46	0·001 084	0·000 730	0·000 494	0·000 335	0·000 228
47	0·000 934	0·000 624	0·000 418	0·000 281	0·000 190
48	0·000 805	0·000 533	0·000 355	0·000 236	0·000 158
49	0·000 694	0·000 456	0·000 300	0·000 199	0·000 132
50	0·000 599	0·000 390	0·000 255	0·000 167	0·000 110

YEAR

APPENDIX A

Present value of 1 due n years hence $v_{\overline{n|}r} = (1+r)^{-n}$

PERCENTAGE

YEAR	21	22	23	24	25
1	0·826 446	0·819 672	0·813 008	0·806 451	0·800 000
2	0·683 013	0·671 862	0·660 982	0·650 364	0·640 000
3	0·564 474	0·550 707	0·537 384	0·524 487	0·512 000
4	0·466 507	0·451 399	0·436 897	0·422 973	0·409 600
5	0·385 543	0·369 999	0·355 201	0·341 107	0·327 680
6	0·318 631	0·303 278	0·288 781	0·275 087	0·262 144
7	0·263 331	0·248 588	0·234 781	0·221 844	0·209 715
8	0·217 629	0·203 761	0·190 879	0·178 906	0·167 772
9	0·179 859	0·167 017	0·155 186	0·144 279	0·134 218
10	0·148 643	0·136 899	0·126 168	0·116 354	0·107 374
11	0·122 846	0·112 212	0·102 575	0·093 834	0·085 899
12	0·101 525	0·091 977	0·083 395	0·075 673	0·068 719
13	0·083 905	0·075 391	0·067 800	0·061 026	0·054 975
14	0·069 343	0·061 796	0·055 122	0·049 215	0·043 980
15	0·057 308	0·050 653	0·044 815	0·039 689	0·035 184
16	0·047 362	0·041 518	0·036 435	0·032 008	0·028 147
17	0·039 142	0·034 032	0·029 622	0·025 812	0·022 518
18	0·032 349	0·027 895	0·024 083	0·020 817	0·018 014
19	0·026 735	0·022 865	0·019 579	0·016 788	0·014 411
20	0·022 095	0·018 741	0·015 918	0·013 538	0·011 529
21	0·018 260	0·015 362	0·012 942	0·010 918	0·009 223
22	0·015 091	0·012 592	0·010 522	0·008 805	0·007 379
23	0·012 472	0·010 321	0·008 554	0·007 101	0·005 903
24	0·010 307	0·008 460	0·006 955	0·005 726	0·004 722
25	0·008 519	0·006 934	0·005 654	0·004 618	0·003 778
26	0·007 040	0·005 684	0·004 597	0·003 724	0·003 022
27	0·005 818	0·004 659	0·003 737	0·003 003	0·002 418
28	0·004 808	0·003 819	0·003 038	0·002 422	0·001 934
29	0·003 974	0·003 130	0·002 470	0·001 953	0·001 547
30	0·003 284	0·002 566	0·002 008	0·001 575	0·001 238
31	0·002 714	0·002 103	0·001 633	0·001 270	0·000 990
32	0·002 243	0·001 724	0·001 327	0·001 024	0·000 792
33	0·001 854	0·001 413	0·001 079	0·000 826	0·000 634
34	0·001 532	0·001 158	0·000 877	0·000 666	0·000 507
35	0·001 266	0·000 949	0·000 713	0·000 537	0·000 406
36	0·001 046	0·000 778	0·000 580	0·000 433	0·000 325
37	0·000 865	0·000 638	0·000 472	0·000 349	0·000 260
38	0·000 715	0·000 523	0·000 383	0·000 282	0·000 208
39	0·000 591	0·000 429	0·000 312	0·000 227	0·000 166
40	0·000 488	0·000 351	0·000 253	0·000 183	0·000 133
41	0·000 403	0·000 288	0·000 206	0·000 148	0·000 106
42	0·000 333	0·000 236	0·000 167	0·000 119	8·51, –5*
43	0·000 276	0·000 193	0·000 136	9·61, –5*	6·81, –5
44	0·000 228	0·000 159	0·000 111	7·75, –5	5·44, –5
45	0·000 188	0·000 130	9·00, –5*	6·25, –5	4·36, –5
46	0·000 156	0·000 107	7·32, –5	5·04, –5	3·48, –5
47	0·000 129	8·73, –5*	5·95, –5	4·07, –5	2·79, –5
48	0·000 106	7·16, –5	4·84, –5	3·28, –5	2·23, –5
49	8·78, –5*	5·87, –5	3·93, –5	2·64, –5	1·78, –5
50	7·26, –5	4·81, –5	3·20, –5	2·13, –5	1·43, –5

* The final digit is the power of 10 by which the given tabular value has to be multiplied (see example on p. 163).

APPENDIX A

Present value of 1 due n years hence $v_{\overline{n}|r} = (1+r)^{-n}$

PERCENTAGE

	26	27	28	29	30
1	0·793 651	0·787 401	0·781 250	0·775 194	0·769 231
2	0·629 881	0·620 001	0·610 351	0·600 925	0·591 716
3	0·499 906	0·488 190	0·476 837	0·465 833	0·455 166
4	0·396 751	0·384 401	0·372 529	0·361 111	0·350 127
5	0·314 881	0·302 678	0·291 038	0·279 931	0·269 329
6	0·249 906	0·238 329	0·227 373	0·217 001	0·207 176
7	0·198 338	0·187 661	0·177 635	0·168 218	0·159 366
8	0·157 411	0·147 764	0·138 778	0·130 401	0·122 589
9	0·124 929	0·116 350	0·108 420	0·101 086	0·094 299
10	0·099 150	0·091 614	0·084 703	0·078 361	0·072 538
11	0·078 691	0·072 137	0·066 174	0·060 745	0·055 798
12	0·062 453	0·056 801	0·051 699	0·047 089	0·042 922
13	0·049 566	0·044 725	0·040 390	0·036 503	0·033 017
14	0·039 338	0·035 217	0·031 554	0·028 297	0·025 398
15	0·031 221	0·027 730	0·024 652	0·021 936	0·019 537
16	0·024 778	0·021 834	0·019 259	0·017 004	0·015 028
17	0·019 665	0·017 192	0·015 046	0·013 182	0·011 560
18	0·015 607	0·013 537	0·011 755	0·010 218	0·008 892
19	0·012 387	0·010 659	0·009 184	0·007 921	0·006 840
20	0·009 831	0·008 393	0·007 175	0·006 141	0·005 262
21	0·007 802	0·006 609	0·005 605	0·004 760	0·004 048
22	0·006 192	0·005 204	0·004 379	0·003 690	0·003 113
23	0·004 914	0·004 097	0·003 421	0·002 860	0·002 395
24	0·003 900	0·003 226	0·002 673	0·002 217	0·001 842
25	0·003 096	0·002 540	0·002 088	0·001 719	0·001 417
26	0·002 457	0·002 000	0·001 631	0·001 332	0·001 090
27	0·001 950	0·001 575	0·001 274	0·001 033	0·000 839
28	0·001 547	0·001 240	0·000 996	0·000 801	0·000 645
29	0·001 228	0·000 977	0·000 778	0·000 621	0·000 496
30	0·000 975	0·000 769	0·000 608	0·000 481	0·000 382
31	0·000 774	0·000 605	0·000 475	0·000 373	0·000 294
32	0·000 614	0·000 477	0·000 371	0·000 289	0·000 226
33	0·000 487	0·000 375	0·000 290	0·000 224	0·000 174
34	0·000 387	0·000 296	0·000 226	0·000 174	0·000 134
35	0·000 307	0·000 233	0·000 177	0·000 135	0·000 103
36	0·000 244	0·000 183	0·000 138	0·000 104	7·91, −5*
37	0·000 193	0·000 144	0·000 108	8·09, −5*	6·08, −5
38	0·000 153	0·000 114	8·43, −5*	6·27, −5	4·68, −5
39	0·000 122	8·95, −5*	6·59, −5	4·86, −5	3·60, −5
40	9·66, −5*	7·04, −5	5·15, −5	3·77, −5	2·77, −5
41	7·67, −5	5·55, −5	4·02, −5	2·92, −5	2·13, −5
42	6·09, −5	4·37, −5	3·14, −5	2·27, −5	1·64, −5
43	4·83, −5	3·44, −5	2·45, −5	1·76, −5	1·26, −5
44	3·83, −5	2·71, −5	1·92, −5	1·36, −5	9·69, −6
45	3·04, −5	2·13, −5	1·50, −5	1·06, −5	7·46, −6
46	2·42, −5	1·68, −5	1·17, −5	8·18, −6	5·74, −6
47	1·92, −5	1·32, −5	9·14, −6	6·34, −6	4·41, −6
48	1·52, −5	1·04, −5	7·14, −6	4·92, −6	3·39, −6
49	1·21, −5	8·20, −6	5·58, −6	3·81, −6	2·61, −6
50	9·58, −6	6·45, −6	4·36, −6	2·95, −6	2·01, −6

YEAR

* The final digit is the power of 10 by which the given tabular value has to be multiplied (see example on p. 163).

APPENDIX A

Present value of 1 due n years hence $v_{\overline{n}|r} = (1+r)^{-n}$

PERCENTAGE

	31	32	33	34	35
1	0·763 359	0·757 576	0·751 880	0·746 268	0·740 741
2	0·582 716	0·573 921	0·565 323	0·556 917	0·548 697
3	0·444 822	0·434 788	0·425 055	0·415 609	0·406 442
4	0·339 558	0·329 385	0·319 590	0·310 156	0·301 068
5	0·259 205	0·249 534	0·240 293	0·231 460	0·223 013
6	0·197 866	0·189 041	0·180 671	0·172 731	0·165 195
7	0·151 043	0·143 213	0·135 843	0·128 904	0·122 367
8	0·115 300	0·108 494	0·102 138	0·096 197	0·090 642
9	0·088 015	0·082 193	0·076 795	0·071 789	0·067 142
10	0·067 187	0·062 267	0·057 741	0·053 574	0·049 735
11	0·051 288	0·047 172	0·043 414	0·039 980	0·036 841
12	0·039 151	0·035 736	0·032 642	0·029 836	0·027 289
13	0·029 886	0·027 073	0·024 543	0·022 266	0·020 214
14	0·022 814	0·020 510	0·018 453	0·016 616	0·014 974
15	0·017 415	0·015 538	0·013 875	0·012 400	0·011 092
16	0·013 294	0·011 771	0·010 432	0·009 254	0·008 216
17	0·010 148	0·008 917	0·007 844	0·006 906	0·006 086
18	0·007 747	0·006 756	0·005 898	0·005 154	0·004 508
19	0·005 913	0·005 118	0·004 434	0·003 846	0·003 339
20	0·004 514	0·003 877	0·003 334	0·002 870	0·002 474
21	0·003 446	0·002 937	0·002 507	0·002 142	0·001 832
22	0·002 630	0·002 225	0·001 885	0·001 598	0·001 357
23	0·002 008	0·001 686	0·001 417	0·001 193	0·001 005
24	0·001 533	0·001 277	0·001 066	0·000 890	0·000 745
25	0·001 170	0·000 967	0·000 801	0·000 664	0·000 552
26	0·000 893	0·000 733	0·000 602	0·000 496	0·000 409
27	0·000 682	0·000 555	0·000 453	0·000 370	0·000 303
28	0·000 520	0·000 421	0·000 341	0·000 276	0·000 224
29	0·000 397	0·000 319	0·000 256	0·000 206	0·000 166
30	0·000 303	0·000 241	0·000 193	0·000 154	0·000 123
31	0·000 232	0·000 183	0·000 145	0·000 115	9·11, −5*
32	0·000 177	0·000 139	0·000 109	8·56, −5*	6·75, −5
33	0·000 135	0·000 105	8·18, −5*	6·39, −5	5·00, −5
34	0·000 103	7·95, −5*	6·15, −5	4·77, −5	3·70, −5
35	7·86, −5*	6·02, −5	4·63, −5	3·56, −5	2·74, −5
36	6·00, −5	4·56, −5	3·48, −5	2·66, −5	2·03, −5
37	4·58, −5	3·46, −5	2·62, −5	1·98, −5	1·51, −5
38	3·50, −5	2·62, −5	1·97, −5	1·48, −5	1·12, −5
39	2·67, −5	1·98, −5	1·48, −5	1·10, −5	8·26, −6
40	2·04, −5	1·50, −5	1·11, −5	8·24, −6	6·12, −6
41	1·56, −5	1·14, −5	8·36, −6	6·15, −6	4·53, −6
42	1·19, −5	8·63, −6	6·28, −6	4·59, −6	3·36, −6
43	9·06, −6	6·54, −6	4·72, −6	3·42, −6	2·49, −6
44	6·92, −6	4·95, −6	3·55, −6	2·55, −6	1·84, −6
45	5·28, −6	3·75, −6	2·67, −6	1·91, −6	1·36, −6
46	4·03, −6	2·84, −6	2·01, −6	1·42, −6	1·01, −6
47	3·08, −6	2·15, −6	1·51, −6	1·06, −6	7·49, −7
48	2·35, −6	1·63, −6	1·14, −6	7·92, −7	5·55, −7
49	1·79, −6	1·24, −6	8·54, −7	5·91, −7	4·11, −7
50	1·37, −6	9·36, −7	6·42, −7	4·41, −7	3·04, −7

YEAR

* The final digit is the power of 10 by which the given tabular value has to be multiplied (see example on p. 163).

APPENDIX A

Present value of 1 due n years hence $v_{\overline{n}|r} = (1+r)^{-n}$

PERCENTAGE

YEAR	36	37	38	39	40
1	0·735 294	0·729 927	0·724 637	0·719 424	0·714 286
2	0·540 657	0·532 793	0·525 099	0·517 571	0·510 204
3	0·397 542	0·388 900	0·380 507	0·372 353	0·364 431
4	0·292 310	0·283 869	0·275 729	0·267 880	0·260 308
5	0·214 934	0·207 203	0·199 804	0·192 719	0·185 934
6	0·158 040	0·151 243	0·144 785	0·138 647	0·132 810
7	0·116 206	0·110 396	0·104 917	0·099 746	0·094 864
8	0·085 445	0·080 581	0·076 027	0·071 760	0·067 760
9	0·062 827	0·058 818	0·055 092	0·051 626	0·048 400
10	0·046 197	0·042 933	0·039 922	0·037 141	0·034 572
11	0·033 968	0·031 338	0·028 929	0·026 720	0·024 694
12	0·024 977	0·022 875	0·020 963	0·019 223	0·017 639
13	0·018 365	0·016 697	0·015 190	0·013 829	0·012 599
14	0·013 504	0·012 187	0·011 008	0·009 949	0·008 999
15	0·009 929	0·008 896	0·007 976	0·007 158	0·006 428
16	0·007 301	0·006 493	0·005 780	0·005 149	0·004 591
17	0·005 368	0·004 740	0·004 188	0·003 705	0·003 280
18	0·003 947	0·003 460	0·003 035	0·002 665	0·002 343
19	0·002 902	0·002 525	0·002 199	0·001 917	0·001 673
20	0·002 134	0·001 843	0·001 594	0·001 379	0·001 195
21	0·001 569	0·001 345	0·001 155	0·000 992	0·000 854
22	0·001 154	0·000 982	0·000 837	0·000 714	0·000 610
23	0·000 848	0·000 717	0·000 606	0·000 514	0·000 436
24	0·000 624	0·000 523	0·000 439	0·000 370	0·000 311
25	0·000 459	0·000 382	0·000 318	0·000 266	0·000 222
26	0·000 337	0·000 279	0·000 231	0·000 191	0·000 159
27	0·000 248	0·000 203	0·000 167	0·000 138	0·000 113
28	0·000 182	0·000 149	0·000 121	9·90, −5*	8·10, −5*
29	0·000 134	0·000 108	8·78, −5*	7·12, −5	5·78, −5
30	9·86, −5*	7·91, −5*	6·36, −5	5·12, −5	4·13, −5
31	7·25, −5	5·78, −5	4·61, −5	3·69, −5	2·95, −5
32	5·33, −5	4·22, −5	3·34, −5	2·65, −5	2·11, −5
33	3·92, −5	3·08, −5	2·42, −5	1·91, −5	1·51, −5
34	2·88, −5	2·25, −5	1·75, −5	1·37, −5	1·08, −5
35	2·12, −5	1·64, −5	1·27, −5	9·87, −6	7·68, −6
36	1·56, −5	1·20, −5	9·21, −6	7·10, −6	5·49, −6
37	1·15, −5	8·74, −6	6·68, −6	5·11, −6	3·92, −6
38	8·42, −6	6·38, −6	4·84, −6	3·68, −6	2·80, −6
39	6·19, −6	4·65, −6	3·51, −6	2·64, −6	2·00, −6
40	4·55, −6	3·40, −6	2·54, −6	1·90, −6	1·43, −6
41	3·35, −6	2·48, −6	1·84, −6	1·37, −6	1·02, −6
42	2·46, −6	1·81, −6	1·33, −6	9·85, −7	7·29, −7
43	1·81, −6	1·32, −6	9·66, −7	7·09, −7	5·21, −7
44	1·33, −6	9·64, −7	7·00, −7	5·10, −7	3·72, −7
45	9·79, −7	7·04, −7	5·07, −7	3·67, −7	2·66, −7
46	7·20, −7	5·14, −7	3·68, −7	2·64, −7	1·90, −7
47	5·29, −7	3·75, −7	2·66, −7	1·90, −7	1·36, −7
48	3·89, −7	2·74, −7	1·93, −7	1·37, −7	9·68, −8
49	2·86, −7	2·00, −7	1·40, −7	9·82, −8	6·91, −8
50	2·10, −7	1·46, −7	1·01, −7	7·07, −8	4·94, −8

* The final digit is the power of 10 by which the given tabular value has to be multiplied (see example on p. 163).

APPENDIX A

Present value of 1 due n years hence $v_{\overline{n}|r} = (1+r)^{-n}$

PERCENTAGE

	41	42	43	44	45
1	0·709 220	0·704 225	0·699 300	0·694 444	0·689 655
2	0·502 992	0·495 933	0·489 021	0·482 253	0·475 624
3	0·356 732	0·349 249	0·341 973	0·334 898	0·328 016
4	0·253 001	0·245 950	0·239 142	0·232 568	0·226 218
5	0·179 434	0·173 204	0·167 232	0·161 505	0·156 012
6	0·127 258	0·121 975	0·116 945	0·112 156	0·107 595
7	0·090 254	0·085 898	0·081 780	0·077 886	0·074 203
8	0·064 010	0·060 491	0·057 189	0·054 088	0·051 175
9	0·045 397	0·042 599	0·039 992	0·037 561	0·035 293
10	0·032 196	0·030 000	0·027 967	0·026 084	0·024 340
11	0·022 834	0·021 126	0·019 557	0·018 114	0·016 786
12	0·016 195	0·014 878	0·013 676	0·012 579	0·011 577
13	0·011 485	0·010 477	0·009 564	0·008 735	0·007 984
14	0·008 146	0·007 378	0·006 688	0·006 066	0·005 506
15	0·005 777	0·005 196	0·004 677	0·004 213	0·003 797
16	0·004 097	0·003 659	0·003 271	0·002 925	0·002 619
17	0·002 906	0·002 577	0·002 287	0·002 032	0·001 806
18	0·002 061	0·001 815	0·001 599	0·001 411	0·001 246
19	0·001 462	0·001 278	0·001 118	0·000 980	0·000 859
20	0·001 037	0·000 900	0·000 782	0·000 680	0·000 592
21	0·000 735	0·000 634	0·000 547	0·000 472	0·000 409
22	0·000 521	0·000 446	0·000 382	0·000 328	0·000 282
23	0·000 370	0·000 314	0·000 267	0·000 228	0·000 194
24	0·000 262	0·000 221	0·000 187	0·000 158	0·000 134
25	0·000 186	0·000 156	0·000 131	0·000 110	9·24, −5*
26	0·000 132	0·000 110	9·15, −5*	7·63, −5*	6·37, −5
27	9·36, −5*	7·73, −5*	6·40, −5	5·30, −5	4·40, −5
28	6·64, −5	5·44, −5	4·47, −5	3·68, −5	3·03, −5
29	4·71, −5	3·83, −5	3·13, −5	2·56, −5	2·09, −5
30	3·34, −5	2·70, −5	2·19, −5	1·77, −5	1·44, −5
31	2·37, −5	1·90, −5	1·53, −5	1·23, −5	9·94, −6
32	1·68, −5	1·34, −5	1·07, −5	8·56, −6	6·86, −6
33	1·19, −5	9·43, −6	7·48, −6	5·94, −6	4·73, −6
34	8·44, −6	6·64, −6	5·23, −6	4·13, −6	3·26, −6
35	5·99, −6	4·68, −6	3·66, −6	2·87, −6	2·25, −6
36	4·25, −6	3·29, −6	2·56, −6	1·99, −6	1·55, −6
37	3·01, −6	2·32, −6	1·79, −6	1·38, −6	1·07, −6
38	2·14, −6	1·63, −6	1·25, −6	9·60, −7	7·38, −7
39	1·52, −6	1·15, −6	8·75, −7	6·67, −7	5·09, −7
40	1·07, −6	8·10, −7	6·12, −7	4·63, −7	3·51, −7
41	7·62, −7	5·70, −7	4·28, −7	3·21, −7	2·42, −7
42	5·40, −7	4·02, −7	2·99, −7	2·23, −7	1·67, −7
43	3·83, −7	2·83, −7	2·09, −7	1·55, −7	1·15, −7
44	2·72, −7	1·99, −7	1·46, −7	1·08, −7	7·94, −8
45	1·93, −7	1·40, −7	1·02, −7	7·48, −8	5·48, −8
46	1·37, −7	9·88, −8	7·15, −8	5·19, −8	3·78, −8
47	9·70, −8	6·96, −8	5·00, −8	3·61, −8	2·60, −8
48	6·88, −8	4·90, −8	3·50, −8	2·50, −8	1·80, −8
49	4·88, −8	3·45, −8	2·45, −8	1·74, −8	1·24, −8
50	3·46, −8	2·43, −8	1·71, −8	1·21, −8	8·54, −9

The left margin is labelled vertically: YEAR

* The final digit is the power of 10 by which the given tabular value has to be multiplied (see example on p. 163).

APPENDIX A

Present value of 1 due n years hence $v_{\overline{n}|r} = (1+r)^{-n}$

PERCENTAGE

	46	47	48	49	50
1	0·684 931	0·680 272	0·675 675	0·671 141	0·666 666
2	0·469 131	0·462 770	0·456 537	0·450 430	0·444 444
3	0·321 322	0·314 809	0·308 471	0·302 302	0·296 296
4	0·220 084	0·214 156	0·208 426	0·202 887	0·197 531
5	0·150 742	0·145 684	0·140 829	0·136 166	0·131 687
6	0·103 248	0·099 105	0·095 154	0·091 386	0·087 791
7	0·070 718	0·067 418	0·064 293	0·061 333	0·058 528
8	0·048 437	0·045 863	0·043 442	0·041 163	0·039 018
9	0·033 176	0·031 199	0·029 352	0·027 626	0·026 012
10	0·022 723	0·021 224	0·019 833	0·018 541	0·017 341
11	0·015 564	0·014 438	0·013 400	0·012 444	0·011 561
12	0·010 660	0·009 822	0·009 054	0·008 351	0·007 707
13	0·007 301	0·006 681	0·006 118	0·005 605	0·005 138
14	0·005 001	0·004 545	0·004 134	0·003 762	0·003 425
15	0·003 425	0·003 092	0·002 793	0·002 525	0·002 284
16	0·002 346	0·002 103	0·001 887	0·001 694	0·001 522
17	0·001 607	0·001 431	0·001 275	0·001 137	0·001 015
18	0·001 101	0·000 973	0·000 862	0·000 763	0·000 677
19	0·000 754	0·000 662	0·000 582	0·000 512	0·000 451
20	0·000 516	0·000 450	0·000 393	0·000 344	0·000 301
21	0·000 354	0·000 306	0·000 266	0·000 231	0·000 200
22	0·000 242	0·000 208	0·000 180	0·000 155	0·000 134
23	0·000 166	0·000 142	0·000 121	0·000 104	8·91, −5*
24	0·000 114	9·65, −5*	8·20, −5*	6·97, −5*	5·94, −5
25	7·78, −5*	6·56, −5	5·54, −5	4·68, −5	3·96, −5
26	5·33, −5	4·46, −5	3·74, −5	3·14, −5	2·64, −5
27	3·65, −5	3·04, −5	2·53, −5	2·11, −5	1·76, −5
28	2·50, −5	2·07, −5	1·71, −5	1·42, −5	1·17, −5
29	1·71, −5	1·41, −5	1·15, −5	9·50, −6	7·82, −6
30	1·17, −5	9·56, −6	7·80, −6	6·37, −6	5·22, −6
31	8·04, −6	6·50, −6	5·27, −6	4·28, −6	3·48, −6
32	5·50, −6	4·42, −6	3·56, −6	2·87, −6	2·32, −6
33	3·77, −6	3·01, −6	2·41, −6	1·93, −6	1·55, −6
34	2·58, −6	2·05, −6	1·63, −6	1·29, −6	1·03, −6
35	1·77, −6	1·39, −6	1·10, −6	8·68, −7	6·87, −7
36	1·21, −6	9·47, −7	7·42, −7	5·82, −7	4·58, −7
37	8·30, −7	6·45, −7	5·02, −7	3·91, −7	3·05, −7
38	5·68, −7	4·38, −7	3·39, −7	2·62, −7	2·03, −7
39	3·89, −7	2·98, −7	2·29, −7	1·76, −7	1·36, −7
40	2·67, −7	2·03, −7	1·55, −7	1·18, −7	9·04, −8
41	1·83, −7	1·38, −7	1·05, −7	7·93, −8	6·03, −8
42	1·25, −7	9·39, −8	7·06, −8	5·32, −8	4·02, −8
43	8·57, −8	6·39, −8	4·77, −8	3·57, −8	2·68, −8
44	5·87, −8	4·35, −8	3·22, −8	2·40, −8	1·79, −8
45	4·02, −8	2·96, −8	2·18, −8	1·61, −8	1·19, −8
46	2·75, −8	2·01, −8	1·47, −8	1·08, −8	7·94, −9
47	1·89, −8	1·37, −8	9·95, −9	7·25, −9	5·29, −9
48	1·29, −8	9·31, −9	6·72, −9	4·86, −9	3·53, −9
49	8·85, −9	6·33, −9	4·54, −9	3·26, −9	2·35, −9
50	6·06, −9	4·31, −9	3·07, −9	2·19, −9	1·57, −9

* The final digit is the power of 10 by which the given tabular value has to be multiplied (see example on p. 163).

APPENDIX B

Present value of 1 p.a. due end-year $a_{\overline{n}|r} = \dfrac{1-(1+r)^{-n}}{r}$

PERCENTAGE

	1	2	3	4	5
1	0·9901	0·9804	0·9709	0·9615	0·9524
2	1·9704	1·9416	1·9135	1·8861	1·8594
3	2·9410	2·8839	2·8286	2·7751	2·7232
4	3·9020	3·8077	3·7171	3·6299	3·5460
5	4·8534	4·7135	4·5797	4·4518	4·3295
6	5·7955	5·6014	5·4172	5·2421	5·0757
7	6·7282	6·4720	6·2303	6·0021	5·7864
8	7·6517	7·3255	7·0197	6·7327	6·4632
9	8·5660	8·1622	7·7861	7·4353	7·1078
10	9·4713	8·9826	8·5302	8·1109	7·7217
11	10·3676	9·7868	9·2526	8·7605	8·3064
12	11·2551	10·5753	9·9540	9·3851	8·8633
13	12·1337	11·3484	10·6350	9·9856	9·3936
14	13·0037	12·1062	11·2961	10·5631	9·8986
15	13·8650	12·8493	11·9379	11·1184	10·3797
16	14·7179	13·5777	12·5611	11·6523	10·8378
17	15·5622	14·2919	13·1661	12·1657	11·2741
18	16·3983	14·9920	13·7535	12·6593	11·6896
19	17·2260	15·6785	14·3238	13·1339	12·0853
20	18·0455	16·3514	14·8775	13·5903	12·4622
21	18·8570	17·0112	15·4150	14·0292	12·8212
22	19·6604	17·6580	15·9369	14·4511	13·1630
23	20·4558	18·2922	16·4436	14·8568	13·4886
24	21·2434	18·9139	16·9355	15·2470	13·7986
25	22·0231	19·5234	17·4131	15·6221	14·0939
26	22·7952	20·1210	17·8768	15·9828	14·3752
27	23·5596	20·7069	18·3270	16·3296	14·6430
28	24·3164	21·2813	18·7641	16·6631	14·8981
29	25·0658	21·8444	19·1884	16·9837	15·1411
30	25·8077	22·3964	19·6004	17·2920	15·3725
31	26·5423	22·9377	20·0004	17·5885	15·5928
32	27·2696	23·4683	20·3888	17·8736	15·8027
33	27·9897	23·9886	20·7658	18·1476	16·0025
34	28·7027	24·4986	21·1318	18·4112	16·1929
35	29·4086	24·9986	21·4872	18·6646	16·3742
36	30·1075	25·4888	21·8322	18·9083	16·5469
37	30·7995	25·9694	22·1672	19·1426	16·7113
38	31·4846	26·4406	22·4925	19·3679	16·8679
39	32·1630	26·9026	22·8082	19·5845	17·0170
40	32·8347	27·3555	23·1148	19·7928	17·1591
41	33·4997	27·7995	23·4124	19·9931	17·2944
42	34·1581	28·2348	23·7014	20·1856	17·4232
43	34·8100	28·6616	23·9819	20·3708	17·5459
44	35·4554	29·0800	24·2543	20·5488	17·6628
45	36·0945	29·4902	24·5187	20·7200	17·7741
46	36·7272	29·8923	24·7754	20·8847	17·8801
47	37·3537	30·2866	25·0247	21·0429	17·9810
48	37·9739	30·6731	25·2667	21·1951	18·0772
49	38·5881	31·0521	25·5017	21·3415	18·1687
50	39·1961	31·4236	25·7298	21·4822	18·2559

YEAR

APPENDIX B

Present value of 1 p.a. due end-year $a_{\overline{n}|r} = \dfrac{1-(1+r)^{-n}}{r}$

PERCENTAGE

YEAR	6	7	8	9	10
1	0·9434	0·9346	0·9259	0·9174	0·9091
2	1·8334	1·8080	1·7833	1·7591	1·7355
3	2·6730	2·6243	2·5771	2·5313	2·4869
4	3·4651	3·3872	3·3121	3·2397	3·1699
5	4·2124	4·1002	3·9927	3·8897	3·7908
6	4·9173	4·7665	4·6229	4·4859	4·3553
7	5·5824	5·3893	5·2064	5·0330	4·8684
8	6·2098	5·9713	5·7466	5·5348	5·3349
9	6·8017	6·5152	6·2469	5·9952	5·7590
10	7·3601	7·0236	6·7101	6·4177	6·1446
11	7·8869	7·4987	7·1390	6·8052	6·4951
12	8·3838	7·9427	7·5361	7·1607	6·8137
13	8·8527	8·3577	7·9038	7·4869	7·1034
14	9·2950	8·7455	8·2442	7·7862	7·3667
15	9·7122	9·1079	8·5595	8·0607	7·6061
16	10·1059	9·4466	8·8514	8·3126	7·8237
17	10·4773	9·7632	9·1216	8·5436	8·0216
18	10·8276	10·0591	9·3719	8·7556	8·2014
19	11·1581	10·3356	9·6036	8·9501	8·3649
20	11·4699	10·5940	9·8181	9·1285	8·5136
21	11·7641	10·8355	10·0168	9·2922	8·6487
22	12·0416	11·0612	10·2007	9·4424	8·7715
23	12·3034	11·2722	10·3711	9·5802	8·8832
24	12·5504	11·4693	10·5288	9·7066	8·9847
25	12·7834	11·6536	10·6748	9·8226	9·0770
26	13·0032	11·8258	10·8100	9·9290	9·1609
27	13·2105	11·9867	10·9352	10·0266	9·2372
28	13·4062	12·1371	11·0511	10·1161	9·3066
29	13·5907	12·2777	11·1584	10·1983	9·3696
30	13·7648	12·4090	11·2578	10·2737	9·4269
31	13·9291	12·5318	11·3498	10·3428	9·4790
32	14·0840	12·6466	11·4350	10·4062	9·5264
33	14·2302	12·7538	11·5139	10·4644	9·5694
34	14·3681	12·8540	11·5869	10·5178	9·6086
35	14·4982	12·9477	11·6546	10·5668	9·6442
36	14·6210	13·0352	11·7172	10·6118	9·6765
37	14·7368	13·1170	11·7752	10·6530	9·7059
38	14·8460	13·1935	11·8289	10·6908	9·7327
39	14·9491	13·2649	11·8786	10·7255	9·7570
40	15·0463	13·3317	11·9246	10·7574	9·7791
41	15·1380	13·3941	11·9672	10·7866	9·7991
42	15·2245	13·4524	12·0067	10·8134	9·8174
43	15·3062	13·5070	12·0432	10·8380	9·8340
44	15·3832	13·5579	12·0771	10·8605	9·8491
45	15·4558	13·6055	12·1084	10·8812	9·8628
46	15·5244	13·6500	12·1374	10·9002	9·8753
47	15·5890	13·6916	12·1643	10·9176	9·8866
48	15·6500	13·7305	12·1891	10·9336	9·8969
49	15·7076	13·7668	12·2122	10·9482	9·9063
50	15·7619	13·8007	12·2335	10·9617	9·9148

APPENDIX B

Present value of 1 p.a. due end-year $a_{\overline{n}|r} = \dfrac{1-(1+r)^{-n}}{r}$

PERCENTAGE

	11	12	13	14	15
1	0·9009	0·8929	0·8850	0·8772	0·8696
2	1·7125	1·6901	1·6681	1·6467	1·6257
3	2·4437	2·4018	2·3612	2·3216	2·2832
4	3·1024	3·0373	2·9745	2·9137	2·8550
5	3·6959	3·6048	3·5172	3·4331	3·3522
6	4·2305	4·1114	3·9975	3·8887	3·7845
7	4·7122	4·5638	4·4226	4·2883	4·1604
8	5·1461	4·9676	4·7988	4·6389	4·4873
9	5·5370	5·3282	5·1317	4·9464	4·7716
10	5·8892	5·6502	5·4262	5·2161	5·0188
11	6·2065	5·9377	5·6869	5·4527	5·2337
12	6·4924	6·1944	5·9176	5·6603	5·4206
13	6·7499	6·4235	6·1218	5·8424	5·5831
14	6·9819	6·6282	6·3025	6·0021	5·7245
15	7·1909	6·8109	6·4624	6·1422	5·8474
16	7·3792	6·9740	6·6039	6·2651	5·9542
17	7·5488	7·1196	6·7291	6·3729	6·0472
18	7·7016	7·2497	6·8399	6·4674	6·1280
19	7·8393	7·3658	6·9380	6·5504	6·1982
20	7·9633	7·4694	7·0248	6·6231	6·2593
21	8·0751	7·5620	7·1015	6·6870	6·3125
22	8·1757	7·6446	7·1695	6·7429	6·3587
23	8·2664	7·7184	7·2297	6·7921	6·3988
24	8·3481	7·7843	7·2829	6·8351	6·4338
25	8·4217	7·8431	7·3300	6·8729	6·4641
26	8·4881	7·8957	7·3717	6·9061	6·4906
27	8·5478	7·9426	7·4086	6·9352	6·5135
28	8·6016	7·9844	7·4412	6·9607	6·5335
29	8·6501	8·0218	7·4701	6·9830	6·5509
30	8·6938	8·0552	7·4957	7·0027	6·5660
31	8·7331	8·0850	7·5183	7·0199	6·5791
32	8·7686	8·1116	7·5383	7·0350	6·5905
33	8·8005	8·1354	7·5560	7·0482	6·6005
34	8·8293	8·1566	7·5717	7·0599	6·6091
35	8·8552	8·1755	7·5856	7·0700	6·6166
36	8·8786	8·1924	7·5979	7·0790	6·6231
37	8·8996	8·2075	7·6087	7·0868	6·6288
38	8·9186	8·2210	7·6183	7·0937	6·6338
39	8·9357	8·2330	7·6268	7·0997	6·6380
40	8·9511	8·2438	7·6344	7·1050	6·6418
41	8·9649	8·2534	7·6410	7·1097	6·6450
42	8·9774	8·2619	7·6469	7·1138	6·6478
43	8·9886	8·2696	7·6522	7·1173	6·6503
44	8·9988	8·2764	7·6568	7·1205	6·6524
45	9·0079	8·2825	7·6609	7·1232	6·6543
46	9·0161	8·2880	7·6645	7·1256	6·6559
47	9·0235	8·2928	7·6677	7·1277	6·6573
48	9·0302	8·2972	7·6705	7·1296	6·6585
49	9·0362	8·3010	7·6730	7·1312	6·6596
50	9·0417	8·3045	7·6752	7·1327	6·6605

YEAR (rows 23–26)

APPENDIX B

Present value of 1 p.a. due end-year $a_{\overline{n}|r} = \dfrac{1-(1+r)^{-n}}{r}$

PERCENTAGE

	16	17	18	19	20
1	0·8621	0·8547	0·8475	0·8403	0·8333
2	1·6052	1·5852	1·5656	1·5465	1·5278
3	2·2459	2·2096	2·1743	2·1399	2·1065
4	2·7982	2·7432	2·6901	2·6386	2·5887
5	3·2743	3·1993	3·1272	3·0576	2·9906
6	3·6847	3·5892	3·4976	3·4098	3·3255
7	4·0386	3·9224	3·8115	3·7057	3·6046
8	4·3436	4·2072	4·0776	3·9544	3·8372
9	4·6065	4·4506	4·3030	4·1633	4·0310
10	4·8332	4·6586	4·4941	4·3389	4·1925
11	5·0286	4·8364	4·6560	4·4865	4·3271
12	5·1971	4·9884	4·7932	4·6105	4·4392
13	5·3423	5·1183	4·9095	4·7147	4·5327
14	5·4675	5·2293	5·0081	4·8023	4·6106
15	5·5755	5·3242	5·0916	4·8759	4·6755
16	5·6685	5·4053	5·1624	4·9377	4·7296
17	5·7487	5·4746	5·2223	4·9897	4·7746
18	5·8178	5·5339	5·2732	5·0333	4·8122
19	5·8775	5·5845	5·3162	5·0700	4·8435
20	5·9288	5·6278	5·3527	5·1009	4·8696
21	5·9731	5·6648	5·3837	5·1268	4·8913
22	6·0113	5·6964	5·4099	5·1486	4·9094
23	6·0442	5·7234	5·4321	5·1668	4·9245
24	6·0726	5·7465	5·4509	5·1822	4·9371
25	6·0971	5·7662	5·4669	5·1951	4·9476
26	6·1182	5·7831	5·4804	5·2060	4·9563
27	6·1364	5·7975	5·4919	5·2151	4·9636
28	6·1520	5·8099	5·5016	5·2228	4·9697
29	6·1656	5·8204	5·5098	5·2292	4·9747
30	6·1772	5·8294	5·5168	5·2347	4·9789
31	6·1872	5·8371	5·5227	5·2392	4·9824
32	6·1959	5·8437	5·5277	5·2430	4·9854
33	6·2034	5·8493	5·5320	5·2462	4·9878
34	6·2098	5·8541	5·5356	5·2489	4·9898
35	6·2153	5·8582	5·5386	5·2512	4·9915
36	6·2201	5·8617	5·5412	5·2531	4·9929
37	6·2242	5·8647	5·5434	5·2547	4·9941
38	6·2278	5·8673	5·5452	5·2561	4·9951
39	6·2309	5·8695	5·5468	5·2572	4·9959
40	6·2335	5·8713	5·5482	5·2582	4·9966
41	6·2358	5·8729	5·5493	5·2590	4·9972
42	6·2377	5·8743	5·5502	5·2596	4·9976
43	6·2394	5·8755	5·5510	5·2602	4·9980
44	6·2409	5·8765	5·5517	5·2607	4·9984
45	6·2421	5·8773	5·5523	5·2611	4·9986
46	6·2432	5·8781	5·5528	5·2614	4·9989
47	6·2442	5·8787	5·5532	5·2617	4·9991
48	6·2450	5·8792	5·5536	5·2619	4·9992
49	6·2457	5·8797	5·5539	5·2621	4·9993
50	6·2463	5·8801	5·5541	5·2623	4·9995

YEAR

APPENDIX B

Present value of 1 p.a. due end-year $a_{\overline{n}|r} = \dfrac{1-(1+r)^{-n}}{r}$

PERCENTAGE

	21	22	23	24	25
1	0·8264	0·8197	0·8130	0·8065	0·8000
2	1·5095	1·4915	1·4740	1·4568	1·4400
3	2·0739	2·0422	2·0114	1·9813	1·9520
4	2·5404	2·4936	2·4483	2·4043	2·3616
5	2·9260	2·8636	2·8035	2·7454	2·6893
6	3·2446	3·1669	3·0923	3·0205	2·9514
7	3·5079	3·4155	3·3270	3·2423	3·1611
8	3·7256	3·6193	3·5179	3·4212	3·3289
9	3·9054	3·7863	3·6731	3·5655	3·4631
10	4·0541	3·9232	3·7993	3·6819	3·5705
11	4·1769	4·0354	3·9018	3·7757	3·6564
12	4·2784	4·1274	3·9852	3·8514	3·7251
13	4·3624	4·2028	4·0530	3·9124	3·7801
14	4·4317	4·2646	4·1082	3·9616	3·8241
15	4·4890	4·3152	4·1530	4·0013	3·8593
16	4·5364	4·3567	4·1894	4·0333	3·8874
17	4·5755	4·3908	4·2190	4·0591	3·9099
18	4·6079	4·4187	4·2431	4·0799	3·9279
19	4·6346	4·4415	4·2627	4·0967	3·9424
20	4·6567	4·4603	4·2786	4·1103	3·9539
21	4·6750	4·4756	4·2916	4·1212	3·9631
22	4·6900	4·4882	4·3021	4·1300	3·9705
23	4·7025	4·4985	4·3106	4·1371	3·9764
24	4·7128	4·5070	4·3176	4·1428	3·9811
25	4·7213	4·5139	4·3232	4·1474	3·9849
26	4·7284	4·5196	4·3278	4·1511	3·9879
27	4·7342	4·5243	4·3316	4·1542	3·9903
28	4·7390	4·5281	4·3346	4·1566	3·9923
29	4·7430	4·5312	4·3371	4·1585	3·9938
30	4·7463	4·5338	4·3391	4·1601	3·9950
31	4·7490	4·5359	4·3407	4·1614	3·9960
32	4·7512	4·5376	4·3421	4·1624	3·9968
33	4·7531	4·5390	4·3431	4·1632	3·9975
34	4·7546	4·5402	4·3440	4·1639	3·9980
35	4·7559	4·5411	4·3447	4·1644	3·9984
36	4·7569	4·5419	4·3453	4·1649	3·9987
37	4·7578	4·5426	4·3458	4·1652	3·9990
38	4·7585	4·5431	4·3462	4·1655	3·9992
39	4·7591	4·5435	4·3465	4·1657	3·9993
40	4·7596	4·5439	4·3467	4·1659	3·9995
41	4·7600	4·5441	4·3469	4·1661	3·9996
42	4·7603	4·5444	4·3471	4·1662	3·9997
43	4·7606	4·5446	4,3472	4·1663	3·9997
44	4·7608	4·5447	4·3473	4·1663	3·9998
45	4·7610	4·5449	4·3474	4·1664	3·9998
46	4·7612	4·5450	4·3475	4·1665	3·9999
47	4·7613	4·5451	4·3476	4·1665	3·9999
48	4·7614	4·5451	4·3476	4·1665	3·9999
49	4·7615	4·5452	4·3477	4·1666	3·9999
50	4·7616	4·5452	4·3477	4·1666	3·9999

YEAR

APPENDIX B

Present value of 1 p.a. due end-year $a_{\overline{n}|r} = \dfrac{1-(1+r)^{-n}}{r}$

PERCENTAGE

	26	27	28	29	30
1	0·7937	0·7874	0·7812	0·7752	0·7692
2	1·4235	1·4074	1·3916	1·3761	1·3609
3	1·9234	1·8956	1·8684	1·8420	1·8161
4	2·3202	2·2800	2·2410	2·2031	2·1662
5	2·6351	2·5827	2·5320	2·4830	2·4356
6	2·8850	2·8210	2·7594	2·7000	2·6427
7	3·0833	3·0087	2·9370	2·8682	2·8021
8	3·2407	3·1564	3·0758	2·9986	2·9247
9	3·3657	3·2728	3·1842	3·0997	3·0190
10	3·4648	3·3644	3·2689	3·1781	3·0915
11	3·5435	3·4365	3·3351	3·2388	3·1473
12	3·6059	3·4933	3·3868	3·2859	3·1903
13	3·6555	3·5381	3·4272	3·3224	3·2233
14	3·6949	3·5733	3·4587	3·3507	3·2487
15	3·7261	3·6010	3·4834	3·3726	3·2682
16	3·7509	3·6228	3·5026	3·3896	3·2832
17	3·7705	3·6400	3·5177	3·4028	3·2948
18	3·7861	3·6536	3·5294	3·4130	3·3037
19	3·7985	3·6642	3·5386	3·4210	3·3105
20	3·8083	3·6726	3·5458	3·4271	3·3158
21	3·8161	3·6792	3·5514	3·4319	3·3198
22	3·8223	3·6844	3·5558	3·4356	3·3230
23	3·8273	3·6885	3·5592	3·4384	3·3254
24	3·8312	3·6918	3·5619	3·4406	3·3272
25	3·8342	3·6943	3·5640	3·4423	3·3286
26	3·8367	3·6963	3·5656	3·4437	3·3297
27	3·8387	3·6979	3·5669	3·4447	3·3305
28	3·8402	3·6991	3·5679	3·4455	3·3312
29	3·8414	3·7001	3·5687	3·4461	3·3317
30	3·8424	3·7009	3·5693	3·4466	3·3321
31	3·8432	3·7015	3·5697	3·4470	3·3324
32	3·8438	3·7019	3·5701	3·4473	3·3326
33	3·8443	3·7023	3·5704	3·4475	3·3328
34	3·8447	3·7026	3·5706	3·4477	3·3329
35	3·8450	3·7028	3·5708	3·4478	3·3330
36	3·8452	3·7030	3·5709	3·4479	3·3331
37	3·8454	3·7032	3·5710	3·4480	3·3331
38	3·8456	3·7033	3·5711	3·4481	3·3332
39	3·8457	3·7034	3·5712	3·4481	3·3332
40	3·8458	3·7034	3·5712	3·4481	3·3332
41	3·8459	3·7035	3·5713	3·4482	3·3333
42	3·8459	3·7035	3·5713	3·4482	3·3333
43	3·8460	3·7036	3·5713	3·4482	3·3333
44	3·8460	3·7036	3·5714	3·4482	3·3333
45	3·8460	3·7036	3·5714	3·4482	3·3333
46	3·8461	3·7036	3·5714	3·4482	3·3333
47	3·8461	3·7037	3·5714	3·4483	3·3333
48	3·8461	3·7037	3·5714	3·4483	3·3333
49	3·8461	3·7037	3·5714	3·4483	3·3333
50	3·8461	3·7037	3·5714	3·4483	3·3333

YEAR

APPENDIX B

Present value of 1 p.a. due end-year $a_{\overline{n}|r} = \dfrac{1-(1+r)^{-n}}{r}$

PERCENTAGE

	31	32	33	34	35
1	0·7634	0·7576	0·7519	0·7463	0·7407
2	1·3461	1·3315	1·3172	1·3032	1·2894
3	1·7909	1·7663	1·7423	1·7188	1·6959
4	2·1305	2·0957	2·0618	2·0290	1·9969
5	2·3897	2·3452	2·3021	2·2604	2·2200
6	2·5875	2·5342	2·4828	2·4331	2·3852
7	2·7386	2·6775	2·6187	2·5620	2·5075
8	2·8539	2·7860	2·7208	2·6582	2·5982
9	2·9419	2·8681	2·7976	2·7300	2·6653
10	3·0091	2·9304	2·8553	2·7836	2·7150
11	3·0604	2·9776	2·8987	2·8236	2·7519
12	3·0995	3·0133	2·9314	2·8534	2·7792
13	3·1294	3·0404	2·9559	2·8757	2·7994
14	3·1522	3·0609	2·9744	2·8923	2·8144
15	3·1696	3·0764	2·9883	2·9047	2·8255
16	3·1829	3·0882	2·9987	2·9140	2·8337
17	3·1931	3·0971	3·0065	2·9209	2·8398
18	3·2008	3·1039	3·0124	2·9260	2·8443
19	3·2067	3·1090	3·0169	2·9299	2·8476
20	3·2112	3·1129	3·0202	2·9327	2·8501
21	3·2147	3·1158	3·0227	2·9349	2·8519
22	3·2173	3·1180	3·0246	2·9365	2·8533
23	3·2193	3·1197	3·0260	2·9377	2·8543
24	3·2209	3·1210	3·0271	2·9386	2·8550
25	3·2220	3·1220	3·0279	2·9392	2·8556
26	3·2229	3·1227	3·0285	2·9397	2·8560
27	3·2236	3·1233	3·0289	2·9401	2·8563
28	3·2241	3·1237	3·0293	2·9404	2·8565
29	3·2245	3·1240	3·0295	2·9406	2·8567
30	3·2248	3·1242	3·0297	2·9407	2·8568
31	3·2251	3·1244	3·0299	2·9408	2·8569
32	3·2252	3·1246	3·0300	2·9409	2·8569
33	3·2254	3·1247	3·0301	2·9410	2·8570
34	3·2255	3·1248	3·0301	2·9410	2·8570
35	3·2256	3·1248	3·0302	2·9411	2·8571
36	3·2256	3·1249	3·0302	2·9411	2·8571
37	3·2257	3·1249	3·0302	2·9411	2·8571
38	3·2257	3·1249	3·0302	2·9411	2·8571
39	3·2257	3·1249	3·0303	2·9411	2·8571
40	3·2257	3·1250	3·0303	2·9412	2·8571
41	3·2258	3·1250	3·0303	2·9412	2·8571
42	3·2258	3·1250	3·0303	2·9412	2·8571
43	3·2258	3·1250	3·0303	2·9412	2·8571
44	3·2258	3·1250	3·0303	2·9412	2·8571
45	3·2258	3·1250	3·0303	2·9412	2·8571
46	3·2258	3·1250	3·0303	2·9412	2·8571
47	3·2258	3·1250	3·0303	2·9412	2·8571
48	3·2258	3·1250	3·0303	2·9412	2·8571
49	3·2258	3·1250	3·0303	2·9412	2·8571
50	3·2258	3·1250	3·0303	2·9412	2·8571

YEAR

APPENDIX B

Present value of 1 p.a. due end-year $a_{\overline{n}|r} = \dfrac{1-(1+r)^{-n}}{r}$

PERCENTAGE

	36	37	38	39	40
1	0·7353	0·7299	0·7246	0·7194	0·7143
2	1·2760	1·2627	1·2497	1·2370	1·2245
3	1·6735	1·6516	1·6302	1·6093	1·5889
4	1·9658	1·9355	1·9060	1·8772	1·8492
5	2·1807	2·1427	2·1058	2·0699	2·0352
6	2·3388	2·2939	2·2506	2·2086	2·1680
7	2·4550	2·4043	2·3555	2·3083	2·2628
8	2·5404	2·4849	2·4315	2·3801	2·3306
9	2·6033	2·5437	2·4866	2·4317	2·3790
10	2·6495	2·5867	2·5265	2·4689	2·4136
11	2·6834	2·6180	2·5555	2·4956	2·4383
12	2·7084	2·6409	2·5764	2·5148	2·4559
13	2·7268	2·6576	2·5916	2·5286	2·4685
14	2·7403	2·6698	2·6026	2·5386	2·4775
15	2·7502	2·6787	2·6106	2·5457	2·4839
16	2·7575	2·6852	2·6164	2·5509	2·4885
17	2·7629	2·6899	2·6206	2·5546	2·4918
18	2·7668	2·6934	2·6236	2·5573	2·4941
19	2·7697	2·6959	2·6258	2·5592	2·4958
20	2·7718	2·6977	2·6274	2·5606	2·4970
21	2·7734	2·6991	2·6285	2·5616	2·4979
22	2·7746	2·7000	2·6294	2·5623	2·4985
23	2·7754	2·7008	2·6300	2·5628	2·4989
24	2·7760	2·7013	2·6304	2·5632	2·4992
25	2·7765	2·7017	2·6307	2·5634	2·4994
26	2·7768	2·7019	2·6310	2·5636	2·4996
27	2·7771	2·7022	2·6311	2·5637	2·4997
28	2·7773	2·7023	2·6313	2·5638	2·4998
29	2·7774	2·7024	2·6313	2·5639	2·4999
30	2·7775	2·7025	2·6314	2·5640	2·4999
31	2·7776	2·7025	2·6315	2·5640	2·4999
32	2·7776	2·7026	2·6315	2·5640	2·4999
33	2·7777	2·7026	2·6315	2·5641	2·5000
34	2·7777	2·7026	2·6315	2·5641	2·5000
35	2·7777	2·7027	2·6315	2·5641	2·5000
36	2·7777	2·7027	2·6316	2·5641	2·5000
37	2·7777	2·7027	2·6316	2·5641	2·5000
38	2·7778	2·7027	2·6316	2·5641	2·5000
39	2·7778	2·7027	2·6316	2·5641	2·5000
40	2·7778	2·7027	2·6316	2·5641	2·5000
41	2·7778	2·7027	2·6316	2·5641	2·5000
42	2·7778	2·7027	2·6316	2·5641	2·5000
43	2·7778	2·7027	2·6316	2·5641	2·5000
44	2·7778	2·7027	2·6316	2·5641	2·5000
45	2·7778	2·7027	2·6316	2·5641	2·5000
46	2·7778	2·7027	2·6316	2·5641	2·5000
47	2·7778	2·7027	2·6316	2·5641	2·5000
48	2·7778	2·7027	2·6316	2·5641	2·5000
49	2·7778	2·7027	2·6316	2·5641	2·5000
50	2·7778	2·7027	2·6316	2·5641	2·5000

YEAR

APPENDIX B

Present value of 1 p.a. due end-year $a_{\overline{n}|r} = \dfrac{1-(1+r)^{-n}}{r}$

PERCENTAGE

	41	42	43	44	45
1	0·7092	0·7042	0·6993	0·6944	0·6897
2	1·2122	1·2002	1·1883	1·1767	1·1653
3	1·5689	1·5494	1·5303	1·5116	1·4933
4	1·8219	1·7954	1·7694	1·7442	1·7195
5	2·0014	1·9686	1·9367	1·9057	1·8755
6	2·1286	2·0905	2·0536	2·0178	1·9831
7	2·2189	2·1764	2·1354	2·0957	2·0573
8	2·2829	2·2369	2·1926	2·1498	2·1085
9	2·3283	2·2795	2·2326	2·1874	2·1438
10	2·3605	2·3095	2·2605	2·2134	2·1681
11	2·3833	2·3307	2·2801	2·2316	2·1849
12	2·3995	2·3455	2·2938	2·2441	2·1965
13	2·4110	2·3560	2·3033	2·2529	2·2045
14	2·4192	2·3634	2·3100	2·2589	2·2100
15	2·4249	2·3686	2·3147	2·2632	2·2138
16	2·4290	2·3722	2·3180	2·2661	2·2164
17	2·4319	2·3748	2·3203	2·2681	2·2182
18	2·4340	2·3766	2·3219	2·2695	2·2195
19	2·4355	2·3779	2·3230	2·2705	2·2203
20	2·4365	2·3788	2·3238	2·2712	2·2209
21	2·4372	2·3794	2·3243	2·2717	2·2213
22	2·4378	2·3799	2·3247	2·2720	2·2216
23	2·4381	2·3802	2·3250	2·2722	2·2218
24	2·4384	2·3804	2·3251	2·2724	2·2219
25	2·4386	2·3806	2·3253	2·2725	2·2220
26	2·4387	2·3807	2·3254	2·2726	2·2221
27	2·4388	2·3808	2·3254	2·2726	2·2221
28	2·4389	2·3808	2·3255	2·2726	2·2222
29	2·4389	2·3809	2·3255	2·2727	2·2222
30	2·4389	2·3809	2·3255	2·2727	2·2222
31	2·4390	2·3809	2·3255	2·2727	2·2222
32	2·4390	2·3809	2·3256	2·2727	2·2222
33	2·4390	2·3809	2·3256	2·2727	2·2222
34	2·4390	2·3809	2·3256	2·2727	2·2222
35	2·4390	2·3809	2·3256	2·2727	2·2222
36	2·4390	2·3809	2·3256	2·2727	2·2222
37	2·4390	2·3809	2·3256	2·2727	2·2222
38	2·4390	2·3809	2·3256	2·2727	2·2222
39	2·4390	2·3809	2·3256	2·2727	2·2222
40	2·4390	2·3810	2·3256	2·2727	2·2222
41	2·4390	2·3810	2·3256	2·2727	2·2222
42	2·4390	2·3810	2·3256	2·2727	2·2222
43	2·4390	2·3810	2·3256	2·2727	2·2222
44	2·4390	2·3810	2·3256	2·2727	2·2222
45	2·4390	2·3810	2·3256	2·2727	2·2222
46	2·4390	2·3810	2·3256	2·2727	2·2222
47	2·4390	2·3810	2·3256	2·2727	2·2222
48	2·4390	2·3810	2·3256	2·2727	2·2222
49	2·4390	2·3810	2·3256	2·2727	2·2222
50	2·4390	2·3810	2·3256	2·2727	2·2222

YEAR

APPENDIX B

Present value of 1 p.a. due end-year $a_{\overline{n}|r} = \dfrac{1-(1+r)^{-n}}{r}$

PERCENTAGE

	46	47	48	49	50
1	0·6849	0·6803	0·6757	0·6711	0·6667
2	1·1541	1·1430	1·1322	1·1216	1·1111
3	1·4754	1·4579	1·4407	1·4239	1·4074
4	1·6955	1·6720	1·6491	1·6268	1·6049
5	1·8462	1·8177	1·7899	1·7629	1·7366
6	1·9495	1·9168	1·8851	1·8543	1·8244
7	2·0202	1·9842	1·9494	1·9156	1·8829
8	2·0686	2·0301	1·9928	1·9568	1·9220
9	2·1018	2·0613	2·0222	1·9844	1·9480
10	2·1245	2·0825	2·0420	2·0030	1·9653
11	2·1401	2·0969	2·0554	2·0154	1·9769
12	2·1507	2·1068	2·0645	2·0238	1·9846
13	2·1580	2·1134	2·0706	2·0294	1·9897
14	2·1630	2·1180	2·0747	2·0331	1·9931
15	2·1665	2·1211	2·0775	2·0357	1·9954
16	2·1688	2·1232	2·0794	2·0374	1·9970
17	2·1704	2·1246	2·0807	2·0385	1·9980
18	2·1715	2·1256	2·0815	2·0393	1·9986
19	2·1723	2·1263	2·0821	2·0398	1·9991
20	2·1728	2·1267	2·0825	2·0401	1·9994
21	2·1731	2·1270	2·0828	2·0403	1·9996
22	2·1734	2·1272	2·0830	2·0405	1·9997
23	2·1736	2·1274	2·0831	2·0406	1·9998
24	2·1737	2·1275	2·0832	2·0407	1·9999
25	2·1737	2·1275	2·0832	2·0407	1·9999
26	2·1738	2·1276	2·0833	2·0408	1·9999
27	2·1738	2·1276	2·0833	2·0408	2·0000
28	2·1739	2·1276	2·0833	2·0408	2·0000
29	2·1739	2·1276	2·0833	2·0408	2·0000
30	2·1739	2·1276	2·0833	2·0408	2·0000
31	2·1739	2·1276	2·0833	2·0408	2·0000
32	2·1739	2·1277	2·0833	2·0408	2·0000
33	2·1739	2·1277	2·0833	2·0408	2·0000
34	2·1739	2·1277	2·0833	2·0408	2·0000
35	2·1739	2·1277	2·0833	2·0408	2·0000
36	2·1739	2·1277	2·0833	2·0408	2·0000
37	2·1739	2·1277	2·0833	2·0408	2·0000
38	2·1739	2·1277	2·0833	2·0408	2·0000
39	2·1739	2·1277	2·0833	2·0408	2·0000
40	2·1739	2·1277	2·0833	2·0408	2·0000
41	2·1739	2·1277	2·0833	2·0408	2·0000
42	2·1739	2·1277	2·0833	2·0408	2·0000
43	2·1739	2·1277	2·0833	2·0408	2·0000
44	2·1739	2·1277	2·0833	2·0408	2·0000
45	2·1739	2·1277	2·0833	2·0408	2·0000
46	2·1739	2·1277	2·0833	2·0408	2·0000
47	2·1739	2·1277	2·0833	2·0408	2·0000
48	2·1739	2·1277	2·0833	2·0408	2·0000
49	2·1739	2·1277	2·0833	2·0408	2·0000
50	2·1739	2·1277	2·0833	2·0408	2·0000

YEAR

APPENDIX C

(Compound rates of decline)

Present value of 1 due n years hence $v_{\overline{n}|-r} = (1-r)^{-n}$

PERCENTAGE

YEAR	1	2	3	4	5
1	1·0101,0*	1·0204,0*	1·0309,0*	1·0417,0*	1·0526,0*
2	1·0203,0	1·0412,0	1·0628,0	1·0851,0	1·1080,0
3	1·0306,0	1·0625,0	1·0957,0	1·1303,0	1·1664,0
4	1·0410,0	1·0842,0	1·1296,0	1·1774,0	1·2277,0
5	1·0515,0	1·1063,0	1·1645,0	1·2264,0	1·2924,0
6	1·0622,0	1·1289,0	1·2005,0	1·2775,0	1·3604,0
7	1·0729,0	1·1519,0	1·2376,0	1·3308,0	1·4320,0
8	1·0837,0	1·1754,0	1·2759,0	1·3862,0	1·5073,0
9	1·0947,0	1·1994,0	1·3154,0	1·4440,0	1·5867,0
10	1·1057,0	1·2239,0	1·3561,0	1·5041,0	1·6702,0
11	1·1169,0	1·2489,0	1·3980,0	1·5668,0	1·7581,0
12	1·1282,0	1·2743,0	1·4412,0	1·6321,0	1·8506,0
13	1·1396,0	1·3004,0	1·4858,0	1·7001,0	1·9480,0
14	1·1511,0	1·3269,0	1·5318,0	1·7709,0	2·0505,0
15	1·1627,0	1·3540,0	1·5792,0	1·8447,0	2·1585,0
16	1·1745,0	1·3816,0	1·6280,0	1·9216,0	2·2721,0
17	1·1863,0	1·4098,0	1·6783,0	2·0017,0	2·3917,0
18	1·1983,0	1·4386,0	1·7302,0	2·0851,0	2·5175,0
19	1·2104,0	1·4679,0	1·7838,0	2·1719,0	2·6500,0
20	1·2226,0	1·4979,0	1·8389,0	2·2624,0	2·7895,0
21	1·2350,0	1·5285,0	1·8958,0	2·3567,0	2·9363,0
22	1·2475,0	1·5596,0	1·9544,0	2·4549,0	3·0909,0
23	1·2601,0	1·5915,0	2·0149,0	2·5572,0	3·2535,0
24	1·2728,0	1·6240,0	2·0772,0	2·6637,0	3·4248,0
25	1·2856,0	1·6571,0	2·1414,0	2·7747,0	3·6050,0
26	1·2986,0	1·6909,0	2·2077,0	2·8903,0	3·7948,0
27	1·3117,0	1·7254,0	2·2760,0	3·0108,0	3·9945,0
28	1·3250,0	1·7606,0	2·3463,0	3·1362,0	4·2047,0
29	1·3384,0	1·7966,0	2·4189,0	3·2669,0	4·4260,0
30	1·3519,0	1·8332,0	2·4937,0	3·4030,0	4·6590,0
31	1·3656,0	1·8706,0	2·5708,0	3·5448,0	4·9042,0
32	1·3793,0	1·9088,0	2·6504,0	3·6925,0	5·1623,0
33	1·3933,0	1·9478,0	2·7323,0	3·8464,0	5·4340,0
34	1·4074,0	1·9875,0	2·8168,0	4·0066,0	5·7200,0
35	1·4216,0	2·0281,0	2·9040,0	4·1736,0	6·0211,0
36	1·4359,0	2·0695,0	2·9938,0	4·3475,0	6·3380,0
37	1·4504,0	2·1117,0	3·0864,0	4·5286,0	6·6715,0
38	1·4651,0	2·1548,0	3·1818,0	4·7173,0	7·0227,0
39	1·4799,0	2·1988,0	3·2802,0	4·9138,0	7·3923,0
40	1·4948,0	2·2437,0	3·3817,0	5·1186,0	7·7814,0
41	1·5099,0	2·2894,0	3·4863,0	5·3319,0	8·1909,0
42	1·5252,0	2·3362,0	3·5941,0	5·5540,0	8·6220,0
43	1·5406,0	2·3838,0	3·7052,0	5·7854,0	9·0758,0
44	1·5561,0	2·4325,0	3·8198,0	6·0265,0	9·5535,0
45	1·5719,0	2·4821,0	3·9380,0	6·2776,0	1·0056,1
46	1·5877,0	2·5328,0	4·0598,0	6·5392,0	1·0586,1
47	1·6038,0	2·5845,0	4·1853,0	6·8116,0	1·1143,1
48	1·6200,0	2·6372,0	4·3148,0	7·0955,0	1·1729,1
49	1·6363,0	2·6911,0	4·4482,0	7·3911,0	1·2346,1
50	1·6529,0	2·7460,0	4·5858,0	7·6991,0	1·2996,1

* The final digit is the power of 10 by which the given tabular value has to be multiplied (see examples on p. 163).

APPENDIX C

(Compound rates of decline)

Present value of 1 due n years hence $v_{\overline{n}|-r} = (1-r)^{-n}$

PERCENTAGE

	6	7	8	9	10
1	1·0638,0*	1·0753,0*	1·0870,0*	1·0989,0*	1·1111,0*
2	1·1317,0	1·1562,0	1·1815,0	1·2076,0	1·2346,0
3	1·2040,0	1·2432,0	1·2842,0	1·3270,0	1·3717,0
4	1·2808,0	1·3368,0	1·3959,0	1·4583,0	1·5242,0
5	1·3626,0	1·4374,0	1·5173,0	1·6025,0	1·6935,0
6	1·4495,0	1·5456,0	1·6492,0	1·7610,0	1·8817,0
7	1·5421,0	1·6620,0	1·7926,0	1·9351,0	2·0908,0
8	1·6405,0	1·7870,0	1·9485,0	2·1265,0	2·3231,0
9	1·7452,0	1·9216,0	2·1179,0	2·3368,0	2·5812,0
10	1·8566,0	2·0662,0	2·3021,0	2·5679,0	2·8680,0
11	1·9751,0	2·2217,0	2·5023,0	2·8219,0	3·1866,0
12	2·1012,0	2·3889,0	2·7199,0	3·1010,0	3·5407,0
13	2·2353,0	2·5687,0	2·9564,0	3·4077,0	3·9341,0
14	2·3780,0	2·7621,0	3·2134,0	3·7447,0	4·3712,0
15	2·5298,0	2·9700,0	3·4929,0	4·1151,0	4·8569,0
16	2·6913,0	3·1935,0	3·7966,0	4·5221,0	5·3966,0
17	2·8630,0	3·4339,0	4·1267,0	4·9693,0	5·9962,0
18	3·0458,0	3·6924,0	4·4856,0	5·4608,0	6·6625,0
19	3·2402,0	3·9703,0	4·8756,0	6·0009,0	7·4027,0
20	3·4470,0	4·2691,0	5·2996,0	6·5944,0	8·2253,0
21	3·6670,0	4·5905,0	5·7604,0	7·2465,0	9·1392,0
22	3·9011,0	4·9360,0	6·2613,0	7·9632,0	1·0155,1
23	4·1501,0	5·3075,0	6·8058,0	8·7508,0	1·1283,1
24	4·4150,0	5·7070,0	7·3976,0	9·6163,0	1·2537,1
25	4·6968,0	6·1366,0	8·0409,0	1·0567,1	1·3930,1
26	4·9966,0	6·5985,0	8·7401,0	1·1612,1	1·5477,1
27	5·3155,0	7·0951,0	9·5001,0	1·2761,1	1·7197,1
28	5·6548,0	7·6292,0	1·0326,1	1·4023,1	1·9108,1
29	6·0158,0	8·2034,0	1·1224,1	1·5410,1	2·1231,1
30	6·3998,0	8·8209,0	1·2200,1	1·6934,1	2·3590,1
31	6·8083,0	9·4848,0	1·3261,1	1·8609,1	2·6211,1
32	7·2428,0	1·0199,1	1·4414,1	2·0449,1	2·9123,1
33	7·7051,0	1·0966,1	1·5668,1	2·2472,1	3·2359,1
34	8·1970,0	1·1792,1	1·7030,1	2·4694,1	3·5955,1
35	8·7202,0	1·2679,1	1·8511,1	2·7136,1	3·9950,1
36	9·2768,0	1·3634,1	2·0120,1	2·9820,1	4·4388,1
37	9·8689,0	1·4660,1	2·1870,1	3·2769,1	4·9320,1
38	1·0499,1	1·5763,1	2·3772,1	3·6010,1	5·4801,1
39	1·1169,1	1·6950,1	2·5839,1	3·9572,1	6·0889,1
40	1·1882,1	1·8226,1	2·8086,1	4·3485,1	6·7655,1
41	1·2640,1	1·9597,1	3·0528,1	4·7786,1	7·5172,1
42	1·3447,1	2·1072,1	3·3183,1	5·2512,1	8·3525,1
43	1·4305,1	2·2659,1	3·6068,1	5·7706,1	9·2805,1
44	1·5219,1	2·4364,1	3·9204,1	6·3413,1	1·0312,2
45	1·6190,1	2·6198,1	4·2614,1	6·9685,1	1·1457,2
46	1·7223,1	2·8170,1	4·6319,1	7·6577,1	1·2730,2
47	1·8323,1	3·0290,1	5·0347,1	8·4150,1	1·4145,2
48	1·9492,1	3·2570,1	5·4725,1	9·2473,1	1·5717,2
49	2·0736,1	3·5022,1	5·9483,1	1·0162,2	1·7463,2
50	2·2060,1	3·7658,1	6·4656,1	1·1167,2	1·9403,2

The row label **YEAR** appears vertically along the left side of the table (rows 23–25).

* The final digit is the power of 10 by which the given tabular value has to be multiplied (see examples on p. 163).

APPENDIX C

(Compound rates of decline)

Present value of 1 due n years hence $v_{\overline{n}|-r} = (1-r)^{-n}$

PERCENTAGE

	11	12	13	14	15
1	1·1236,0*	1·1364,0*	1·1494,0*	1·1628,0*	1·1765,0*
2	1·2625,0	1·2913,0	1·3212,0	1·3521,0	1·3841,0
3	1·4185,0	1·4674,0	1·5186,0	1·5722,0	1·6283,0
4	1·5938,0	1·6675,0	1·7455,0	1·8281,0	1·9157,0
5	1·7908,0	1·8949,0	2·0063,0	2·1257,0	2·2537,0
6	2·0121,0	2·1533,0	2·3061,0	2·4718,0	2·6515,0
7	2·2608,0	2·4469,0	2·6507,0	2·8742,0	3·1194,0
8	2·5403,0	2·7806,0	3·0468,0	3·3420,0	3·6699,0
9	2·8542,0	3·1598,0	3·5021,0	3·8861,0	4·3175,0
10	3·2070,0	3·5907,0	4·0254,0	4·5187,0	5·0794,0
11	3·6034,0	4·0803,0	4·6269,0	5·2543,0	5·9757,0
12	4·0487,0	4·6367,0	5·3183,0	6·1097,0	7·0303,0
13	4·5491,0	5·2690,0	6·1129,0	7·1043,0	8·2709,0
14	5·1114,0	5·9875,0	7·0264,0	8·2608,0	9·7305,0
15	5·7431,0	6·8039,0	8·0763,0	9·6056,0	1·1448,1
16	6·4530,0	7·7317,0	9·2831,0	1·1169,1	1·3468,1
17	7·2505,0	8·7861,0	1·0670,1	1·2988,1	1·5844,1
18	8·1467,0	9·9842,0	1·2265,1	1·5102,1	1·8641,1
19	9·1536,0	1·1346,1	1·4097,1	1·7560,1	2·1930,1
20	1·0285,1	1·2893,1	1·6204,1	2·0419,1	2·5800,1
21	1·1556,1	1·4651,1	1·8625,1	2·3743,1	3·0353,1
22	1·2984,1	1·6649,1	2·1408,1	2·7608,1	3·5709,1
23	1·4589,1	1·8919,1	2·4607,1	3·2102,1	4·2011,1
24	1·6392,1	2·1499,1	2·8284,1	3·7328,1	4·9425,1
25	1·8418,1	2·4431,1	3·2510,1	4·3405,1	5·8147,1
26	2·0695,1	2·7762,1	3·7368,1	5·0471,1	6·8408,1
27	2·3253,1	3·1548,1	4·2952,1	5·8687,1	8·0480,1
28	2·6126,1	3·5850,1	4·9370,1	6·8241,1	9·4683,1
29	2·9356,1	4·0738,1	5·6747,1	7·9350,1	1·1139,2
30	3·2984,1	4·6293,1	6·5226,1	9·2267,1	1·3105,2
31	3·7060,1	5·2606,1	7·4973,1	1·0729,2	1·5417,2
32	4·1641,1	5·9780,1	8·6176,1	1·2475,2	1·8138,2
33	4·6788,1	6·7932,1	9·9052,1	1·4506,2	2·1339,2
34	5·2570,1	7·7195,1	1·1385,2	1·6868,2	2·5105,2
35	5·9068,1	8·7722,1	1·3087,2	1·9613,2	2·9535,2
36	6·6368,1	9·9684,1	1·5042,2	2·2806,2	3·4747,2
37	7·4571,1	1·1328,2	1·7290,2	2·6519,2	4·0879,2
38	8·3788,1	1·2872,2	1·9873,2	3·0836,2	4·8093,2
39	9·4143,1	1·4628,2	2·2843,2	3·5856,2	5·6580,2
40	1·0578,2	1·6622,2	2·6256,2	4·1693,2	6·6565,2
41	1·1885,2	1·8889,2	3·0179,2	4·8480,2	7·8311,2
42	1·3354,2	2·1465,2	3·4689,2	5·6372,2	9·2131,2
43	1·5005,2	2·4392,2	3·9872,2	6·5549,2	1·0839,3
44	1·6859,2	2·7718,2	4·5830,2	7·6220,2	1·2752,3
45	1·8943,2	3·1498,2	5·2679,2	8·8628,2	1·5002,3
46	2·1284,2	3·5793,2	6·0550,2	1·0306,3	1·7649,3
47	2·3915,2	4·0674,2	6·9598,2	1·1983,3	2·0764,3
48	2·6871,2	4·6220,2	7·9997,2	1·3934,3	2·4428,3
49	3·0192,2	5·2523,2	9·1951,2	1·6202,3	2·8739,3
50	3·3923,2	5·9685,2	1·0569,3	1·8840,3	3·3811,3

* The final digit is the power of 10 by which the given tabular value has to be multiplied (see examples on p. 163).

APPENDIX C

(Compound rates of decline)

Present value of 1 due n years hence $v_{n|-r} = (1-r)^{-n}$

PERCENTAGE

	16	17	18	19	20
1	1·1905,0*	1·2048,0*	1·2195,0*	1·2346,0*	1·2500,0*
2	1·4172,0	1·4516,0	1·4872,0	1·5242,0	1·5625,0
3	1·6872,0	1·7489,0	1·8137,0	1·8817,0	1·9531,0
4	2·0086,0	2·1071,0	2·2118,0	2·3231,0	2·4414,0
5	2·3911,0	2·5387,0	2·6973,0	2·8680,0	3·0518,0
6	2·8466,0	3·0587,0	3·2894,0	3·5407,0	3·8147,0
7	3·3888,0	3·6851,0	4·0115,0	4·3712,0	4·7684,0
8	4·0343,0	4·4399,0	4·8920,0	5·3966,0	5·9605,0
9	4·8027,0	5·3493,0	5·9659,0	6·6625,0	7·4506,0
10	5·7175,0	6·4449,0	7·2755,0	8·2253,0	9·3132,0
11	6·8066,0	7·7650,0	8·8725,0	1·0155,1	1·1642,1
12	8·1031,0	9·3554,0	1·0820,1	1·2537,1	1·4552,1
13	9·6465,0	1·1272,1	1·3195,1	1·5477,1	1·8190,1
14	1·1484,1	1·3580,1	1·6092,1	1·9108,1	2·2737,1
15	1·3671,1	1·6362,1	1·9624,1	2·3590,1	2·8422,1
16	1·6275,1	1·9713,1	2·3932,1	2·9123,1	3·5527,1
17	1·9375,1	2·3750,1	2·9185,1	3·5955,1	4·4409,1
18	2·3066,1	2·8615,1	3·5592,1	4·4388,1	5·5511,1
19	2·7460,1	3·4476,1	4·3405,1	5·4801,1	6·9389,1
20	3·2690,1	4·1537,1	5·2933,1	6·7655,1	8·6736,1
21	3·8917,1	5·0045,1	6·4552,1	8·3525,1	1·0842,2
22	4·6329,1	6·0295,1	7·8722,1	1·0312,2	1·3553,2
23	5·5154,1	7·2645,1	9·6002,1	1·2730,2	1·6941,2
24	6·5659,1	8·7524,1	1·1708,2	1·5717,2	2·1176,2
25	7·8166,1	1·0545,2	1·4278,2	1·9403,2	2·6470,2
26	9·3055,1	1·2705,2	1·7412,2	2·3955,2	3·3087,2
27	1·1078,2	1·5307,2	2·1234,2	2·9574,2	4·1359,2
28	1·3188,2	1·8442,2	2·5895,2	3·6511,2	5·1699,2
29	1·5700,2	2·2220,2	3·1579,2	4·5075,2	6·4623,2
30	1·8691,2	2·6771,2	3·8511,2	5·5648,2	8·0779,2
31	2·2251,2	3·2254,2	4·6965,2	6·8701,2	1·0097,3
32	2·6489,2	3·8860,2	5·7274,2	8·4816,2	1·2622,3
33	3·1534,2	4·6819,2	6·9846,2	1·0471,3	1·5777,3
34	3·7541,2	5·6409,2	8·5178,2	1·2927,3	1·9722,3
35	4·4691,2	6·7962,2	1·0388,3	1·5960,3	2·4652,3
36	5·3204,2	8·1882,2	1·2668,3	1·9703,3	3·0815,3
37	6·3338,2	9·8653,2	1·5449,3	2·4325,3	3·8519,3
38	7·5403,2	1·1886,3	1·8840,3	3·0031,3	4·8148,3
39	8·9765,2	1·4320,3	2·2975,3	3·7075,3	6·0185,3
40	1·0686,3	1·7253,3	2·8019,3	4·5772,3	7·5232,3
41	1·2722,3	2·0787,3	3·4169,3	5·6509,3	9·4040,3
42	1·5145,3	2·5045,3	4·1669,3	6·9764,3	1·1755,4
43	1·8030,3	3·0175,3	5·0816,3	8·6128,3	1·4694,4
44	2·1464,3	3·6355,3	6·1971,3	1·0633,4	1·8367,4
45	2·5552,3	4·3801,3	7·5575,3	1·3127,4	2·2959,4
46	3·0420,3	5·2772,3	9·2164,3	1·6206,4	2·8699,4
47	3·6214,3	6·3581,3	1·1240,4	2·0008,4	3·5873,4
48	4·3112,3	7·6604,3	1·3707,4	2·4701,4	4·4842,4
49	5·1323,3	9·2294,3	1·6716,4	3·0495,4	5·6052,4
50	6·1099,3	1·1120,4	2·0385,4	3·7649,4	7·0065,4

YEAR

* The final digit is the power of 10 by which the given tabular value has to be multiplied (see examples on p. 163).

APPENDIX C

(Compound rates of decline)

Present value of 1 due n years hence $v_{\overline{n}|-r} = (1-r)^{-n}$

PERCENTAGE

	21	22	23	24	25
1	1·2658,0*	1·2821,0*	1·2987,0*	1·3158,0*	1·3333,0*
2	1·6023,0	1·6437,0	1·6866,0	1·7313,0	1·7778,0
3	2·0282,0	2·1073,0	2·1904,0	2·2780,0	2·3704,0
4	2·5674,0	2·7016,0	2·8447,0	2·9974,0	3·1605,0
5	3·2499,0	3·4636,0	3·6944,0	3·9440,0	4·2140,0
6	4·1137,0	4·4405,0	4·7979,0	5·1894,0	5·6187,0
7	5·2073,0	5·6930,0	6·2311,0	6·8282,0	7·4915,0
8	6·5915,0	7·2987,0	8·0923,0	8·9844,0	9·9887,0
9	8·3437,0	9·3573,0	1·0510,1	1·1822,1	1·3318,1
10	1·0562,1	1·1996,1	1·3649,1	1·5555,1	1·7758,1
11	1·3369,1	1·5380,1	1·7726,1	2·0467,1	2·3677,1
12	1·6923,1	1·9718,1	2·3020,1	2·6930,1	3·1569,1
13	2·1421,1	2·5280,1	2·9897,1	3·5434,1	4·2092,1
14	2·7116,1	3·2410,1	3·8827,1	4·6624,1	5·6123,1
15	3·4324,1	4·1551,1	5·0424,1	6·1347,1	7·4831,1
16	4·3448,1	5·3270,1	6·5486,1	8·0720,1	9·9775,1
17	5·4997,1	6·8295,1	8·5047,1	1·0621,2	1·3303,2
18	6·9617,1	8·7558,1	1·1045,2	1·3975,2	1·7738,2
19	8·8122,1	1·1225,2	1·4344,2	1·8388,2	2·3650,2
20	1·1155,2	1·4392,2	1·8629,2	2·4195,2	3·1534,2
21	1·4120,2	1·8451,2	2·4193,2	3·1836,2	4·2045,2
22	1·7873,2	2·3655,2	3·1420,2	4·1889,2	5·6060,2
23	2·2624,2	3·0327,2	4·0805,2	5·5117,2	7·4747,2
24	2·8638,2	3·8880,2	5·2994,2	7·2523,2	9·9662,2
25	3·6251,2	4·9847,2	6·8823,2	9·5425,2	1·3288,3
26	4·5888,2	6·3906,2	8·9380,2	1·2556,3	1·7718,3
27	5·8086,2	8·1931,2	1·1608,3	1·6521,3	2·3624,3
28	7·3526,2	1·0504,3	1·5075,3	2·1738,3	3·1498,3
29	9·3071,2	1·3467,3	1·9578,3	2·8603,3	4·1998,3
30	1·1781,3	1·7265,3	2·5426,3	3·7635,3	5·5997,3
31	1·4913,3	2·2134,3	3·3021,3	4·9520,3	7·4662,3
32	1·8877,3	2·8377,3	4·2884,3	6·5158,3	9·9550,3
33	2·3895,3	3·6381,3	5·5694,3	8·5734,3	1·3273,4
34	3·0247,3	4·6643,3	7·2329,3	1·1281,4	1·7698,4
35	3·8287,3	5·9798,3	9·3934,3	1·4843,4	2·3597,4
36	4·8465,3	7·6665,3	1·2199,4	1·9530,4	3·1463,4
37	6·1348,3	9·8288,3	1·5843,4	2·5698,4	4·1950,4
38	7·7655,3	1·2601,4	2·0576,4	3·3813,4	5·5934,4
39	9·8298,3	1·6155,4	2·6722,4	4·4491,4	7·4578,4
40	1·2443,4	2·0712,4	3·4703,4	5·8540,4	9·9437,4
41	1·5750,4	2·6553,4	4·5069,4	7·7027,4	1·3258,5
42	1·9937,4	3·4043,4	5·8531,4	1·0135,5	1·7678,5
43	2·5237,4	4·3645,4	7·6015,4	1·3336,5	2·3570,5
44	3·1945,4	5·5955,4	9·8721,4	1·7547,5	3·1427,5
45	4·0437,4	7·1737,4	1·2821,5	2·3088,5	4·1903,5
46	5·1186,4	9·1970,4	1·6650,5	3·0379,5	5·5870,5
47	6·4793,4	1·1791,5	2·1624,5	3·9972,5	7·4494,5
48	8·2016,4	1·5117,5	2·8083,5	5·2595,5	9·9325,5
49	1·0382,5	1·9380,5	3·6472,5	6·9204,5	1·3243,6
50	1·3142,5	2·4847,5	4·7366,5	9·1058,5	1·7658,6

* The final digit is the power of 10 by which the given tabular value has to be multiplied (see examples on p. 163).

APPENDIX D

(Compound rates of decline)

Present value of 1 p.a. due end-year $a_{\overline{n}|-r} = \dfrac{(1-r)^{-n}-1}{r}$

PERCENTAGE

	1	2	3	4	5
1	1·0101,0*	1·0204,0*	1·0309,0*	1·0417,0*	1·0526,0*
2	2·0304,0	2·0616,0	2·0937,0	2·1267,0	2·1607,0
3	3·0610,0	3·1241,0	3·1894,0	3·2570,0	3·3270,0
4	4·1020,0	4·2083,0	4·3190,0	4·4344,0	4·5548,0
5	5·1536,0	5·3146,0	5·4835,0	5·6608,0	5·8471,0
6	6·2157,0	6·4434,0	6·6840,0	6·9384,0	7·2075,0
7	7·2886,0	7·5954,0	7·9217,0	8·2691,0	8·6395,0
8	8·3723,0	8·7708,0	9·1976,0	9·6553,0	1·0147,1
9	9·4670,0	9·9702,0	1·0513,1	1·1099,1	1·1733,1
10	1·0573,1	1·1194,1	1·1869,1	1·2603,1	1·3404,1
11	1·1690,1	1·2443,1	1·3267,1	1·4170,1	1·5162,1
12	1·2818,1	1·3717,1	1·4708,1	1·5802,1	1·7012,1
13	1·3957,1	1·5018,1	1·6194,1	1·7502,1	1·8960,1
14	1·5108,1	1·6344,1	1·7726,1	1·9273,1	2·1011,1
15	1·6271,1	1·7698,1	1·9305,1	2·1118,1	2·3169,1
16	1·7446,1	1·9080,1	2·0933,1	2·3040,1	2·5441,1
17	1·8632,1	2·0490,1	2·2611,1	2·5041,1	2·7833,1
18	1·9830,1	2·1928,1	2·4342,1	2·7126,1	3·0351,1
19	2·1041,1	2·3396,1	2·6125,1	2·9298,1	3·3001,1
20	2·2263,1	2·4894,1	2·7964,1	3·1561,1	3·5790,1
21	2·3498,1	2·6423,1	2·9860,1	3·3917,1	3·8727,1
22	2·4746,1	2·7982,1	3·1815,1	3·6372,1	4·1817,1
23	2·6006,1	2·9574,1	3·3829,1	3·8930,1	4·5071,1
24	2·7279,1	3·1198,1	3·5907,1	4·1593,1	4·8496,1
25	2·8564,1	3·2855,1	3·8048,1	4·4368,1	5·2101,1
26	2·9863,1	3·4546,1	4·0256,1	4·7258,1	5·5896,1
27	3·1175,1	3·6271,1	4·2532,1	5·0269,1	5·9890,1
28	3·2500,1	3·8032,1	4·4878,1	5·3405,1	6·4095,1
29	3·3838,1	3·9828,1	4·7297,1	5·6672·1	6·8521,1
30	3·5190,1	4·1662,1	4·9791,1	6·0075,1	7·3180,1
31	3·6555,1	4·3532,1	5·2362,1	6·3620,1	7·8084,1
32	3·7935,1	4·5441,1	5·5012,1	6·7312,1	8·3246,1
33	3·9328,1	4·7389,1	5·7744,1	7·1159,1	8·8680,1
34	4·0735,1	4·9376,1	6·0561,1	7·5165,1	9·4400,1
35	4·2157,1	5·1405,1	6·3465,1	7·9339,1	1·0042,2
36	4·3593,1	5·3474,1	6·6459,1	8·3686,1	1·0676,2
37	4·5043,1	5·5586,1	6·9545,1	8·8215,1	1·1343,2
38	4·6508,1	5·7741,1	7·2727,1	9·2932,1	1·2045,2
39	4·7988,1	5·9939,1	7·6007,1	9·7846,1	1·2785,2
40	4·9483,1	6·2183,1	7·9389,1	1·0296,2	1·3563,2
41	5·0993,1	6·4472,1	8·2875,1	1·0830,2	1·4382,2
42	5·2518,1	6·6809,1	8·6469,1	1·1385,2	1·5244,2
43	5·4059,1	6·9192,1	9·0174,1	1·1964,2	1·6152,2
44	5·5615,1	7·1625,1	9·3994,1	1·2566,2	1·7107,2
45	5·7187,1	7·4107,1	9·7932,1	1·3194,2	1·8113,2
46	5·8775,1	7·6640,1	1·0199,2	1·3848,2	1·9171,2
47	6·0378,1	7·9224,1	1·0618,2	1·4529,2	2·0285,2
48	6·1998,1	8·1862,1	1·1049,2	1·5239,2	2·1458,2
49	6·3635,1	8·4553,1	1·1494,2	1·5978,2	2·2693,2
50	6·5288,1	8·7299,1	1·1953,2	1·6748,2	2·3993,2

(Left margin label: YEAR)

* The final digit is the power of 10 by which the given tabular value has to be multiplied (see examples on p. 163).

APPENDIX D

(Compound rates of decline)

Present value of 1 p.a. due end-year $a_{\overline{n}|-r} = \dfrac{(1-r)^{-n}-1}{r}$

PERCENTAGE

	6	7	8	9	10
1	1·0638,0*	1·0753,0*	1·0870,0*	1·0989,0*	1·1111,0*
2	2·1956,0	2·2315,0	2·2684,0	2·3065,0	2·3457,0
3	3·3995,0	3·4747,0	3·5526,0	3·6335,0	3·7174,0
4	4·6804,0	4·8115,0	4·9485,0	5·0918,0	5·2416,0
5	6·0429,0	6·2489,0	6·4658,0	6·6942,0	6·9351,0
6	7·4925,0	7·7945,0	8·1150,0	8·4552,0	8·8168,0
7	9·0346,0	9·4565,0	9·9076,0	1·0390,1	1·0908,1
8	1·0675,1	1·1244,1	1·1856,1	1·2517,1	1·3231,1
9	1·2420,1	1·3165,1	1·3974,1	1·4854,1	1·5812,1
10	1·4277,1	1·5231,1	1·6276,1	1·7422,1	1·8680,1
11	1·6252,1	1·7453,1	1·8778,1	2·0244,1	2·1866,1
12	1·8353,1	1·9842,1	2·1498,1	2·3345,1	2·5407,1
13	2·0589,1	2·2411,1	2·4455,1	2·6752,1	2·9341,1
14	2·2966,1	2·5173,1	2·7668,1	3·0497,1	3·3712,1
15	2·5496,1	2·8143,1	3·1161,1	3·4612,1	3·8569,1
16	2·8188,1	3·1336,1	3·4957,1	3·9134,1	4·3966,1
17	3·1051,1	3·4770,1	3·9084,1	4·4103,1	4·9962,1
18	3·4096,1	3·8463,1	4·3570,1	4·9564,1	5·6625,1
19	3·7337,1	4·2433,1	4·8445,1	5·5565,1	6·4027,1
20	4·0784,1	4·6702,1	5·3745,1	6·2159,1	7·2253,1
21	4·4451,1	5·1293,1	5·9505,1	6·9406,1	8·1392,1
22	4·8352,1	5·6229,1	6·5767,1	7·7369,1	9·1546,1
23	5·2502,1	6·1536,1	7·2573,1	8·6120,1	1·0283,2
24	5·6917,1	6·7243,1	7·9970,1	9·5736,1	1·1537,2
25	6·1614,1	7·3380,1	8·8011,1	1·0630,2	1·2930,2
26	6·6610,1	7·9978,1	9·6751,1	1·1792,2	1·4477,2
27	7·1926,1	8·7073,1	1·0625,2	1·3068,2	1·6197,2
28	7·7581,1	9·4702,1	1·1658,2	1·4470,2	1·8108,2
29	8·3596,1	1·0291,2	1·2780,2	1·6011,2	2·0231,2
30	8·9996,1	1·1173,2	1·4000,2	1·7704,2	2·2590,2
31	9·6804,1	1·2121,2	1·5326,2	1·9565,2	2·5211,2
32	1·0405,2	1·3141,2	1·6768,2	2·1610,2	2·8123,2
33	1·1175,2	1·4238,2	1·8334,2	2·3857,2	3·1359,2
34	1·1995,2	1·5417,2	2·0037,2	2·6327,2	3·4955,2
35	1·2867,2	1·6685,2	2·1889,2	2·9040,2	3·8950,2
36	1·3795,2	1·8048,2	2·3901,2	3·2022,2	4·3388,2
37	1·4782,2	1·9514,2	2·6088,2	3·5299,2	4·8320,2
38	1·5831,2	2·1090,2	2·8465,2	3·8900,2	5·3801,2
39	1·6948,2	2·2785,2	3·1049,2	4·2858,2	5·9889,2
40	1·8136,2	2·4608,2	3·3857,2	4·7206,2	6·6655,2
41	1·9401,2	2·6568,2	3·6910,2	5·1985,2	7·4172,2
42	2·0745,2	2·8675,2	4·0228,2	5·7236,2	8·2525,2
43	2·2176,2	3·0941,2	4·3835,2	6·3007,2	9·1805,2
44	2·3698,2	3·3377,2	4·7756,2	6·9348,2	1·0212,3
45	2·5317,2	3·5997,2	5·2017,2	7·6316,2	1·1357,3
46	2·7039,2	3·8814,2	5·6649,2	8·3974,2	1·2630,3
47	2·8871,2	4·1843,2	6·1684,2	9·2389,2	1·4045,3
48	3·0820,2	4·5100,2	6·7156,2	1·0164,3	1·5617,3
49	3·2894,2	4·8602,2	7·3104,2	1·1180,3	1·7363,3
50	3·5100,2	5·2368,2	7·9570,2	1·2296,3	1·9303,3

YEAR (rows 21–25 left margin)

* The final digit is the power of 10 by which the given tabular value has to be multiplied (see examples on p. 163).

APPENDIX D

(Compound rates of decline)

Present value of 1 p.a. due end-year $a_{\overline{n}|-r} = \dfrac{(1-r)^{-n}-1}{r}$

PERCENTAGE

YEAR	11	12	13	14	15
1	1·1236,0*	1·1364,0*	1·1494,0*	1·1628,0*	1·1765,0*
2	2·3861,0	2·4277,0	2·4706,0	2·5149,0	2·5606,0
3	3·8046,0	3·8951,0	3·9892,0	4·0871,0	4·1889,0
4	5·3984,0	5·5626,0	5·7347,0	5·9152,0	6·1046,0
5	7·1892,0	7·4575,0	7·7410,0	8·0409,0	8·3583,0
6	9·2013,0	9·6108,0	1·0047,1	1·0513,1	1·1010,1
7	1·1462,1	1·2058,1	1·2698,1	1·3387,1	1·4129,1
8	1·4002,1	1·4838,1	1·5745,1	1·6729,1	1·7799,1
9	1·6857,1	1·7998,1	1·9247,1	2·0615,1	2·2116,1
10	2·0064,1	2·1589,1	2·3272,1	2·5134,1	2·7196,1
11	2·3667,1	2·5669,1	2·7899,1	3·0388,1	3·3172,1
12	2·7716,1	3·0306,1	3·3217,1	3·6498,1	4·0202,1
13	3·2265,1	3·5575,1	3·9330,1	4·3602,1	4·8473,1
14	3·7376,1	4·1562,1	4·6357,1	5·1863,1	5·8203,1
15	4·3120,1	4·8366,1	5·4433,1	6·1468,1	6·9651,1
16	4·9572,1	5·6098,1	6·3716,1	7·2638,1	8·3119,1
17	5·6823,1	6·4884,1	7·4386,1	8·5625,1	9·8963,1
18	6·4970,1	7·4868,1	8·6651,1	1·0073,2	1·1760,2
19	7·4123,1	8·6214,1	1·0075,2	1·1829,2	1·3953,2
20	8·4408,1	9·9107,1	1·1695,2	1·3871,2	1·6533,2
21	9·5964,1	1·1376,2	1·3558,2	1·6245,2	1·9569,2
22	1·0895,2	1·3041,2	1·5698,2	1·9006,2	2·3140,2
23	1·2354,2	1·4933,2	1·8159,2	2·2216,2	2·7341,2
24	1·3993,2	1·7082,2	2·0988,2	2·5949,2	3·2283,2
25	1·5835,2	1·9525,2	2·4239,2	3·0289,2	3·8098,2
26	1·7904,2	2·2302,2	2·7975,2	3·5336,2	4·4939,2
27	2·0230,2	2·5456,2	3·2271,2	4·1205,2	5·2987,2
28	2·2842,2	2·9041,2	3·7207,2	4·8029,2	6·2455,2
29	2·5778,2	3·3115,2	4·2882,2	5·5964,2	7·3594,2
30	2·9076,2	3·7745,2	4·9405,2	6·5191,2	8·6699,2
31	3·2782,2	4·3005,2	5·6902,2	7·5919,2	1·0212,3
32	3·6946,2	4·8983,2	6·5520,2	8·8395,2	1·2025,3
33	4·1625,2	5·5776,2	7·5425,2	1·0290,3	1·4159,3
34	4·6882,2	6·3496,2	8·6810,2	1·1977,3	1·6670,3
35	5·2789,2	7·2268,2	9·9897,2	1·3938,3	1·9623,3
36	5·9426,2	8·2236,2	1·1494,3	1·6219,3	2·3098,3
37	6·6883,2	9·3564,2	1·3223,3	1·8871,3	2·7186,3
38	7·5261,2	1·0644,3	1·5210,3	2·1954,3	3·1995,3
39	8·4676,2	1·2106,3	1·7494,3	2·5540,3	3·7653,3
40	9·5254,2	1·3769,3	2·0120,3	2·9709,3	4·4310,3
41	1·0714,3	1·5658,3	2·3138,3	3·4557,3	5·2141,3
42	1·2049,3	1·7804,3	2·6607,3	4·0194,3	6·1354,3
43	1·3550,3	2·0243,3	3·0594,3	4·6749,3	7·2193,3
44	1·5236,3	2·3015,3	3·5177,3	5·4371,3	8·4945,3
45	1·7130,3	2·6165,3	4·0445,3	6·3234,3	9·9946,3
46	1·9258,3	2·9744,3	4·6500,3	7·3540,3	1·1760,4
47	2·1650,3	3·3811,3	5·3460,3	8·5523,3	1·3836,4
48	2·4337,3	3·8434,3	6·1460,3	9·9457,3	1·6279,4
49	2·7356,3	4·3686,3	7·0655,3	1·1566,4	1·9153,4
50	3·0749,3	4·9654,3	8·1224,3	1·3450,4	2·2534,4

* The final digit is the power of 10 by which the given tabular value has to be multiplied (see examples on p. 163).

APPENDIX D

(Compound rates of decline)

Present value of 1 p.a. due end-year $a_{\overline{n}|-r} = \dfrac{(1-r)^{-n}-1}{r}$

PERCENTAGE

	16	17	18	19	20
1	1·1905,0*	1·2048,0*	1·2195,0*	1·2346,0*	1·2500,0*
2	2·6077,0	2·6564,0	2·7067,0	2·7587,0	2·8125,0
3	4·2949,0	4·4053,0	4·5204,0	4·6404,0	4·7656,0
4	6·3034,0	6·5124,0	6·7322,0	6·9635,0	7·2070,0
5	8·6946,0	9·0511,0	9·4295,0	9·8314,0	1·0259,1
6	1·1541,1	1·2110,1	1·2719,1	1·3372,1	1·4073,1
7	1·4930,1	1·5795,1	1·6730,1	1·7743,1	1·8842,1
8	1·8964,1	2·0235,1	2·1622,1	2·3140,1	2·4802,1
9	2·3767,1	2·5584,1	2·7588,1	2·9802,1	3·2253,1
10	2·9484,1	3·2029,1	3·4864,1	3·8028,1	4·1566,1
11	3·6291,1	3·9794,1	4·3736,1	4·8182,1	5·3208,1
12	4·4394,1	4·9149,1	5·4556,1	6·0719,1	6·7760,1
13	5·4041,1	6·0421,1	6·7752,1	7·6196,1	8·5949,1
14	6·5524,1	7·4001,1	8·3844,1	9·5304,1	1·0869,2
15	7·9196,1	9·0363,1	1·0347,2	1·1889,2	1·3711,2
16	9·5471,1	1·1008,2	1·2740,2	1·4802,2	1·7264,2
17	1·1485,2	1·3383,2	1·5659,2	1·8397,2	2·1704,2
18	1·3791,2	1·6244,2	1·9218,2	2·2836,2	2·7256,2
19	1·6537,2	1·9692,2	2·3558,2	2·8316,2	3·4194,2
20	1·9806,2	2·3845,2	2·8851,2	3·5082,2	4·2868,2
21	2·3698,2	2·8850,2	3·5307,2	4·3434,2	5·3710,2
22	2·8331,2	3·4879,2	4·3179,2	5·3746,2	6·7263,2
23	3·3846,2	4·2144,2	5·2779,2	6·6476,2	8·4203,2
24	4·0412,2	5·0896,2	6·4487,2	8·2193,2	1·0538,3
25	4·8229,2	6·1441,2	7·8764,2	1·0160,3	1·3185,3
26	5·7534,2	7·4146,2	9·6176,2	1·2555,3	1·6494,3
27	6·8612,2	8·9453,2	1·1741,3	1·5512,3	2·0630,3
28	8·1800,2	1·0790,3	1·4330,3	1·9163,3	2·5799,3
29	9·7500,2	1·3011,3	1·7488,3	2·3671,3	3·2262,3
30	1·1619,3	1·5689,3	2·1339,3	2·9236,3	4·0340,3
31	1·3844,3	1·8914,3	2·6036,3	3·6106,3	5·0437,3
32	1·6493,3	2·2800,3	3·1763,3	4·4588,3	6·3059,3
33	1·9646,3	2·7482,3	3·8748,3	5·5059,3	7·8836,3
34	2·3401,3	3·3123,3	4·7266,3	6·7986,3	9·8558,3
35	2·7870,3	3·9919,3	5·7653,3	8·3946,3	1·2321,4
36	3·3190,3	4·8107,3	7·0321,3	1·0365,4	1·5402,4
37	3·9524,3	5·7972,3	8·5770,3	1·2797,4	1·9254,4
38	4·7064,3	6·9858,3	1·0461,4	1·5801,4	2·4069,4
39	5·6041,3	8·4179,3	1·2758,4	1·9508,4	3·0088,4
40	6·6727,3	1·0143,4	1·5560,4	2·4085,4	3·7611,4
41	7·9449,3	1·2222,4	1·8977,4	2·9736,4	4·7015,4
42	9·4594,3	1·4726,4	2·3144,4	3·6712,4	5·8770,4
43	1·1262,4	1·7744,4	2·8226,4	4·5325,4	7·3463,4
44	1·3409,4	2·1379,4	3·4423,4	5·5958,4	9·1830,4
45	1·5964,4	2·5760,4	4·1980,4	6·9086,4	1·1479,5
46	1·9006,4	3·1037,4	5·1197,4	8·5292,4	1·4349,5
47	2·2627,4	3·7395,4	6·2436,4	1·0530,5	1·7936,5
48	2·6939,4	4·5055,4	7·6143,4	1·3000,5	2·2420,5
49	3·2071,4	5·4285,4	9·2859,4	1·6050,5	2·8025,5
50	3·8181,4	6·5404,4	1·1324,5	1·9815,5	3·5032,5

YEAR

* The final digit is the power of 10 by which the given tabular value has to be multiplied (see examples on p. 163).

APPENDIX D

(Compound rates of decline)

Present value of 1 p.a. due end-year $a_{\overline{n|}-r} = \dfrac{(1-r)^{-n}-1}{r}$

PERCENTAGE

YEAR	21	22	23	24	25
1	1·2658,0*	1·2821,0*	1·2987,0*	1·3158,0*	1·3333,0*
2	2·8681,0	2·9257,0	2·9853,0	3·0471,0	3·1111,0
3	4·8964,0	5·0330,0	5·1757,0	5·3251,0	5·4815,0
4	7·4638,0	7·7346,0	8·0205,0	8·3225,0	8·6420,0
5	1·0714,1	1·1198,1	1·1715,1	1·2266,1	1·2856,1
6	1·4827,1	1·5639,1	1·6513,1	1·7456,1	1·8475,1
7	2·0035,1	2·1332,1	2·2744,1	2·4284,1	2·5966,1
8	2·6626,1	2·8630,1	3·0836,1	3·3269,1	3·5955,1
9	3·4970,1	3·7988,1	4·1346,1	4·5090,1	4·9273,1
10	4·5531,1	4·9984,1	5·4995,1	6·0645,1	6·7031,1
11	5·8900,1	6·5364,1	7·2720,1	8·1112,1	9·0708,1
12	7·5823,1	8·5082,1	9·5741,1	1·0804,2	1·2228,2
13	9·7245,1	1·1036,2	1·2564,2	1·4348,2	1·6437,2
14	1·2436,2	1·4277,2	1·6446,2	1·9010,2	2·2049,2
15	1·5868,2	1·8432,2	2·1489,2	2·5145,2	2·9532,2
16	2·0213,2	2·3759,2	2·8037,2	3·3217,2	3·9510,2
17	2·5713,2	3·0589,2	3·6542,2	4·3838,2	5·2813,2
18	3·2675,2	3·9345,2	4·7587,2	5·7813,2	7·0551,2
19	4·1487,2	5·0570,2	6·1931,2	7·6201,2	9·4201,2
20	5·2641,2	6·4962,2	8·0560,2	1·0040,3	1·2573,3
21	6·6761,2	8·3412,2	1·0475,3	1·3223,3	1·6778,3
22	8·4635,2	1·0707,3	1·3617,3	1·7412,3	2·2384,3
23	1·0726,3	1·3739,3	1·7698,3	2·2924,3	2·9859,3
24	1·3590,3	1·7627,3	2·2997,3	3·0176,3	3·9825,3
25	1·7215,3	2·2612,3	2·9879,3	3·9719,3	5·3113,3
26	2·1804,3	2·9003,3	3·8817,3	5·2274,3	7·0831,3
27	2·7612,3	3·7196,3	5·0425,3	6·8795,3	9·4454,3
28	3·4965,3	4·7700,3	6·5500,3	9·0533,3	1·2595,4
29	4·4272,3	6·1166,3	8·5078,3	1·1914,4	1·6795,4
30	5·6053,3	7·8431,3	1·1050,4	1·5677,4	2·2395,4
31	7·0966,3	1·0057,4	1·4353,4	2·0629,4	2·9861,4
32	8·9843,3	1·2894,4	1·8641,4	2·7145,4	3·9816,4
33	1·1374,4	1·6532,4	2·4210,4	3·5718,4	5·3089,4
34	1·4398,4	2·1197,4	3·1443,4	4·6999,4	7·0787,4
35	1·8227,4	2·7177,4	4·0837,4	6·1842,4	9·4384,4
36	2·3074,4	3·4843,4	5·3036,4	8·1372,4	1·2585,5
37	2·9208,4	4·4672,4	6·8879,4	1·0707,5	1·6780,5
38	3·6974,4	5·7273,4	8·9455,4	1·4088,5	2·2373,5
39	4·6804,4	7·3428,4	1·1618,5	1·8537,5	2·9831,5
40	5·9246,4	9·4140,4	1·5088,5	2·4391,5	3·9775,5
41	7·4997,4	1·2069,5	1·9595,5	3·2094,5	5·3033,5
42	9·4934,4	1·5474,5	2·5448,5	4·2229,5	7·0711,5
43	1·2017,5	1·9838,5	3·3050,5	5·5565,5	9·4281,5
44	1·5212,5	2·5434,5	4·2922,5	7·3112,5	1·2571,6
45	1·9255,5	3·2607,5	5·5742,5	9·6200,5	1·6761,6
46	2·4374,5	4·1804,5	7·2393,5	1·2658,6	2·2348,6
47	3·0853,5	5·3595,5	9·4017,5	1·6655,6	2·9798,6
48	3·9055,5	6·8712,5	1·2210,6	2·1915,6	3·9730,6
49	4·9437,5	8·8093,5	1·5857,6	2·8835,6	5·2973,6
50	6·2578,5	1·1294,6	2·0594,6	3·7941,6	7·0631,6

* The final digit is the power of 10 by which the given tabular value has to be multiplied (see examples on p. 163).

APPENDIX E

(*a*) Present value, S, of investment incentives on a principal of unity (columns (2), (3) and (4)):

$$S = \frac{P}{(1+r)^k} + \frac{(1-P)DT(1+r)}{(1+r)^z(r+D)}$$

(*b*) Effective net of tax factor y (column (5)):

$$y = 1 - \frac{T}{(1+r)^z}, \text{ i.e., } 1 - T(1+r)^{-z}.$$

P = cash grant;

D = annual allowance on a reducing balance basis;

T = corporation tax at 40%;

k = 18 months time-lag between incurring of capital expenditure and receipt of cash grant;

z = time-lag between company's financial year end and date of corporation tax payment;

r = rate of discount.

APPENDIX E

PLANT QUALIFYING FOR CASH GRANTS—NATIONAL

$z = 9$ months, $T = 40\%$

(1)	(2)	(3)	(4)	(5)
r	$P = 25\%$ $D = 15\%$	$P = 25\%$ $D = 20\%$	$P = 25\%$ $D = 25\%$	$1 - T(1+r)^{-z}$
1	0·5282	0·5327	0·5355	0·6030
2	0·5087	0·5168	0·5218	0·6059
3	0·4910	0·5020	0·5090	0·6088
4	0·4749	0·4882	0·4969	0·6116
5	0·4601	0·4753	0·4858	0·6144
6	0·4465	0·4632	0·4746	0·6171
7	0·4339	0·4519	0·4642	0·6198
8	0·4222	0·4412	0·4544	0·6224
9	0·4113	0·4311	0·4451	0·6250
10	0·4010	0·4215	0·4361	0·6276
11	0·3914	0·4124	0·4276	0·6301
12	0·3824	0·4038	0·4194	0·6326
13	0·3738	0·3956	0·4116	0·6350
14	0·3657	0·3877	0·4041	0·6374
15	0·3581	0·3802	0·3969	0·6398
16	0·3508	0·3731	0·3899	0·6421
17	0·3438	0·3662	0·3833	0·6444
18	0·3372	0·3596	0·3768	0·6467
19	0·3308	0·3533	0·3706	0·6489
20	0·3247	0·3472	0·3646	0·6511
21	0·3189	0·3413	0·3588	0·6533
22	0·3133	0·3357	0·3532	0·6554
23	0·3080	0·3302	0·3478	0·6575
24	0·3028	0·3250	0·3426	0·6596
25	0·2978	0·3199	0·3375	0·6616
26	0·2930	0·3150	0·3326	0·6637
27	0·2884	0·3102	0·3278	0·6656
28	0·2839	0·3056	0·3232	0·6676
29	0·2796	0·3011	0·3186	0·6695
30	0·2754	0·2968	0·3143	0·6714
31	0·2714	0·2926	0·3100	0·6733
32	0·2675	0·2885	0·3059	0·6752
33	0·2637	0·2846	0·3019	0·6770
34	0·2600	0·2807	0·2979	0·6788
35	0·2564	0·2770	0·2941	0·6806
36	0·2529	0·2733	0·2904	0·6824
37	0·2495	0·2698	0·2868	0·6841
38	0·2462	0·2663	0·2832	0·6858
39	0·2430	0·2630	0·2798	0·6875
40	0·2399	0·2597	0·2764	0·6892
41	0·2369	0·2565	0·2731	0·6909
42	0·2339	0·2534	0·2699	0·6925
43	0·2310	0·2503	0·2668	0·6941
44	0·2282	0·2474	0·2637	0·6957
45	0·2255	0·2445	0·2608	0·6973
46	0·2228	0·2416	0·2578	0·6988
47	0·2202	0·2389	0·2550	0·7004
48	0·2176	0·2362	0·2522	0·7019
49	0·2151	0·2335	0·2494	0·7034
50	0·2127	0·2309	0·2468	0·7049

RATE OF DISCOUNT

APPENDIX E

PLANT QUALIFYING FOR CASH GRANTS—NATIONAL

$z = 12$ months, $T = 40\%$

(1) r	(2) $P = 25\%$ $D = 15\%$	(3) $P = 25\%$ $D = 20\%$	(4) $P = 25\%$ $D = 25\%$	(5) $1 - T(1+r)^{-z}$
1	0·5275	0·5320	0·5348	0·6040
2	0·5074	0·5154	0·5205	0·6078
3	0·4892	0·5000	0·5070	0·6117
4	0·4726	0·4857	0·4943	0·6154
5	0·4574	0·4724	0·4824	0·6190
6	0·4434	0·4598	0·4710	0·6226
7	0·4304	0·4481	0·4602	0·6262
8	0·4184	0·4370	0·4500	0·6296
9	0·4072	0·4266	0·4403	0·6330
10	0·3967	0·4167	0·4310	0·6364
11	0·3869	0·4073	0·4221	0·6396
12	0·3776	0·3984	0·4136	0·6429
13	0·3688	0·3899	0·4055	0·6460
14	0·3606	0·3819	0·3977	0·6491
15	0·3527	0·3741	0·3902	0·6522
16	0·3453	0·3668	0·3830	0·6552
17	0·3382	0·3597	0·3761	0·6581
18	0·3314	0·3529	0·3695	0·6610
19	0·3249	0·3464	0·3630	0·6639
20	0·3188	0·3402	0·3568	0·6667
21	0·3128	0·3342	0·3509	0·6694
22	0·3071	0·3284	0·3451	0·6721
23	0·3017	0·3228	0·3395	0·6748
24	0·2964	0·3174	0·3341	0·6774
25	0·2914	0·3122	0·3289	0·6800
26	0·2865	0·3072	0·3238	0·6825
27	0·2818	0·3023	0·3189	0·6850
28	0·2773	0·2976	0·3141	0·6875
29	0·2729	0,2931	0·3095	0·6899
30	0·2687	0·2887	0·3050	0·6923
31	0·2646	0·2844	0·3007	0·6947
32	0·2606	0·2802	0·2964	0·6970
33	0·2567	0·2762	0·2923	0·6992
34	0·2530	0·2723	0·2883	0·7015
35	0·2494	0·2685	0·2844	0·7037
36	0·2459	0·2648	0·2806	0·7059
37	0·2424	0·2612	0·2769	0·7080
38	0·2391	0·2577	0·2733	0·7101
39	0·2359	0·2542	0·2697	0·7122
40	0·2327	0·2509	0·2663	0·7143
41	0·2297	0·2477	0·2630	0·7163
42	0·2267	0·2445	0·2597	0·7183
43	0·2238	0·2414	0·2565	0·7203
44	0·2209	0·2384	0·2534	0·7222
45	0·2182	0·2355	0·2503	0·7241
46	0·2155	0·2326	0·2473	0·7260
47	0·2129	0·2298	0·2444	0·7279
48	0·2103	0·2271	0·2416	0·7297
49	0·2078	0·2244	0·2388	0·7315
50	0·2053	0·2218	0·2361	0·7333

RATE OF DISCOUNT

APPENDIX E

PLANT QUALIFYING FOR CASH GRANTS—NATIONAL

$z = 18$ months, $T = 40\%$

(1)	(2)	(3)	(4)	(5)
	$P = 25\%$	$P = 25\%$	$P = 25\%$	
r	$D = 15\%$	$D = 20\%$	$D = 25\%$	$1 - T(1+r)^{-z}$
1	0·5262	0·5306	0·5333	0·6059
2	0·5048	0·5127	0·5177	0·6117
3	0·4855	0·4962	0·5031	0·6173
4	0·4680	0·4809	0·4893	0·6229
5	0·4519	0·4666	0·4763	0·6282
6	0·4372	0·4532	0·4641	0·6335
7	0·4236	0·4407	0·4525	0·6386
8	0·4110	0·4289	0·4414	0·6436
9	0·3993	0·4179	0·4310	0·6485
10	0·3883	0·4074	0·4210	0·6533
11	0·3781	0·3975	0·4115	0·6580
12	0·3684	0·3881	0·4025	0·6625
13	0·3593	0·3792	0·3938	0·6670
14	0·3507	0·3707	0·3855	0·6714
15	0·3426	0·3626	0·3776	0·6757
16	0·3349	0·3548	0·3699	0·6798
17	0·3276	0·3475	0·3626	0·6839
18	0·3206	0·3404	0·3556	0·6879
19	0·3139	0·3336	0·3488	0·6919
20	0·3076	0·3271	0·3423	0·6957
21	0·3015	0·3209	0·3361	0·6995
22	0·2956	0·3149	0·3300	0·7032
23	0·2900	0·3091	0·3242	0·7068
24	0·2847	0·3035	0·3185	0·7103
25	0·2795	0·2981	0·3130	0·7138
26	0·2745	0·2930	0·3078	0·7172
27	0·2698	0·2880	0·3027	0·7205
28	0·2651	0·2831	0·2977	0·7238
29	0·2607	0·2784	0·2929	0·7270
30	0·2564	0·2739	0·2883	0·7301
31	0·2522	0·2695	0·2838	0·7332
32	0·2482	0·2653	0·2794	0·7362
33	0·2443	0·2612	0·2751	0·7392
34	0·2405	0·2572	0·2710	0·7421
35	0·2368	0·2533	0·2670	0·7450
36	0·2333	0·2495	0·2631	0·7478
37	0·2298	0·2458	0·2593	0·7506
38	0·2265	0·2423	0·2556	0·7533
39	0·2232	0·2388	0·2519	0·7559
40	0·2201	0·2354	0·2484	0·7585
41	0·2170	0·2322	0·2450	0·7611
42	0·2140	0·2290	0·2417	0·7636
43	0·2111	0·2258	0·2384	0·7661
44	0·2082	0·2228	0·2353	0·7685
45	0·2055	0·2198	0·2322	0·7709
46	0·2028	0·2170	0·2291	0·7733
47	0·2001	0·2141	0·2262	0·7756
48	0·1976	0·2114	0·2233	0·7778
49	0·1951	0·2087	0·2205	0·7801
50	0·1926	0·2061	0·2177	0·7823

RATE OF DISCOUNT

APPENDIX E

$z = 21$ months, $T = 40\%$

(1)	(2)	(3)	(4)	(5)
r	$P = 25\%$ $D = 15\%$	$P = 25\%$ $D = 20\%$	$P = 25\%$ $D = 25\%$	$1 - T(1+r)^{-z}$
1	0·5255	0·5299	0·5326	0·6069
2	0·5035	0·5114	0·5164	0·6136
3	0·4837	0·4943	0·5011	0·6202
4	0·4657	0·4785	0·4868	0·6265
5	0·4493	0·4637	0·4734	0·6327
6	0·4342	0·4500	0·4607	0·6388
7	0·4203	0·4371	0·4487	0·6447
8	0·4074	0·4250	0·4373	0·6504
9	0·3954	0·4136	0·4265	0·6560
10	0·3843	0·4029	0·4162	0·6615
11	0·3738	0·3928	0·4064	0·6668
12	0·3640	0·3831	0·3971	0·6720
13	0·3548	0·3740	0·3882	0·6770
14	0·3460	0·3653	0·3797	0·6820
15	0·3378	0·3571	0·3716	0·6868
16	0·3300	0·3492	0·3638	0·6915
17	0·3225	0·3417	0·3563	0·6961
18	0·3155	0·3345	0·3491	0·7006
19	0·3087	0·3276	0·3422	0·7050
20	0·3023	0·3210	0·3355	0·7093
21	0·2962	0·3147	0·3292	0·7135
22	0·2903	0·3086	0·3230	0·7176
23	0·2847	0·3027	0·3170	0·7216
24	0·2792	0·2971	0·3113	0·7255
25	0·2740	0·2917	0·3058	0·7293
26	0·2690	0·2864	0·3004	0·7331
27	0·2642	0·2814	0·2952	0·7367
28	0·2596	0·2765	0·2902	0·7403
29	0·2551	0·2718	0·2854	0·7438
30	0·2508	0·2672	0·2807	0.7473
31	0·2466	0·2628	0·2761	0·7506
32	0·2426	0·2585	0·2717	0·7539
33	0·2387	0·2544	0·2674	0·7572
34	0·2349	0·2504	0·2632	0·7603
35	0·2312	0·2465	0·2592	0·7634
36	0·2277	0·2427	0·2553	0·7665
37	0·2242	0·2390	0·2514	0·7694
38	0·2209	0·2355	0·2477	0·7723
39	0·2176	0·2320	0·2441	0·7752
40	0·2145	0·2286	0·2406	0·7780
41	0·2114	0·2253	0·2371	0·7808
42	0·2084	0·2221	0·2338	0·7835
43	0·2055	0·2190	0·2305	0·7861
44	0·2027	0·2160	0·2274	0·7887
45	0·1999	0·2130	0·2243	0·7912
46	0·1973	0·2102	0·2212	0·7937
47	0·1946	0·2073	0·2183	0·7962
48	0·1921	0·2046	0·2154	0·7986
49	0·1896	0·2019	0·2126	0·8009
50	0·1872	0·1993	0·2099	0·8033

RATE OF DISCOUNT

APPENDIX E

PLANT QUALIFYING FOR CASH GRANTS—DEVELOPMENT AREA

$z = 9$ months, $T = 40\%$

(1)	(2)	(3)	(4)	(5)
	$P = 45\%$ $D = 15\%$	$P = 45\%$ $D = 20\%$	$P = 45\%$ $D = 25\%$	$1-T(1+r)^{-z}$
1	0·6501	0·6534	0·6554	0·6030
2	0·6319	0·6378	0·6415	0·6059
3	0·6152	0·6232	0·6284	0·6088
4	0·5997	0·6094	0·6158	0·6116
5	0·5853	0·5964	0·6038	0·6144
6	0·5718	0·5841	0·5924	0·6171
7	0·5591	0·5723	0·5814	0·6198
8	0·5472	0·5611	0·5708	0·6224
9	0·5359	0·5505	0·5607	0·6250
10	0·5252	0·5403	0·5510	0·6276
11	0·5151	0·5305	0·5416	0·6301
12	0·5054	0·5211	0·5326	0·6326
13	0·4961	0·5121	0·5239	0·6350
14	0·4873	0·5034	0·5154	0·6374
15	0·4788	0·4951	0·5073	0·6398
16	0·4707	0·4870	0·4994	0·6421
17	0·4628	0·4793	0·4918	0·6444
18	0·4553	0·4717	0·4844	0·6467
19	0·4480	0·4645	0·4772	0·6489
20	0·4410	0·4575	0·4702	0·6511
21	0·4342	0·4506	0·4635	0·6533
22	0·4277	0·4440	0·4569	0·6554
23	0·4213	0·4376	0·4505	0·6575
24	0·4152	0·4314	0·4443	0·6596
25	0·4092	0·4254	0·4383	0·6616
26	0·4034	0·4195	0·4324	0·6637
27	0·3978	0·4138	0·4267	0·6656
28	0·3924	0·4082	0·4211	0·6676
29	0·3871	0·4028	0·4157	0·6695
30	0·3819	0·3976	0·4104	0·6714
31	0·3769	0·3924	0·4052	0·6733
32	0·3720	0·3874	0·4001	0·6752
33	0·3672	0·3825	0·3952	0·6770
34	0·3626	0·3778	0·3904	0·6788
35	0·3580	0·3731	0·3857	0·6806
36	0·3536	0·3686	0·3811	0·6824
37	0·3493	0·3641	0·3766	0·6841
38	0·3451	0·3598	0·3722	0·6858
39	0·3409	0·3556	0·3679	0·6875
40	0·3369	0·3514	0·3637	0·6892
41	0·3330	0·3474	0·3596	0·6909
42	0·3291	0·3434	0·3555	0·6925
43	0·3254	0·3395	0·3516	0·6941
44	0·3217	0·3357	0·3477	0·6957
45	0·3181	0·3320	0·3439	0·6973
46	0·3146	0·3284	0·3402	0·6988
47	0·3111	0·3248	0·3366	0·7004
48	0·3077	0·3213	0·3330	0·7019
49	0·3044	0·3179	0·3295	0·7034
50	0·3011	0·3145	0·3261	0·7049

RATE OF DISCOUNT

14

APPENDIX E

PLANT QUALIFYING FOR CASH GRANTS—DEVELOPMENT AREA

$z = 12$ months, $T = 40\%$

(1)	(2)	(3)	(4)	(5)
r	$P = 45\%$ $D = 15\%$	$P = 45\%$ $D = 20\%$	$P = 45\%$ $D = 25\%$	$1-T(1+r)^{-z}$
1	0·6496	0·6529	0·6549	0·6040
2	0·6309	0·6368	0·6405	0·6078
3	0·6138	0·6218	0·6269	0·6117
4	0·5980	0·6076	0·6139	0·6154
5	0·5832	0·5942	0·6016	0·6190
6	0·5695	0·5816	0·5898	0·6226
7	0·5566	0·5695	0·5784	0·6262
8	0·5444	0·5581	0·5676	0·6296
9	0·5329	0·5472	0·5572	0·6330
10	0·5221	0·5367	0·5472	0·6364
11	0·5117	0·5267	0·5376	0·6396
12	0·5019	0·5172	0·5283	0·6429
13	0·4925	0·5080	0·5194	0·6460
14	0·4835	0·4991	0·5107	0·6491
15	0·4749	0·4906	0·5024	0·6522
16	0·4666	0·4824	0·4943	0·6552
17	0·4587	0·4745	0·4865	0·0581
18	0·4511	0·4669	0·4790	0·6610
19	0·4437	0·4595	0·4717	0·6639
20	0·4366	0·4523	0·4645	0·6667
21	0·4298	0·4454	0·4577	0·6694
22	0·4231	0·4387	0·4510	0·6721
23	0·4167	0·4322	0·4445	0·6748
24	0·4105	0·4259	0·4381	0·6774
25	0·4045	0·4198	0·4320	0·6800
26	0·3987	0·4138	0·4260	0·6825
27	0·3930	0·4080	0·4202	0·6850
28	0·3875	0·4024	0·4145	0·6875
29	0·3821	0·3969	0·4090	0·6899
30	0·3769	0·3916	0·4036	0·6923
31	0·3719	0·3864	0·3983	0·6947
32	0·3669	0·3813	0·3932	0·6970
33	0·3621	0·3764	0·3882	0·6992
34	0·3575	0·3716	0·3833	0·7015
35	0·3529	0·3669	0·3786	0·7037
36	0·3484	0·3623	0·3739	0·7059
37	0·3441	0·3578	0·3693	0·7080
38	0·3398	0·3534	0·3649	0·7101
39	0·3357	0·3492	0·3605	0·7122
40	0·3317	0·3450	0·3563	0·7143
41	0·3277	0·3409	0·3521	0·7163
42	0·3238	0·3369	0·3480	0·7183
43	0·3200	0·3330	0·3440	0·7203
44	0·3163	0·3292	0·3401	0·7222
45	0·3127	0·3254	0·3363	0·7241
46	0·3092	0·3218	0·3325	0·7260
47	0·3057	0·3182	0·3289	0·7279
48	0·3023	0·3146	0·3253	0·7297
49	0·2990	0·3112	0·3217	0·7315
50	0·2957	0·3078	0·3183	0·7333

RATE OF DISCOUNT

APPENDIX E

PLANT QUALIFYING FOR CASH GRANTS—DEVELOPMENT AREA

$z = 18$ months, $T = 40\%$

(1)	(2)	(3)	(4)	(5)
r	$P = 45\%$ $D = 15\%$	$P = 45\%$ $D = 20\%$	$P = 45\%$ $D = 25\%$	$1-T(1+r)^{-z}$
1	0·6486	0·6518	0·6538	0·6059
2	0·6290	0·6349	0·6385	0·6117
3	0·6111	0·6190	0·6240	0·6173
4	0·5946	0·6041	0·6103	0·6229
5	0·5793	0·5900	0·5972	0·6282
6	0·5650	0·5767	0·5847	0·6335
7	0·5516	0·5641	0·5727	0·6386
8	0·5390	0·5521	0·5613	0·6436
9	0·5271	0·5408	0·5504	0·6485
10	0·5159	0·5299	0·5399	0·6533
11	0·5053	0·5195	0·5298	0·6580
12	0·4951	0·5096	0·5201	0·6625
13	0·4855	0·5001	0·5108	0·6670
14	0·4763	0·4909	0·5018	0·6714
15	0·4675	0·4821	0·4931	0·6757
16	0·4590	0·4737	0·4847	0·6798
17	0·4509	0·4655	0·4766	0·6839
18	0·4431	0·4577	0·4688	0·6879
19	0·4356	0·4501	0·4612	0·6919
20	0·4284	0·4427	0·4539	0·6957
21	0·4214	0·4357	0·4468	0·6995
22	0·4147	0·4288	0·4399	0·7032
23	0·4082	0·4221	0·4332	0·7068
24	0·4019	0·4157	0·4267	0·7103
25	0·3958	0·4094	0·4204	0·7138
26	0·3899	0·4034	0·4142	0·7172
27	0·3841	0·3975	0·4083	0·7205
28	0·3786	0·3918	0·4025	0·7238
29	0·3732	0·3862	0·3968	0·7270
30	0·3679	0·3808	0·3913	0·7301
31	0·3628	0·3755	0·3859	0·7332
32	0·3578	0·3704	0·3807	0·7362
33	0·3530	0·3654	0·3756	0·7392
34	0·3483	0·3605	0·3706	0·7421
35	0·3437	0·3557	0·3658	0·7450
36	0·3392	0·3511	0·3610	0·7478
37	0·3348	0·3466	0·3564	0·7506
38	0·3306	0·3422	0·3519	0·7533
39	0·3264	0·3378	0·3475	0·7559
40	0·3224	0·3336	0·3432	0·7585
41	0·3184	0·3295	0·3390	0·7611
42	0·3145	0·3255	0·3348	0·7636
43	0·3107	0·3216	0·3308	0·7661
44	0·3070	0·3177	0·3268	0·7685
45	0·3034	0·3139	0·3230	0·7709
46	0·2999	0·3103	0·3192	0·7733
47	0·2964	0·3067	0·3155	0·7756
48	0·2930	0·3031	0·3119	0·7778
49	0·2897	0·2997	0·3083	0·7801
50	0·2864	0·2963	0·3048	0·7823

RATE OF DISCOUNT

APPENDIX E

PLANT QUALIFYING FOR CASH GRANTS—DEVELOPMENT AREA

$z = 21$ months, $T = 40\%$

(1)	(2)	(3)	(4)	(5)
r	$P = 45\%$ $D = 15\%$	$P = 45\%$ $D = 20\%$	$P = 45\%$ $D = 25\%$	$1 - T(1+r)^{-z}$
1	0·6480	0·6513	0·6533	0·6069
2	0·6281	0·6339	0·6375	0·6136
3	0·6098	0·6176	0·6226	0·6202
4	0·5929	0·6023	0·6084	0·6265
5	0·5773	0·5879	0·5950	0·6327
6	0·5628	0·5743	0·5822	0·6388
7	0·5491	0·5615	0·5699	0·6447
8	0·5364	0·5493	0·5583	0·6504
9	0·5243	0·5377	0·5471	0·6560
10	0·5129	0·5266	0·5364	0·6615
11	0·5022	0·5160	0·5261	0·6668
12	0·4919	0·5059	0·5162	0·6720
13	0·4822	0·4963	0·5067	0·6770
14	0·4728	0·4870	0·4975	0·6820
15	0·4639	0·4781	0·4887	0·6868
16	0·4554	0·4695	0·4802	0·6915
17	0·4472	0·4613	0·4720	0·6961
18	0·4394	0·4533	0·4640	0·7006
19	0·4318	0·4457	0·4564	0·7050
20	0·4246	0·4383	0·4489	0·7093
21	0·4175	0·4311	0·4417	0·7135
22	0·4108	0·4242	0·4348	0·7176
23	0·4042	0·4175	0·4280	0·7216
24	0·3979	0·4110	0·4214	0·7255
25	0·3918	0·4047	0·4150	0·7293
26	0·3858	0·3986	0·4088	0·7331
27	0·3801	0·3927	0·4028	0·7367
28	0·3745	0·3869	0·3970	0·7403
29	0·3691	0·3813	0·3913	0·7438
30	0·3638	0·3759	0·3857	0·7473
31	0·3587	0·3706	0·3803	0·7506
32	0·3537	0·3654	0·3751	0·7539
33	0·3489	0·3604	0·3700	0·7572
34	0·3442	0·3555	0·3650	0·7603
35	0·3396	0·3508	0·3601	0·7634
36	0·3351	0·3461	0·3553	0·7665
37	0·3307	0·3416	0·3507	0·7694
38	0·3265	0·3372	0·3462	0·7723
39	0·3223	0·3328	0·3417	0·7752
40	0·3183	0·3286	0·3374	0·7780
41	0·3143	0·3245	0·3332	0·7808
42	0·3104	0·3205	0·3290	0·7835
43	0·3067	0·3166	0·3250	0·7861
44	0·3030	0·3127	0·3211	0·7887
45	0·2994	0·3090	0·3172	0·7912
46	0·2958	0·3053	0·3134	0·7937
47	0·2924	0·3017	0·3097	0·7962
48	0·2890	0·2982	0·3061	0·7986
49	0·2857	0·2947	0·3025	0·8009
50	0·2824	0·2913	0·2991	0·8033

RATE OF DISCOUNT

APPENDIX E

(a) Present value S_1 of investment incentives on a principal of unity (columns (2), (3) and (4)):

$$S_1 = \frac{T}{(1+r)^z}\left[\frac{Rr+D(1+r)}{r+D}\right].$$

(b) Effective net of tax factor, y, (column (5)): $y = 1-T(1+r)^{-z}$.

$R = 30\%$ initial allowance;
$D = $ annual allowance on a reducing balance basis;
$T = $ corporation tax at 40%;
$z = $ time-lag between company's financial year-end and date of corporation tax payment;
$r = $ rate of discount.

APPENDIX E

PLANT NOT QUALIFYING FOR CASH GRANTS

$z = 9$ months, $T = 40\%$

(1)	(2)	(3)	(4)	(5)
r	$R = 30\%$ $D = 15\%$	$R = 30\%$ $D = 20\%$	$R = 30\%$ $D = 25\%$	$1-T(1+r)^{-z}$
1	0·3834	0·3876	0·3902	0·6030
2	0·3686	0·3762	0·3810	0·6059
3	0·3554	0·3657	0·3724	0·6088
4	0·3434	0·3560	0·3643	0·6116
5	0·3326	0·3471	0·3567	0·6144
6	0·3227	0·3387	0·3495	0·6171
7	0·3137	0·3309	0·3428	0·6198
8	0·3053	0·3236	0·3364	0·6224
9	0·2976	0·3168	0·3303	0·6250
10	0·2905	0·3103	0·3245	0·6276
11	0·2838	0·3043	0·3190	0·6301
12	0·2776	0·2985	0·3138	0·6326
13	0·2718	0·2931	0·3088	0·6350
14	0·2663	0·2879	0·3040	0·6374
15	0·2611	0·2830	0·2994	0·6398
16	0·2563	0·2783	0·2950	0·6421
17	0·2517	0·2739	0·2908	0·6444
18	0·2473	0·2696	0·2868	0·6467
19	0·2432	0·2656	0·2829	0·6489
20	0·2392	0·2617	0·2791	0·6511
21	0·2355	0·2579	0·2755	0·6533
22	0·2319	0·2543	0·2720	0·6554
23	0·2285	0·2509	0·2686	0·0575
24	0·2252	0·2476	0·2654	0·6596
25	0·2220	0·2444	0·2622	0·6616
26	0·2190	0·2413	0·2592	0·6637
26	0·2161	0·2383	0·2562	0·6656
28	0·2134	0·2354	0·2534	0·6676
29	0·2107	0·2327	0·2506	0·6695
30	0·2081	0·2300	0·2479	0·6714
31	0·2056	0·2274	0·2453	0·6733
32	0·2032	0·2249	0·2428	0·6752
33	0·2009	0·2224	0·2403	0·6770
34	0·1986	0·2201	0·2379	0·6788
35	0·1964	0·2178	0·2355	0·6800
36	0·1943	0·2155	0·2333	0·6824
37	0·1923	0·2134	0·2310	0·6841
38	0·1903	0·2112	0·2289	0·6858
39	0·1883	0·2092	0·2268	0·6875
40	0·1865	0·2072	0·2247	0·6892
41	0·1847	0·2052	0·2227	0·0909
42	0·1829	0·2033	0·2208	0·6925
43	0·1812	0·2015	0·2188	0·6941
44	0·1795	0·1997	0·2170	0·6957
45	0·1778	0·1979	0·2151	0·6973
46	0·1763	0·1962	0·2134	0·6988
47	0·1747	0·1945	0·2116	0·7004
48	0·1732	0·1929	0·2099	0·7019
49	0·1717	0·1913	0·2082	0·7034
50	0·1703	0·1897	0·2066	0·7049

RATE OF DISCOUNT

APPENDIX E

PLANT NOT QUALIFYING FOR CASH GRANTS

$z = 12$ months, $T = 40\%$

(1)	(2)	(3)	(4)	(5)
r	$R = 30\%$ $D = 15\%$	$R = 30\%$ $D = 20\%$	$R = 30\%$ $D = 25\%$	$1-T(1+r)^{-z}$
1	0·3824	0·3866	0·3892	0·6040
2	0·3668	0·3743	0·3791	0·6078
3	0·3528	0·3630	0·3696	0·6117
4	0·3401	0·3526	0·3607	0·6154
5	0·3286	0·3429	0·3524	0·6190
6	0·3181	0·3338	0·3445	0·6226
7	0·3084	0·3254	0·3370	0·6262
8	0·2995	0·3175	0·3300	0·6296
9	0·2913	0·3100	0·3233	0·6330
10	0·2836	0·3030	0·3169	0·6364
11	0·2765	0·2964	0·3108	0·6396
12	0·2698	0·2902	0·3050	0·6429
13	0·2636	0·2843	0·2995	0·6460
14	0·2577	0·2786	0·2942	0·6491
15	0·2522	0·2733	0·2891	0·6522
16	0·2469	0·2682	0·2843	0·6552
17	0·2420	0·2633	0·2796	0·6581
18	0·2373	0·2587	0·2751	0·6610
19	0·2328	0·2543	0·2708	0·6639
20	0·2286	0·2500	0·2667	0·6667
21	0·2245	0·2459	0·2627	0·6694
22	0·2206	0·2420	0·2588	0·6721
23	0·2169	0·2382	0·2551	0·6748
24	0·2134	0·2346	0·2515	0·6774
25	0·2100	0·2311	0·2480	0·6800
26	0·2067	0·2277	0·2446	0·6825
27	0·2036	0·2245	0·2414	0·6850
28	0·2006	0·2214	0·2382	0·6875
29	0·1977	0·2183	0·2351	0·6899
30	0·1949	0·2154	0·2322	0·6923
31	0·1922	0·2125	0·2293	0·6947
32	0·1896	0·2098	0·2265	0·6970
33	0·1870	0·2071	0·2237	0·6992
34	0·1846	0·2045	0·2211	0·7015
35	0·1822	0·2020	0·2185	0·7037
36	0·1799	0·1996	0·2160	0·7059
37	0·1777	0·1972	0·2136	0·7080
38	0·1756	0·1949	0·2112	0·7101
39	0·1735	0·1927	0·2089	0·7122
40	0·1714	0·1905	0·2066	0·7143
41	0·1695	0·1884	0·2044	0·7163
42	0·1675	0·1863	0·2022	0·7183
43	0·1657	0·1843	0·2001	0·7203
44	0·1638	0·1823	0·1981	0·7222
45	0·1621	0·1804	0·1961	0·7241
46	0·1603	0·1785	0·1941	0·7260
47	0·1587	0·1767	0·1922	0·7279
48	0·1570	0·1749	0·1903	0·7297
49	0·1554	0·1731	0·1885	0·7315
50	0·1538	0·1714	0·1867	0·7333

RATE OF DISCOUNT

APPENDIX E

$z = 18$ months, $T = 40\%$

(1)	(2)	(3)	(4)	(5)
	$R = 30\%$	$R = 30\%$	$R = 30\%$	
r	$D = 15\%$	$D = 20\%$	$D = 25\%$	$1 - T(1+r)^{-z}$
1	0·3805	0·3847	0·3873	0·6059
2	0·3632	0·3706	0·3754	0·6117
3	0·3476	0·3577	0·3642	0·6173
4	0·3335	0·3457	0·3537	0·6229
5	0·3207	0·3346	0·3439	0·6282
6	0·3089	0·3242	0·3346	0·6335
7	0·2982	0·3145	0·3258	0·6386
8	0·2882	0·3055	0·3175	0·6436
9	0·2790	0·2970	0·3096	0·6485
10	0·2704	0·2889	0·3021	0·6533
11	0·2624	0·2814	0·2950	0·6580
12	0·2550	0·2742	0·2882	0·6625
13	0·2480	0·2674	0·2817	0·6670
14	0·2414	0·2610	0·2755	0·6714
15	0·2352	0·2548	0·2696	0·6757
16	0·2293	0·2490	0·2639	0·6798
17	0·2237	0·2435	0·2585	0·6839
18	0·2184	0·2382	0·2533	0·6879
19	0·2134	0·2331	0·2483	0·6919
20	0·2087	0·2282	0·2434	0·6957
21	0·2041	0·2236	0·2388	0·6995
22	0·1998	0·2191	0·2343	0·7032
23	0·1956	0·2148	0·2300	0·7068
24	0·1916	0·2107	0·2258	0·7103
25	0·1878	0·2067	0·2218	0·7138
26	0·1842	0·2029	0·2179	0·7172
27	0·1807	0·1992	0·2142	0·7205
28	0·1773	0·1957	0·2105	0·7238
29	0·1740	0·1922	0·2070	0·7270
30	0·1709	0·1889	0·2036	0·7301
31	0·1679	0·1857	0·2003	0·7332
32	0·1650	0·1826	0·1971	0·7362
33	0·1622	0·1796	0·1940	0·7392
34	0·1595	0·1767	0·1910	0·7421
35	0·1568	0·1739	0·1881	0·7450
36	0·1543	0·1711	0·1852	0·7478
37	0·1518	0·1685	0·1825	0·7506
38	0·1494	0·1659	0·1798	0·7533
39	0·1471	0·1634	0·1772	0·7559
40	0·1449	0·1610	0·1746	0·7585
41	0·1427	0·1586	0·1721	0·7611
42	0·1406	0·1563	0·1697	0·7636
43	0·1385	0·1541	0·1674	0·7661
44	0·1365	0·1519	0·1651	0·7685
45	0·1346	0·1498	0·1628	0·7709
46	0·1327	0·1477	0·1606	0·7733
47	0·1309	0·1457	0·1585	0·7756
48	0·1291	0·1438	0·1564	0·7778
49	0·1273	0·1418	0·1544	0·7801
50	0·1256	0·1400	0·1524	0·7823

RATE OF DISCOUNT

APPENDIX E

$z = 21$ months, $T = 40\%$

(1)	(2)	(3)	(4)	(5)
	$R = 30\%$ $D = 15\%$	$R = 30\%$ $D = 20\%$	$R = 30\%$ $D = 25\%$	$1 - T(1+r)^{-2}$
r				
1	0·3796	0·3837	0·3863	0·6069
2	0·3614	0·3688	0·3735	0·6136
3	0·3450	0·3551	0·3615	0·6202
4	0·3302	0·3423	0·3503	0·6265
5	0·3168	0·3305	0·3397	0·6327
6	0·3045	0·3195	0·3298	0·6388
7	0·2932	0·3093	0·3204	0·6447
8	0·2827	0·2997	0·3115	0·6504
9	0·2731	0·2906	0·3030	0·6560
10	0·2641	0·2821	0·2950	0·6615
11	0·2557	0·2741	0·2874	0·6668
12	0·2479	0·2665	0·2802	0·6720
13	0·2405	0·2594	0·2733	0·6770
14	0·2336	0·2526	0·2667	0·6820
15	0·2271	0·2461	0·2604	0·6868
16	0·2209	0·2399	0·2543	0·6915
17	0·2151	0·2341	0·2485	0·6961
18	0·2096	0·2285	0·2430	0·7006
19	0·2043	0·2232	0·2377	0·7050
20	0·1994	0·2180	0·2326	0·7093
21	0·1946	0·2132	0·2277	0·7135
22	0·1901	0·2085	0·2229	0·7176
23	0·1857	0·2040	0·2184	0·7216
24	0·1816	0·1997	0·2140	0·7255
25	0·1776	0·1955	0·2098	0·7293
26	0·1738	0·1915	0·2057	0·7331
27	0·1702	0·1877	0·2018	0·7367
28	0·1667	0·1839	0·1979	0·7403
29	0·1633	0·1804	0·1943	0·7438
30	0·1601	0·1769	0·1907	0·7473
31	0·1569	0·1736	0·1872	0·7506
32	0·1539	0·1704	0·1839	0·7539
33	0·1510	0·1672	0·1807	0·7572
34	0·1482	0·1642	0·1775	0·7603
35	0·1455	0·1613	0·1745	0·7634
36	0·1429	0·1585	0·1715	0·7665
37	0·1403	0·1557	0·1686	0·7694
38	0·1379	0·1531	0·1659	0·7723
39	0·1355	0·1505	0·1632	0·7752
40	0·1332	0·1480	0·1605	0·7780
41	0·1310	0·1456	0·1580	0·7808
42	0·1288	0·1432	0·1555	0·7835
43	0·1267	0·1409	0·1530	0·7861
44	0·1246	0·1387	0·1507	0·7887
45	0·1227	0·1365	0·1484	0·7912
46	0·1207	0·1344	0·1461	0·7937
47	0·1188	0·1323	0·1440	0·7962
48	0·1170	0·1303	0·1418	0·7986
49	0·1152	0·1284	0·1397	0·8009
50	0·1135	0·1265	0·1377	0·8033

RATE OF DISCOUNT

APPENDIX E

INDUSTRIAL BUILDINGS

(a) *National* Initial plus annual allowances on a straight-line basis. Present value S_2 of investment incentives on a principal of unity (column (2)):

$$S_2 = \frac{T}{(1+r)^z}\left\{(R+D)+D\left[\frac{1-(1+r)^{-20}}{r}\right]\right\}$$

(b) (i) *Development area* Cash grant at 25% plus initial allowance at 15% and annual allowances at 4% (on a straight-line basis) on the balance of expenditure (column (3)).

(ii) *Development area* Cash grant at 35% plus initial allowance at 15% and annual allowances at 4% (on a straight-line basis) on the balance of expenditure (column (4)).

Present value S_3 of (b)(i) and (ii) on a principal of unity:

$$S_3 = \frac{P}{(1+r)^k} + \frac{T(1-P)}{(1+r)^z}\left\{(R+D)+D\left[\frac{1-(1+r)^{-20}}{r}\right]\right\}.$$

(c) Effective net of tax factor y (column (5)): $y = 1-T(1+r)^{-z}$.

$P =$ cash grant;
$R =$ initial allowance at 15%;
$D =$ annual allowance at 4% on a straight line basis;
$T =$ corporation tax at 40%;
$k = 18$ months time-lag between incurring of capital expenditure and receipt of cash-grant;
$z =$ time-lag between company's financial year-end and date of corporation tax payment;
$r =$ rate of discount.

APPENDIX E

INDUSTRIAL BUILDINGS

$z = 9$ months, $T = 40\%$

(1)	(2)	(3)	(4)	(5)
r	$R = 15\%$ $D = 4\%$	$P = 25\%$ $R = 15\%$ $D = 4\%$	$P = 35\%$ $R = 15\%$ $D = 4\%$	$1 - T(1+r)^{-z}$
1	0·36202	0·51781	0·58013	0·6030
2	0·33265	0·49217	0·55598	0·6059
3	0·30715	0·46952	0·53447	0·6088
4	0·28494	0·44942	0·51521	0·6116
5	0·26550	0·43148	0·49788	0·6144
6	0·24842	0·41539	0·48218	0·6171
7	0·23336	0·40089	0·46790	0·6198
8	0·22002	0·38776	0·45485	0·6224
9	0·20816	0·37580	0·44286	0·6250
10	0·19758	0·36488	0·43180	0·6276
11	0·18810	0·35485	0·42155	0·6301
12	0·17958	0·34560	0·41201	0·6326
13	0·17189	0·33705	0·40311	0·6350
14	0·16494	0·32910	0·39476	0·6374
15	0·15862	0·32168	0·38691	0·6398
16	0·15286	0·31475	0·37950	0·6421
17	0·14760	0·30824	0·37250	0·6444
18	0·14277	0·30212	0·36585	0·6467
19	0·13834	0·29634	0·35954	0·6489
20	0·13424	0·29086	0·35351	0·6511
21	0·13046	0·28567	0·34776	0·6533
22	0·12695	0·28073	0·34225	0·6554
23	0·12368	0·27603	0·33697	0·6575
24	0·12064	0·27154	0·33189	0·6596
25	0·11780	0·26724	0·32701	0·6616
26	0·11514	0·26312	0·32231	0·6637
27	0·11265	0·25916	0·31777	0·6656
28	0·11030	0·25536	0·31338	0·6676
29	0·10809	0·25170	0·30914	0·6695
30	0·10600	0·24817	0·30503	0·6714
31	0·10403	0·24476	0·30105	0·6733
32	0·10216	0·24146	0·29719	0·6752
33	0·10038	0·23828	0·29344	0·6770
34	0·09870	0·23519	0·28979	0·6788
35	0·09709	0·23220	0·28625	0·6806
36	0·09556	0·22930	0·28279	0·6824
37	0·09410	0·22648	0·27943	0·6841
38	0·09271	0·22374	0·27616	0·6858
39	0·09137	0·22108	0·27296	0·6875
40	0·09009	0·21849	0·26985	0·6892
41	0·08886	0·21597	0·26681	0·6909
42	0·08768	0·21351	0·26384	0·6925
43	0·08655	0·21111	0·26093	0·6941
44	0·08546	0·20877	0·25809	0·6957
45	0·08441	0·20649	0·25532	0·6973
46	0·08339	0·20426	0·25260	0·6988
47	0·08242	0·20208	0·24995	0·7004
48	0·08147	0·19995	0·24735	0·7019
49	0·08056	0·19787	0·24480	0·7034
50	0·07967	0·19584	0·24230	0·7049

RATE OF DISCOUNT

APPENDIX E

$$z = 12 \text{ months}, \quad T = 40\%$$

(1)	(2)	(3)	(4)	(5)
	$R = 15\%$ $D = 4\%$	$P = 25\%$ $R = 15\%$ $D = 4\%$	$P = 35\%$ $R = 15\%$ $D = 4\%$	$1 - T(1+r)^{-z}$
1	0·36112	0·51713	0·57954	0·6040
2	0·33100	0·49094	0·55491	0·6078
3	0·30489	0·46783	0·53300	0·6117
4	0·28216	0·44734	0·51341	0·6154
5	0·26228	0·42907	0·49578	0·6190
6	0·24483	0·41270	0·47985	0·6226
7	0·22944	0·39796	0·46536	0·6262
8	0·21582	0·38461	0·45213	0·6296
9	0·20372	0·37248	0·43998	0·6330
10	0·19292	0·36139	0·42878	0·6364
11	0·18326	0·35122	0·41840	0·6396
12	0·17456	0·34184	0·40875	0·6429
13	0·16672	0·33317	0·39974	0·6460
14	0·15962	0·32511	0·39130	0·6491
15	0·15317	0·31760	0·38337	0·6522
16	0·14729	0·31057	0·37589	0·6552
17	0·14192	0·30398	0·36881	0·6581
18	0·13699	0·29778	0·36209	0·6610
19	0·13245	0·29192	0·35571	0·6639
20	0·12826	0·28638	0·34962	0·6667
21	0·12439	0·28112	0·34381	0·6694
22	0·12079	0·27612	0·33825	0·6721
23	0·11745	0·27135	0·33291	0·6748
24	0·11433	0·26680	0·32779	0·6774
25	0·11141	0·26244	0·32286	0·6800
26	0·10868	0·25827	0·31810	0·6825
27	0·10611	0·25426	0·31352	0·6850
28	0·10370	0·25041	0·30909	0·6875
29	0·10142	0·24670	0·30481	0·6899
30	0·09927	0·24312	0·30066	0·6923
31	0·09724	0·23966	0·29664	0·6947
32	0·09531	0·23633	0·29273	0·6970
33	0·09348	0·23310	0·28895	0·6992
34	0·09173	0·22997	0·28526	0·7015
35	0·09007	0·22694	0·28168	0·7037
36	0·08849	0·22400	0·27820	0·7059
37	0·08698	0·22114	0·27480	0·7080
38	0·08553	0·21836	0·27150	0·7101
39	0·08415	0·21566	0·26827	0·7122
40	0·08282	0·21304	0·26512	0·7143
41	0·08155	0·21048	0·26205	0·7163
42	0·08032	0·20799	0·25905	0·7183
43	0·07915	0·20556	0·25612	0·7203
44	0·07801	0·20319	0·25325	0·7222
45	0·07692	0·20087	0·25045	0·7241
46	0·07587	0·19861	0·24771	0·7260
47	0·07485	0·19641	0·24503	0·7279
48	0·07387	0·19425	0·24240	0·7297
49	0·07291	0·19214	0·23983	0·7315
50	0·07199	0·19008	0·23731	0·7333

RATE OF DISCOUNT

APPENDIX E

$$z = 18 \text{ months}, \quad T = 40\%$$

(1)	(2)	(3)	(4)	(5)
r	$R = 15\%$ $D = 4\%$	$P = 25\%$ $R = 15\%$ $D = 4\%$	$P = 35\%$ $R = 15\%$ $D = 4\%$	$1 - T(1+r)^{-z}$
1	0·35933	0·51579	0·57838	0·6059
2	0·32774	0·48849	0·55279	0·6117
3	0·30042	0·46447	0·53009	0·6173
4	0·27668	0·44323	0·50984	0·6229
5	0·25596	0·42433	0·49167	0·6282
6	0·23780	0·40743	0·47528	0·6335
7	0·22181	0·39223	0·46040	0·6386
8	0·20768	0·37850	0·44683	0·6436
9	0·19513	0·36603	0·43439	0·6485
10	0·18395	0·35466	0·42294	0·6533
11	0·17394	0·34423	0·41234	0·6580
12	0·16495	0·33463	0·40250	0·6625
13	0·15684	0·32575	0·39332	0·6670
14	0·14950	0·31752	0·38472	0·6714
15	0·14283	0·30984	0·37665	0·6757
16	0·13676	0·30267	0·36904	0·6798
17	0·13120	0·29595	0·36184	0·6839
18	0·12611	0·28962	0·35502	0·6879
19	0·12142	0·28365	0·34854	0·6919
20	0·11709	0·27800	0·34236	0·6957
21	0·11308	0·27264	0·33646	0·6995
22	0·10936	0·26754	0·33082	0·7032
23	0·10590	0·26269	0·32541	0·7068
24	0·10267	0·25805	0·32021	0·7103
25	0·09965	0·25362	0·31521	0·7138
26	0·09682	0·24937	0·31040	0·7172
27	0·09416	0·24530	0·30575	0·7205
28	0·09166	0·24138	0·30126	0·7238
29	0·08930	0·23760	0·29692	0·7270
30	0·08707	0·23397	0·29272	0·7301
31	0·08496	0·23045	0·28865	0·7332
32	0·08295	0·22706	0·28471	0·7362
33	0·08105	0·22378	0·28087	0·7392
34	0·07925	0·22060	0·27715	0·7421
35	0·07752	0·21753	0·27353	0·7450
36	0·07588	0·21454	0·27000	0·7478
37	0·07431	0·21164	0·26657	0·7506
38	0·07281	0·20882	0·26323	0·7533
39	0·07138	0·20608	0·25997	0·7559
40	0·07000	0·20342	0·25679	0·7585
41	0·06868	0·20083	0·25368	0·7611
42	0·06741	0·19830	0·25065	0·7636
43	0·06619	0·19584	0·24770	0·7661
44	0·06501	0·19343	0·24480	0·7685
45	0·06388	0·19109	0·24198	0·7709
46	0·06279	0·18880	0·23921	0·7733
47	0·06173	0·18657	0·23650	0·7756
48	0·06072	0·18439	0·23386	0·7778
49	0·05973	0·18226	0·23126	0·7801
50	0·05878	0·18017	0·22872	0·7823

RATE OF DISCOUNT

APPENDIX E

$z = 21$ months, $T = 40\%$

(1)	(2)	(3)	(4)	(5)
		$P = 25\%$	$P = 35\%$	
	$R = 15\%$	$R = 15\%$	$R = 15\%$	
r	$D = 4\%$	$D = 4\%$	$D = 4\%$	$1-T(1+r)^{-z}$
1	0·35843	0·51512	0·57780	0·6069
2	0·32612	0·48728	0·55174	0·6136
3	0·29821	0·46281	0·52866	0·6202
4	0·27398	0·44120	0·50809	0·6265
5	0·25286	0·42200	0·48966	0·6327
6	0·23436	0·40485	0·47304	0·6388
7	0·21809	0·38944	0·45798	0·6447
8	0·20372	0·37553	0·44426	0·6504
9	0·19097	0·36291	0·43169	0·6560
10	0·17962	0·35141	0·42012	0·6615
11	0·16946	0·34087	0·40943	0·6668
12	0·16034	0·33117	0·39951	0·6720
13	0·15212	0·32221	0·39025	0·6770
14	0·14468	0·31390	0·38159	0·6820
15	0·13793	0·30617	0·37346	0·6868
16	0·13178	0·29894	0·36580	0·6915
17	0·12615	0·29216	0·35856	0·6961
18	0·12099	0·28578	0·35170	0·7006
19	0·11625	0·27977	0·34518	0·7050
20	0·11187	0·27408	0·33897	0·7093
21	0·10782	0·26869	0·33304	0·7135
22	0·10405	0·26357	0·32737	0·7176
23	0·10056	0·25868	0·32193	0·7216
24	0·09729	0·25402	0·31672	0·7255
25	0·09424	0·24957	0·31170	0·7293
26	0·09138	0·24530	0·30686	0·7331
27	0·08870	0·24120	0·30220	0·7367
28	0·08617	0·23726	0·29770	0·7403
29	0·08379	0·23347	0·29334	0·7438
30	0·08154	0·22982	0·28913	0·7473
31	0·07941	0·22630	0·28505	0·7506
32	0·07739	0·22289	0·28109	0·7539
33	0·07548	0·21960	0·27725	0·7572
34	0·07366	0·21641	0·27351	0·7603
35	0·07192	0·21332	0·26988	0·7634
36	0·07027	0·21033	0·26635	0·7665
37	0·06869	0·20742	0·26291	0·7694
38	0·06718	0·20460	0·25956	0·7723
39	0·06573	0·20185	0·25630	0·7752
40	0·06435	0·19918	0·25312	0·7780
41	0·06302	0·19659	0·25001	0·7808
42	0·06175	0·19406	0·24698	0·7835
43	0·06052	0·19159	0·24402	0·7861
44	0·05935	0·18919	0·24112	0·7887
45	0·05821	0·18684	0·23829	0·7912
46	0·05712	0·18455	0·23553	0·7937
47	0·05607	0·18232	0·23282	0·7962
48	0·05505	0·18014	0·23017	0·7986
49	0·05407	0·17800	0·22758	0·8009
50	0·05312	0·17592	0·22504	0·8033

RATE OF DISCOUNT

APPENDIX F

Equity cut-off rates. Values of i_e derived from the formula:

$$1 = \frac{i_e(1-p)(1-d)}{r_e-pi_e} - \frac{t}{n}\left\{\frac{[(1+r_e)^n-1]pi_e}{r_e(1+r_e)^{n-1}(r_e-pi_e)}\right\}.$$

$i_e = $ equity cut-off rate net of corporation tax;
$p = $ plough back ratio;
$r_e = $ net of all taxes rate of return to equity shareholders;
$n = $ rate of share turnover;
$d = $ income tax at 41·25%;
$t = $ capital gains tax at 20·625%.

APPENDIX F

$$n = 2$$

$p=0{\cdot}1$	0·2	0·3	0·4	0·5
r_e				
2	3·29	3·18	3·08	2·98	2·89
3	4·93	4·77	4·61	4·47	4·33
4	6·57	6·35	6·15	5·96	5·78
5	8·22	7·94	7·68	7·44	7·21
6	9·86	9·53	9·21	8·92	8·65
7	11·50	11·11	10·75	10·41	10·09
8	13·14	12·69	12·28	11·89	11·52
9	14·78	14·28	13·81	13·36	12·95
10	16·42	15·86	15·33	14·84	14·38
11	18·06	17·44	16·86	16·32	15·81
12	19·70	19·02	18·39	17·79	17·24
13	21·34	20·60	19·91	19·27	18·66
14	22·97	22·18	21·43	20·74	20·09
15	24·61	23·76	22·96	22·21	21·51
16	26·25	25·33	24·48	23·68	22·93
17	27·89	26·91	26·00	25·15	24·35
18	29·52	28·49	27·52	26·62	25·77
19	31·16	30·06	29·04	28·08	27·19
20	32·80	31·64	30·56	29·55	28·60

$$n = 2$$

$p=0{\cdot}6$	0·7	0·8	0·9	1·0
r_e				
2	2·81	2·73	*****	*****	*****
3	4·21	4·09	*****	*****	*****
4	5·61	5·44	*****	*****	*****
5	7·00	6·80	*****	*****	*****
6	8·39	8·15	*****	*****	*****
7	9·79	9·50	*****	*****	*****
8	11·18	10·85	*****	*****	*****
9	12·56	12·20	*****	*****	*****
10	13·95	13·54	*****	*****	*****
11	15·33	14·88	*****	*****	*****
12	16·72	16·22	*****	*****	*****
13	18·10	17·56	*****	*****	*****
14	19·48	18·90	*****	*****	*****
15	20·85	20·23	*****	*****	*****
16	22·23	21·57	*****	*****	*****
17	23·60	22·90	*****	*****	*****
18	24·98	24·23	*****	*****	*****
19	26·35	25·56	*****	*****	*****
20	27·72	26·89	*****	*****	*****

REQUIRED RETURN FOR EQUITY SHAREHOLDERS

APPENDIX F

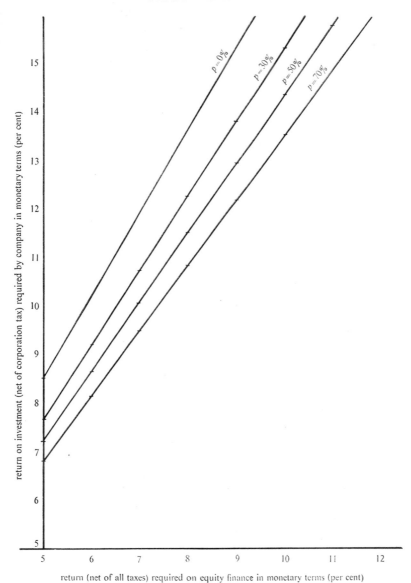

Fig. 12 Equity cut-off rates for capital budgeting in the corporation tax regime

$$\text{rate of share turnover} \frac{1}{n} = \frac{1}{2} \text{ p.a.}$$

proportion of profits retained $= p$.

15

APPENDIX F

$n = 3$

r_e	$p=0.1$	0.2	0.3	0.4	0.5
2	3·29	3·18	3·07	2·98	2·89
3	4·93	4·76	4·61	4·46	4·33
4	6·57	6·35	6·14	5·94	5·76
5	8·21	7·93	7·67	7·42	7·19
6	9·85	9·51	9·19	8·89	8·62
7	11·49	11·09	10·71	10·37	10·04
8	13·12	12·66	12·24	11·84	11·46
9	14·76	14·24	13·75	13·30	12·88
10	16·39	15·81	15·27	14·77	14·29
11	18·03	17·39	16·79	16·23	15·70
12	19·66	18·96	18·30	17·69	17·11
13	21·30	20·53	19·81	19·14	18·52
14	22·93	22·10	21·32	20·60	19·92
15	24·56	23·66	22·83	22·05	21·32
16	26·19	25·23	24·33	23·50	22·72
17	27·82	26·79	25·84	24·95	24·12
18	29·45	28·36	27·34	26·40	25·51
19	31·08	29·92	28·84	27·84	26·90
20	32·71	31·48	30·34	29·28	28·29

$n = 3$

r_e	$p=0.6$	0.7	0.8	0.9	1.0
2	2·80	2·72	*****	*****	*****
3	4·20	4·08	*****	*****	*****
4	5·59	5·42	*****	*****	*****
5	6·97	6·77	*****	*****	*****
6	8·36	8·11	*****	*****	*****
7	9·73	9·45	*****	*****	*****
8	11·11	10·78	*****	*****	*****
9	12·48	12·11	*****	*****	*****
10	13·85	13·43	*****	*****	*****
11	15·21	14·75	*****	*****	*****
12	16·57	16·07	*****	*****	*****
13	17·93	17·38	*****	*****	*****
14	19·29	18·69	*****	*****	*****
15	20·64	20·00	*****	*****	*****
16	21·99	21·31	*****	*****	*****
17	23·34	22·61	*****	*****	*****
18	24·69	23·91	*****	*****	*****
19	26·03	25·21	*****	*****	*****
20	27·37	26·50	*****	*****	*****

REQUIRED RETURN FOR EQUITY SHAREHOLDERS

APPENDIX F

$$n = 4$$

$p=0\cdot1$	0·2	0·3	0·4	0·5
r_e				
2	3·29	3·17	3·07	2·97	2·88
3	4·93	4·76	4·60	4·45	4·32
4	6·57	6·34	6·13	5·93	5·74
5	8·20	7·92	7·65	7·40	7·17
6	9·84	9·49	9·17	8·87	8·58
7	11·47	11·07	10·68	10·33	10·00
8	13·11	12·64	12·20	11·79	11·40
9	14·74	14·20	13·71	13·24	12·81
10	16·37	15·77	15·21	14·69	14·21
11	18·00	17·34	16·72	16·14	15·60
12	19·63	18·90	18·22	17·59	17·00
13	21·26	20·46	19·72	19·03	18·39
14	22·89	22·02	21·22	20·47	19·77
15	24·52	23·58	22·71	21·90	21·15
16	26·14	25·14	24·20	23·34	22·53
17	27·77	26·69	25·70	24·77	23·91
18	29·39	28·25	27·18	26·20	25·28
19	31·02	29·80	28·67	27·63	26·66
20	32·64	31·35	30·16	29·05	28·02

$$n = 4$$

$p=0\cdot6$	0·7	0·8	0·9	1·0
r_e				
2	2·80	2·72	*****	*****	*****
3	4·19	4·06	*****	*****	*****
4	5·57	5·41	*****	*****	*****
5	6·95	6·74	*****	*****	*****
6	8·32	8·07	*****	*****	*****
7	9·68	9·39	*****	*****	*****
8	11·04	10·71	*****	*****	*****
9	12·40	12·02	*****	*****	*****
10	13·75	13·33	*****	*****	*****
11	15·10	14·63	*****	*****	*****
12	16·44	15·93	*****	*****	*****
13	17·78	17·22	*****	*****	*****
14	19·12	18·51	*****	*****	*****
15	20·45	19·80	*****	*****	*****
16	21·78	21·08	*****	*****	*****
17	23·11	22·36	*****	*****	*****
18	24·43	23·63	*****	*****	*****
19	25·75	24·90	*****	*****	*****
20	27·07	26·17	*****	*****	*****

REQUIRED RETURN FOR EQUITY SHAREHOLDERS

APPENDIX F

$$n = 5$$

	$p=0.1$	0.2	0.3	0.4	0.5
r_e					
2	3·28	3·17	3·07	2·97	2·88
3	4·92	4·75	4·60	4·45	4·31
4	6·56	6·33	6·12	5·92	5·73
5	8·20	7·91	7·63	7·38	7·14
6	9·83	9·48	9·15	8·84	8·55
7	11·46	11·04	10·66	10·29	9·95
8	13·09	12·61	12·16	11·74	11·35
9	14·72	14·17	13·66	13·19	12·74
10	16·35	15·73	15·16	14·63	14·13
11	17·98	17·29	16·65	16·06	15·51
12	19·60	18·85	18·15	17·50	16·89
13	21·23	20·40	19·64	18·93	18·26
14	22·85	21·95	21·12	20·35	19·63
15	24·48	23·50	22·61	21·77	21·00
16	26·10	25·05	24·09	23·19	22·36
17	27·72	26·60	25·57	24·61	23·72
18	29·34	28·14	27·04	26·03	25·08
19	30·96	29·69	28·52	27·44	26·44
20	32·58	31·23	29·99	28·85	27·79

$$n = 5$$

	$p=0.6$	0.7	0.8	0.9	1.0
r_e					
2	2·79	2·71	*****	*****	*****
3	4·18	4·05	*****	*****	*****
4	5·55	5·39	*****	*****	*****
5	6·92	6·71	*****	*****	*****
6	8·28	8·03	*****	*****	*****
7	9·64	9·34	*****	*****	*****
8	10·98	10·64	*****	*****	*****
9	12·33	11·94	*****	*****	*****
10	13·67	13·23	*****	*****	*****
11	15·00	14·52	*****	*****	*****
12	16·32	15·80	*****	*****	*****
13	17·65	17·07	*****	*****	*****
14	18·97	18·34	*****	*****	*****
15	20·28	19·61	*****	*****	*****
16	21·59	20·87	*****	*****	*****
17	22·90	22·13	*****	*****	*****
18	24·20	23·39	*****	*****	*****
19	25·51	24·64	*****	*****	*****
20	26·80	25·89	*****	*****	*****

REQUIRED RETURN FOR EQUITY SHAREHOLDERS

APPENDIX F

$n = 6$

$p=0\cdot1$	0·2	0·3	0·4	0·5
r_e				
2	3·28	3·17	3·07	2·97	2·88
3	4·92	4·75	4·59	4·44	4·30
4	6·56	6·32	6·11	5·90	5·71
5	8·19	7·89	7·62	7·36	7·12
6	9·82	9·46	9·13	8·81	8·52
7	11·45	11·02	10·63	10·26	9·91
8	13·08	12·59	12·13	11·70	11·30
9	14·71	14·14	13·62	13·13	12·68
10	16·33	15·70	15·11	14·56	14·06
11	17·96	17·25	16·60	15·99	15·43
12	19·58	18·80	18·08	17·41	16·79
13	21·20	20·35	19·56	18·83	18·15
14	22·82	21·89	21·04	20·24	19·51
15	24·44	23·43	22·51	21·66	20·86
16	26·06	24·98	23·98	23·06	22·21
17	27·67	26·52	25·45	24·47	23·56
18	29·29	28·05	26·92	25·87	24·90
19	30·90	29·59	28·38	27·27	26·24
20	32·52	31·13	29·85	28·67	27·58

$n = 6$

$p=0\cdot6$	0·7	0·8	0·9	1·0
r_e				
2	2·79	2·71	*****	*****	*****
3	4·17	4·04	*****	*****	*****
4	5·54	5·37	*****	*****	*****
5	6·90	6·68	*****	*****	*****
6	8·25	7·99	*****	*****	*****
7	9·59	9·29	*****	*****	*****
8	10·93	10·58	*****	*****	*****
9	12·26	11·86	*****	*****	*****
10	13·58	13·14	*****	*****	*****
11	14·90	14·41	*****	*****	*****
12	16·22	15·68	*****	*****	*****
13	17·52	16·94	*****	*****	*****
14	18·83	18·19	*****	*****	*****
15	20·13	19·44	*****	*****	*****
16	21·42	20·69	*****	*****	*****
17	22·72	21·93	21·20	*****	*****
18	24·00	23·17	22·39	*****	*****
19	25·29	24·40	23·58	*****	*****
20	26·57	25·63	24·76	*****	*****

REQUIRED RETURN FOR EQUITY SHAREHOLDERS

APPENDIX F

$n = 7$

r_e	$p=0.1$	0.2	0.3	0.4	0.5
2	3·28	3·17	3·06	2·96	2·87
3	4·92	4·75	4·58	4·43	4·29
4	6·55	6·32	6·10	5·89	5·70
5	8·19	7·88	7·60	7·34	7·10
6	9·81	9·45	9·11	8·79	8·49
7	11·44	11·01	10·60	10·23	9·88
8	13·07	12·56	12·09	11·66	11·25
9	14·69	14·11	13·58	13·08	12·62
10	16·31	15·66	15·06	14·51	13·99
11	17·93	17·21	16·54	15·92	15·35
12	19·55	18·75	18·02	17·33	16·70
13	21·17	20·30	19·49	18·74	18·05
14	22·79	21·83	20·96	20·15	19·40
15	24·40	23·37	22·42	21·55	20·74
16	26·02	24·91	23·89	22·95	22·08
17	27·63	26·44	25·35	24·34	23·41
18	29·24	27·97	26·81	25·73	24·74
19	30·86	29·50	28·26	27·12	26·07
20	32·47	31·03	29·72	28·51	27·40

$n = 7$

r_e	$p=0.6$	0.7	0.8	0.9	1.0
2	2·78	2·70	*****	*****	*****
3	4·16	4·03	*****	*****	*****
4	5·52	5·35	*****	*****	*****
5	6·87	6·66	*****	*****	*****
6	8·21	7·96	*****	*****	*****
7	9·55	9·24	*****	*****	*****
8	10·88	10·52	*****	*****	*****
9	12·19	11·79	*****	*****	*****
10	13·51	13·06	*****	*****	*****
11	14·81	14·32	*****	*****	*****
12	16·12	15·57	*****	*****	*****
13	17·41	16·81	*****	*****	*****
14	18·70	18·05	17·45	*****	*****
15	19·99	19·29	18·64	*****	*****
16	21·27	20·52	19·82	*****	*****
17	22·55	21·75	21·01	*****	*****
18	23·83	22·97	22·18	*****	*****
19	25·10	24·19	23·35	*****	*****
20	26·37	25·41	24·52	*****	*****

REQUIRED RETURN FOR EQUITY SHAREHOLDERS

APPENDIX F

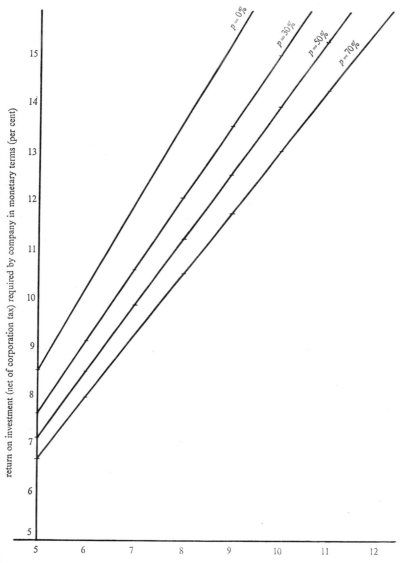

Fig. 13 Equity cut-off rates for capital budgeting in the corporation tax regime

$$\text{rate of share turnover} \frac{1}{n} = \frac{1}{7} \text{ p.a.}$$

proportion of profits retained $= p$.

APPENDIX F

$n = 8$

$p=0.1$	0.2	0.3	0.4	0.5
r_e				
2	3·28	3·17	3·06	2·96	2·87
3	4·92	4·74	4·58	4·43	4·28
4	6·55	6·31	6·09	5·88	5·69
5	8·18	7·87	7·59	7·33	7·08
6	9·81	9·43	9·09	8·76	8·46
7	11·43	10·99	10·58	10·20	9·84
8	13·06	12·54	12·06	11·62	11·21
9	14·68	14·09	13·54	13·04	12·57
10	16·30	15·63	15·02	14·45	13·93
11	17·91	17·17	16·49	15·86	15·28
12	19·53	18·71	17·96	17·26	16·62
13	21·15	20·25	19·42	18·66	17·96
14	22·76	21·78	20·88	20·06	19·29
15	24·37	23·31	22·34	21·45	20·63
16	25·98	24·84	23·80	22·84	21·95
17	27·59	26·37	25·25	24·23	23·28
18	29·20	27·90	26·70	25·61	24·60
19	30·81	29·42	28·15	26·99	25·92
20	32·42	30·95	29·60	28·37	27·23

$n = 8$

$p=0.6$	0.7	0.8	0.9	1.0
r_e				
2	2·78	2·70	*****	*****	*****
3	4·15	4·02	*****	*****	*****
4	5·50	5·33	*****	*****	*****
5	6·85	6·63	*****	*****	*****
6	8·18	7·92	*****	*****	*****
7	9·51	9·20	*****	*****	*****
8	10·83	10·47	*****	*****	*****
9	12·13	11·73	*****	*****	*****
10	13·44	12·98	*****	*****	*****
11	14·73	14·23	*****	*****	*****
12	16·02	15·47	14·95	*****	*****
13	17·31	16·70	16·14	*****	*****
14	18·59	17·93	17·32	*****	*****
15	19·86	19·15	18·49	*****	*****
16	21·13	20·37	19·67	*****	*****
17	22·40	21·59	20·83	*****	*****
18	23·67	22·80	22·00	*****	*****
19	24·93	24·01	23·16	*****	*****
20	26·19	25·22	24·32	*****	*****

REQUIRED RETURN FOR EQUITY SHAREHOLDERS

APPENDIX F

$n = 9$

$p=0\cdot1$	$0\cdot2$	$0\cdot3$	$0\cdot4$	$0\cdot5$
r_e				
2	3·28	3·17	3·06	2·96	2·86
3	4·92	4·74	4·57	4·42	4·27
4	6·55	6·30	6·08	5·87	5·67
5	8·17	7·86	7·58	7·31	7·06
6	9·80	9·42	9·07	8·74	8·44
7	11·42	10·97	10·55	10·17	9·81
8	13·04	12·52	12·03	11·58	11·17
9	14·66	14·06	13·51	12·99	12·52
10	16·28	15·60	14·98	14·40	13·87
11	17·90	17·14	16·44	15·80	15·21
12	19·51	18·67	17·90	17·20	16·54
13	21·12	20·20	19·36	18·59	17·87
14	22·73	21·73	20·82	19·98	19·20
15	24·34	23·26	22·27	21·36	20·52
16	25·95	24·79	23·72	22·74	21·84
17	27·56	26·31	25·17	24·12	23·16
18	29·17	27·83	26·61	25·50	24·47
19	30·77	29·35	28·06	26·87	25·78
20	32·38	30·87	29·50	28·24	27·09

$n = 9$

$p=0\cdot6$	$0\cdot7$	$0\cdot8$	$0\cdot9$	$1\cdot0$
r_e				
2	2·78	2·69	*****	*****	*****
3	4·14	4·01	*****	*****	*****
4	5·49	5·32	*****	*****	*****
5	6·83	6·61	*****	*****	*****
6	8·15	7·89	*****	*****	*****
7	9·47	9·16	*****	*****	*****
8	10·78	10·42	*****	*****	*****
9	12·08	11·67	*****	*****	*****
10	13·37	12·91	12·48	*****	*****
11	14·66	14·15	13·67	*****	*****
12	15·94	15·37	14·85	*****	*****
13	17·21	16·60	16·03	*****	*****
14	18·48	17·82	17·20	*****	*****
15	19·75	19·03	18·36	*****	*****
16	21·01	20·24	19·52	*****	*****
17	22·27	21·45	20·68	*****	*****
18	23·52	22·65	21·83	*****	*****
19	24·78	23·85	22·98	*****	*****
20	26·03	25·04	24·13	*****	*****

REQUIRED RETURN FOR EQUITY SHAREHOLDERS

APPENDIX F

$n = 10$

REQUIRED RETURN FOR EQUITY SHAREHOLDERS

$p=0\cdot1$	$0\cdot2$	$0\cdot3$	$0\cdot4$	$0\cdot5$
r_e				
2	3·28	3·16	3·06	2·95	2·86
3	4·91	4·73	4·57	4·41	4·27
4	6·54	6·30	6·07	5·86	5·66
5	8·17	7·85	7·56	7·29	7·04
6	9·79	9·41	9·05	8·72	8·41
7	11·41	10·95	10·53	10·14	9·77
8	13·03	12·50	12·00	11·55	11·13
9	14·65	14·04	13·47	12·95	12·47
10	16·27	15·57	14·94	14·35	13·81
11	17·88	17·11	16·40	15·75	15·14
12	19·49	18·64	17·85	17·14	16·47
13	21·10	20·16	19·31	18·52	17·80
14	22·71	21·69	20·76	19·90	19·11
15	24·32	23·21	22·20	21·28	20·43
16	25·92	24·73	23·65	22·65	21·74
17	27·53	26·25	25·09	24·03	23·05
18	29·14	27·77	26·53	25·40	24·36
19	30·74	29·29	27·97	26·76	25·66
20	32·34	30·80	29·41	28·13	26·96

$n = 10$

$p=0\cdot6$	$0\cdot7$	$0\cdot8$	$0\cdot9$	$1\cdot0$
r_e				
2	2·77	2·69	*****	*****	*****
3	4·13	4·00	*****	*****	*****
4	5·47	5·30	*****	*****	*****
5	6·81	6·59	*****	*****	*****
6	8·13	7·86	*****	*****	*****
7	9·43	9·12	*****	*****	*****
8	10·73	10·37	*****	*****	*****
9	12·03	11·61	11·22	*****	*****
10	13·31	12·84	12·41	*****	*****
11	14·59	14·07	13·59	*****	*****
12	15·86	15·29	14·76	*****	*****
13	17·13	16·50	15·92	*****	*****
14	18·39	17·71	17·09	*****	*****
15	19·64	18·92	18·24	*****	*****
16	20·90	20·12	19·39	*****	*****
17	22·15	21·32	20·54	*****	*****
18	23·40	22·51	21·69	*****	*****
19	24·64	23·70	22·83	*****	*****
20	25·88	24·89	23·97	*****	*****

APPENDIX F

$$n = 11$$

$p=0.1$	0·2	0·3	0·4	0·5
r_e				
2	3·28	3·16	3·05	2·95	2·86
3	4·91	4·73	4·56	4·41	4·26
4	6·54	6·29	6·06	5·85	5·65
5	8·16	7·85	7·55	7·28	7·02
6	9·79	9·39	9·03	8·70	8·39
7	11·41	10·94	10·51	10·11	9·74
8	13·02	12·48	11·98	11·52	11·09
9	14·64	14·01	13·44	12·91	12·43
10	16·25	15·55	14·90	14·31	13·76
11	17·86	17·08	16·36	15·70	15·09
12	19·47	18·60	17·81	17·08	16·41
13	21·08	20·13	19·26	18·46	17·72
14	22·69	21·65	20·70	19·83	19·04
15	24·29	23·17	22·14	21·21	20·34
16	25·90	24·69	23·58	22·57	21·65
17	27·50	26·20	25·02	23·94	22·95
18	29·11	27·72	26·46	25·31	24·25
19	30·71	29·23	27·89	26·67	25·55
20	32·31	30·74	29·32	28·03	26·84

(Left margin: REQUIRED RETURN FOR EQUITY SHAREHOLDERS)

$$n = 11$$

$p=0.6$	0·7	0·8	0·9	1·0
r_e				
2	2·77	2·68	*****	*****	*****
3	4·12	3·99	*****	*****	*****
4	5·46	5·29	*****	*****	*****
5	6·79	6·56	*****	*****	*****
6	8·10	7·83	*****	*****	*****
7	9·40	9·08	*****	*****	*****
8	10·69	10·32	9·98	*****	*****
9	11·98	11·55	11·16	*****	*****
10	13·25	12·78	12·34	*****	*****
11	14·52	14·00	13·51	*****	*****
12	15·79	15·21	14·67	*****	*****
13	17·04	16·42	15·83	*****	*****
14	18·30	17·62	16·98	*****	*****
15	19·55	18·81	18·13	*****	*****
16	20·80	20·01	19·28	*****	*****
17	22·04	21·20	20·42	*****	*****
18	23·28	22·38	21·55	*****	*****
19	24·52	23·57	22·69	*****	*****
20	25·75	24·75	23·82	*****	*****

APPENDIX F

$n = 12$

$p=0{\cdot}1$	0·2	0·3	0·4	0·5
r_e				
2	3·28	3·16	3·05	2·95	2·85
3	4·91	4·73	4·56	4·40	4·25
4	6·54	6·28	6·05	5·84	5·63
5	8·16	7·84	7·54	7·26	7·01
6	9·78	9·38	9·02	8·68	8·36
7	11·40	10·92	10·49	10·09	9·71
8	13·01	12·46	11·95	11·49	11·05
9	14·63	13·99	13·41	12·88	12·39
10	16·24	15·52	14·87	14·27	13·71
11	17·85	17·05	16·32	15·65	15·03
12	19·45	18·57	17·77	17·03	16·35
13	21·06	20·09	19·21	18·40	17·66
14	22·67	21·61	20·65	19·77	18·96
15	24·27	23·13	22·09	21·14	20·27
16	25·87	24·64	23·52	22·50	21·57
17	27·48	26·16	24·96	23·86	22·86
18	29·08	27·67	26·39	25·22	24·16
19	30·68	29·18	27·82	26·58	25·45
20	32·28	30·69	29·25	27·94	26·74

$n = 12$

$p=0{\cdot}6$	0·7	0·8	0·9	1·0
r_e				
2	2·76	2·68	*****	*****	*****
3	4·11	3·98	*****	*****	*****
4	5·45	5·27	*****	*****	*****
5	6·77	6·54	*****	*****	*****
6	8·07	7·80	*****	*****	*****
7	9·37	9·04	8·74	*****	*****
8	10·65	10·28	9·93	*****	*****
9	11·93	11·50	11·11	*****	*****
10	13·20	12·72	12·28	*****	*****
11	14·46	13·93	13·44	*****	*****
12	15·72	15·14	14·60	*****	*****
13	16·97	16·34	15·75	*****	*****
14	18·22	17·53	16·89	*****	*****
15	19·46	18·72	18·03	*****	*****
16	20·70	19·91	19·17	*****	*****
17	21·94	21·09	20·30	*****	*****
18	23·18	22·27	21·44	*****	*****
19	24·41	23·45	22·56	*****	*****
20	25·64	24·63	23·69	*****	*****

REQUIRED RETURN FOR EQUITY SHAREHOLDERS

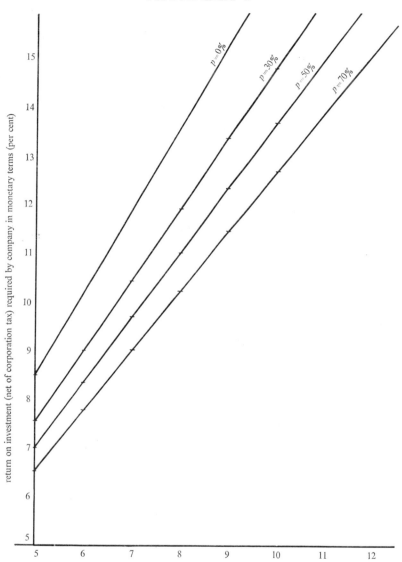

Fig. 14 Equity cut-off rates for capital budgeting in the corporation tax regime

$$\text{rate of share turnover} \frac{1}{n} = \frac{1}{12} \text{ p.a.}$$

$$\text{proportion of profits retained} = p.$$

APPENDIX F

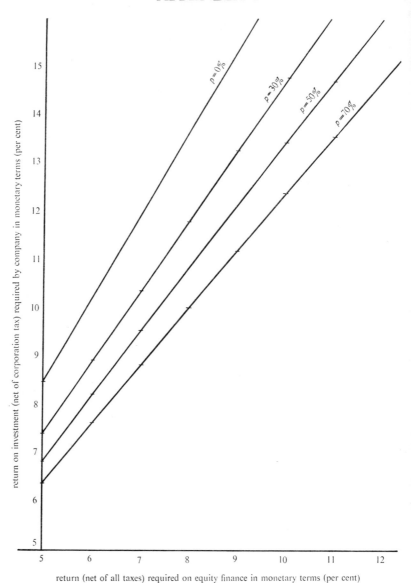

Fig. 15 Equity cut-off rates for capital budgeting in the corporation tax regime

$$\text{rate of share turnover} \frac{1}{n} = \frac{1}{20} \text{ p.a.}$$

proportion of profits retained $= p$.

APPENDIX F

$n = 20$

$p=0\cdot1$	0·2	0·3	0·4	0·5
r_e				
2	3·27	3·15	3·03	2·93	2·83
3	4·89	4·70	4·52	4·35	4·20
4	6·51	6·24	5·99	5·76	5·55
5	8·13	7·78	7·45	7·16	6·88
6	9·74	9·30	8·91	8·54	8·21
7	11·34	10·83	10·35	9·92	9·52
8	12·95	12·34	11·79	11·29	10·82
9	14·55	13·86	13·23	12·65	12·12
10	16·15	15·37	14·66	14·01	13·41
11	17·75	16·88	16·08	15·36	14·70
12	19·35	18·38	17·51	16·71	15·99
13	20·95	19·89	18·93	18·06	17·27
14	22·55	21·39	20·35	19·41	18·55
15	24·14	22·90	21·77	20·75	19·82
16	25·74	24·40	23·19	22·10	21·10
17	27·33	25·90	24·61	23·44	22·37
18	28·93	27·40	26·02	24·78	23·65
19	30·52	28·90	27·44	26·12	24·92
20	32·12	30·40	28·85	27·46	26·19

$n = 20$

$p=0\cdot6$	0·7	0·8	0·9	1·0
r_e				
2	2·73	2·65	*****	*****	*****
3	4·05	3·92	*****	*****	*****
4	5·35	5·17	4·99	*****	*****
5	6·63	6·40	6·18	*****	*****
6	7·90	7·61	7·34	*****	*****
7	9·15	8·81	8·50	*****	*****
8	10·40	10·00	9·64	*****	*****
9	11·64	11·19	10·77	*****	*****
10	12·87	12·37	11·90	*****	*****
11	14·10	13·54	13·02	*****	*****
12	15·32	14·71	14·14	*****	*****
13	16·54	15·87	15·26	*****	*****
14	17·76	17·04	16·37	*****	*****
15	18·98	18·20	17·48	*****	*****
16	20·19	19·36	18·59	*****	*****
17	21·40	20·51	19·69	*****	*****
18	22·62	21·67	20·80	20·00	*****
19	23·83	22·82	21·90	21·05	*****
20	25·04	23·98	23·01	22·11	*****

REQUIRED RETURN FOR EQUITY SHAREHOLDERS

APPENDIX F

$n = 30$

$p=0.1$	0.2	0.3	0.4	0.5
r_e				
2	3·26	3·13	3·01	2·90	2·80
3	4·88	4·67	4·48	4·30	4·14
4	6·49	6·20	5·93	5·69	5·46
5	8·10	7·72	7·38	7·06	6·77
6	9·70	9·23	8·81	8·42	8·07
7	11·30	10·74	10·24	9·78	9·36
8	12·90	12·25	11·66	11·13	10·64
9	14·49	13·75	13·08	12·47	11·92
10	16·09	15·25	14·50	13·81	13·19
11	17·68	16·75	15·91	15·15	14·46
12	19·28	18·25	17·32	16·49	15·73
13	20·87	19·75	18·74	17·83	17·00
14	22·46	21·24	20·15	19·16	18·27
15	24·06	22·74	21·56	20·50	19·54
16	25·65	24·24	22·97	21·83	20·80
17	27·24	25·73	24·38	23·17	22·07
18	28·83	27·23	25·79	24·50	23·34
19	30·43	28·73	27·20	25·84	24·60
20	32·02	30·22	28·62	27·17	25·87

$n = 30$

$p=0.6$	0.7	0.8	0.9	1.0
r_e				
2	2·70	2·61	*****	*****	*****
3	3·99	3·85	3·72	*****	*****
4	5·26	5·07	4·89	*****	*****
5	6·51	6·26	6·03	*****	*****
6	7·74	7·44	7·17	*****	*****
7	8·97	8·62	8·29	*****	*****
8	10·19	9·78	9·40	*****	*****
9	11·41	10·94	10·52	*****	*****
10	12·62	12·10	11·62	*****	*****
11	13·83	13·26	12·73	*****	*****
12	15·04	14·41	13·83	13·29	*****
13	16·25	15·56	14·93	14·34	*****
14	17·45	16·71	16·03	15·40	*****
15	18·66	17·86	17·12	16·45	*****
16	19·86	19·01	18·22	17·50	*****
17	21·07	20·16	19·32	18·55	*****
18	22·27	21·30	20·42	19·60	*****
19	23·48	22·45	21·51	20·65	*****
20	24·68	23·60	22·61	21·70	*****

APPENDIX F

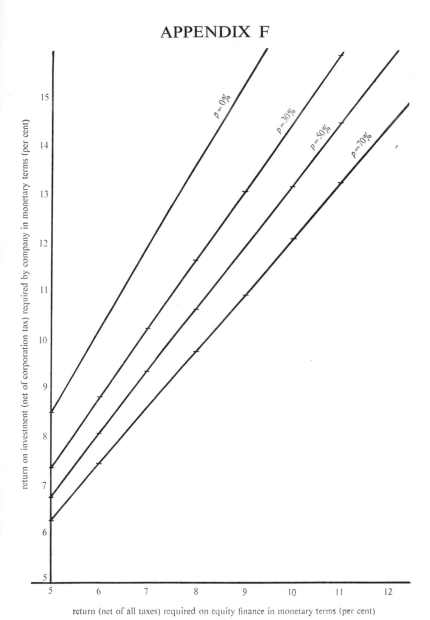

Fig. 16   Equity cut-off rates for capital budgeting in the corporation tax regime

$$\text{rate of share turnover} \frac{1}{n} = \frac{1}{30} \text{ p.a.}$$

proportion of profits retained $= p$.

16

Although the Government has announced that cash grants of 25 and 45% on eligible plant expenditure will remain effective until the end of 1968, it is likely that the time-lag, k (currently 12 months), between the incurring of such expenditure and the payment of cash grants to business firms will be reduced to 6 months in the interim period. As those of the tables in Appendix E which embody the present value of a cash grant employ a (cash grant) time-lag of $k = 18$ months, additional sets of tables of present values of investment incentives on eligible plant expenditure with $k = 6$ months (NATIONAL *and* DEVELOPMENT AREAS) are included in this addendum.

For the reason that the present values of investment incentives are, as revealed by Appendix E, relatively insensitive to the time-lag, z, between a company's year-end and the date on which it makes its corporation tax payments, it is not necessary to reproduce the four values of z shown in Appendix E. Thus the value of z used in this addendum is $z = 18$ months—the most common value of z encountered in practice.

Present values of investment incentives for values of k falling between 6 months and 18 months can be obtained by interpolating between the respective appropriate values in Appendix E and this addendum.

For completeness present value of industrial buildings allowances with, where appropriate, $k = 6$ months are also given in the following addendum

ADDENDUM TO APPENDIX E

(6 months cash grant time-lag)

PLANT QUALIFYING FOR CASH GRANTS

(a) Present value, S, of investment incentives on a principal of unity (columns (2), (3) and (4)):

$$S = \frac{P}{(1+r)^k} + \frac{(1-P)DT(1+r)}{(1+r)^z(r+D)}$$

(b) Effective net of tax factor Y (column (5)):

$$Y = 1 - \frac{T}{(1+r)^z}, \text{ i.e., } 1 - T(1+r)^{-z}.$$

P = cash grant;
D = annual allowance on a reducing balance basis;
T = corporation tax at 40%;
k = 6 months time-lag between incurring of capital expenditure and receipt of cash grant;
z = time-lag between company's financial year-end and date of corporation tax payment;
r = rate of discount.

ADDENDUM TO APPENDIX E

(6 months cash grant time-lag)

INDUSTRIAL BUILDINGS

(*a*) *National* Initial plus annual allowances on a straight-line basis. Present value S_2 of investment incentives on a principal of unity (column (2)):

$$S_2 = \frac{T}{(1+r)^z}\left\{(R+D)+D\left[\frac{1-(1+r)^{-20}}{r}\right]\right\}$$

(*b*) (i) *Development area* Cash grant at 25% plus initial allowance at 15% and annual allowances at 4% (on a straight-line basis) on the balance of expenditure (column (3)).

(ii) *Development area* Cash grant at 35% plus initial allowance at 15% and annual allowances at 4% (on a straight-line basis) on the balance of expenditure (column (4)).

Present value S_3 of (*b*)(i) and (ii) on a principal of unity:

$$S_3 = \frac{P}{(1+r)^k} + \frac{T(1-P)}{(1+r)^z}\left\{(R+D)+D\left[\frac{1-(1+r)^{-20}}{r}\right]\right\}.$$

(*c*) Effective net of tax factor y (column (5)): $y = 1-T(1+r)^{-z}$.

P = cash grant;
R = initial allowance at 15%;
D = annual allowance at 4% on a straight line basis;
T = corporation tax at 40%;
k = 6 months time-lag between incurring of capital expenditure and receipt of cash-grant;
z = time-lag between company's financial year-end and date of corporation tax payment;
r = rate of discount.

ADDENDUM TO APPENDIX E

INDUSTRIAL BUILDINGS

$$k = 6 \text{ months}, \ z = 18 \text{ months}, \ T = 40\%$$

(1)	(2)	(3)	(4)	(5)
		$P = 25\%$	$P = 35\%$	
	$R = 15\%$	$R = 15\%$	$R = 15\%$	
r	$D = 4\%$	$D = 4\%$	$D = 4\%$	$1 - T(1+r)^{-z}$
1	0·35933	0·51825	0·58182	0·6059
2	0·32774	0·49334	0·55958	0·6117
3	0·30042	0·47165	0·54014	0·6173
4	0·27668	0·45265	0·52304	0·6229
5	0·25596	0·43595	0·50794	0·6282
6	0·23780	0·42117	0·49452	0·6335
7	0·22181	0·40804	0·48253	0·6386
8	0·20768	0·39632	0·47178	0·6436
9	0·19513	0·38580	0·46207	0·6485
10	0·18395	0·37633	0·45328	0·6533
11	0·17394	0·36774	0·44527	0·6580
12	0·16495	0·35994	0·43793	0·6625
13	0·15684	0·38281	0·43120	0·6670
14	0·14950	0·34627	0·42498	0·6714
15	0·14283	0·34025	0·41922	0·6757
16	0·13676	0·33469	0·41386	0·6798
17	0·13120	0·32953	0·40886	0·6839
18	0·12611	0·32472	0·40417	0·6879
19	0·12142	0·32024	0·39976	0·6919
20	0·11709	0·31603	0·39561	0·6957
21	0·11308	0·31208	0·39168	0·6995
22	0·10936	0·30836	0·38796	0·7032
23	0·10590	0·30484	0·38442	0·7068
24	0·10267	0·30151	0·38104	0·7103
25	0·09965	0·29834	0·37782	0·7138
26	0·09682	0·29533	0·37474	0·7172
27	0·09416	0·29246	0·37178	0·7205
28	0·09166	0·28971	0·36894	0·7238
29	0·08930	0·28709	0·36620	0·7270
30	0·08707	0·28456	0·36356	0·7301
31	0·08496	0·28214	0·36102	0·7332
32	0·08295	0·27981	0·35856	0·7362
33	0·08105	0·27757	0·35617	0·7392
34	0·07925	0·27540	0·35386	0·7421
35	0·07752	0·27331	0·35162	0·7450
36	0·07588	0·27128	0·34945	0·7478
37	0·07431	0·26932	0·34733	0·7506
38	0·07281	0·26742	0·34527	0·7533
39	0·07138	0·26558	0·34326	0·7559
40	0·07000	0·26379	0·34130	0·7585
41	0·06868	0·26205	0·33939	0·7611
42	0·06741	0·26035	0·33753	0·7636
43	0·06619	0·25870	0·33571	0·7661
44	0·06501	0·25709	0·33392	0·7685
45	0·06388	0·25552	0·33218	0·7709
46	0·06279	0·25399	0·33047	0·7733
47	0·06173	0·25250	0·32880	0·7756
48	0·06072	0·25104	0·32716	0·7778
49	0·05973	0·24961	0·32556	0·7801
50	0·05878	0·24821	0·32398	0·7823

RATE OF DISCOUNT

ADDENDUM TO APPENDIX E

PLANT QUALIFYING FOR CASH GRANTS—NATIONAL

$k = 6$ months, $z = 18$ months, $T = 40\%$

(1)	(2)	(3)	(4)	(5)
	$P = 25\%$ $D = 15\%$	$P = 25\%$ $D = 20\%$	$P = 25\%$ $D = 25\%$	$1 - T(1+r)^{-z}$
r				
1	0·5286	0·5331	0·5358	0·6059
2	0·5096	0·5176	0·5226	0·6117
3	0·4927	0·5034	0·5103	0·6173
4	0·4774	0·4903	0·4987	0·6229
5	0·4636	0·4782	0·4880	0·6282
6	0·4510	0·4670	0·4778	0·6335
7	0·4394	0·4565	0·4683	0·6386
8	0·4288	0·4468	0·4593	0·6436
9	0·4190	0·4376	0·4507	0·6485
10	0·4100	0·4291	0·4427	0·6533
11	0·4016	0·4210	0·4350	0·6580
12	0·3937	0·4134	0·4278	0·6625
13	0·3864	0·4062	0·4208	0·6670
14	0·3795	0·3994	0·4143	0·6714
15	0·3730	0·3930	0·4080	0·6757
16	0·3669	0·3869	0·4020	0·6798
17	0·3611	0·3810	0·3962	0·6839
18	0·3557	0·3755	0·3907	0·6879
19	0·3505	0·3702	0·3854	0·6919
20	0·3456	0·3651	0·3804	0·6957
21	0·3409	0·3603	0·3755	0·6995
22	0·3365	0·3557	0·3708	0·7032
23	0·3322	0·3512	0·3663	0·7068
24	0·3281	0·3470	0·3620	0·7103
25	0·3242	0·3429	0·3578	0·7138
26	0·3205	0·3389	0·3537	0·7172
27	0·3169	0·3351	0·3498	0·7205
28	0·3135	0·3315	0·3460	0·7238
29	0·3102	0·3279	0·3424	0·7270
30	0·3070	0·3245	0·3389	0·7301
31	0·3039	0·3212	0·3354	0·7332
32	0·3009	0·3180	0·3321	0·7362
33	0·2981	0·3149	0·3289	0·7392
34	0·2953	0·3120	0·3258	0·7421
35	0·2926	0·3091	0·3227	0·7450
36	0·2900	0·3062	0·3198	0·7478
37	0·2875	0·3035	0·3169	0·7506
38	0·2851	0·3009	0·3142	0·7533
39	0·2827	0·2983	0·3114	0·7559
40	0·2804	0·2958	0·3088	0·7585
41	0·2782	0·2934	0·3062	0·7611
42	0·2760	0·2910	0·3037	0·7636
43	0·2739	0·2887	0·3013	0·7661
44	0·2719	0·2865	0·2989	0·7685
45	0·2699	0·2843	0·2966	0·7709
46	0·2680	0·2821	0·2943	0·7733
47	0·2661	0·2801	0·2921	0·7750
48	0·2642	0·2780	0·2900	0·7778
49	0·2624	0·2760	0·2878	0·7801
50	0·2607	0·2741	0·2858	0·7823

RATE OF DISCOUNT

ADDENDUM TO APPENDIX E

PLANT QUALIFYING FOR CASH GRANTS—DEVELOPMENT AREA

$k = 6$ months, $z = 18$ months, $T = 40\%$

(1)	(2)	(3)	(4)	(5)
	$P = 45\%$	$P = 45\%$	$P = 45\%$	
r	$D = 15\%$	$D = 20\%$	$D = 25\%$	$1 - T(1+r)^{-z}$
1	0·6530	0·6563	0·6583	0·6059
2	0·6378	0·6436	0·6473	0·6117
3	0·6240	0·6319	0·6396	0·6173
4	0·6116	0·6210	0·6272	0·6229
5	0·6002	0·6109	0·6181	0·6282
6	0·5897	0·6015	0·6094	0·6335
7	0·5800	0·5926	0·6012	0·6386
8	0·5711	0·5842	0·5934	0·6436
9	0·5627	0·5763	0·5860	0·6485
10	0·5549	0·5689	0·5789	0·6533
11	0·5476	0·5618	0·5721	0·6580
12	0·5407	0·5551	0·5657	0·6625
13	0·5342	0·5488	0·5595	0·6670
14	0·5280	0·5427	0·5535	0·6714
15	0·5222	0·5369	0·5478	0·6757
16	0·5167	0·5313	0·5424	0·6798
17	0·5114	0·5260	0·5371	0·6839
18	0·5063	0·5209	0·5320	0·6879
19	0·5015	0·5159	0·5271	0·6919
20	0·4969	0·5112	0·5224	0·6957
21	0·4924	0·5067	0·5178	0·6995
22	0·4882	0·5023	0·5134	0·7032
23	0·4841	0·4980	0·5091	0·7068
24	0·4801	0·4939	0·5049	0·7103
25	0·4763	0·4899	0·5009	0·7138
26	0·4726	0·4861	0·4970	0·7172
27	0·4690	0·4824	0·4932	0·7205
28	0·4656	0·4788	0·4895	0·7238
29	0·4622	0·4753	0·4859	0·7270
30	0·4590	0·4719	0·4824	0·7301
31	0·4558	0·4685	0·4790	0·7332
32	0·4528	0·4653	0·4757	0·7362
33	0·4498	0·4622	0·4724	0·7392
34	0·4469	0·4591	0·4693	0·7421
35	0·4441	0·4562	0·4662	0·7450
36	0·4414	0·4532	0·4632	0·7478
37	0·4387	0·4504	0·4603	0·7506
38	0·4361	0·4476	0·4574	0·7533
39	0·4335	0·4449	0·4546	0·7559
40	0·4310	0·4423	0·4518	0·7585
41	0·4286	0·4397	0·4491	0·7611
42	0·4262	0·4372	0·4465	0·7636
43	0·4239	0·4347	0·4439	0·7661
44	0·4216	0·4323	0·4414	0·7685
45	0·4194	0·4299	0·4390	0·7709
46	0·4172	0·4276	0·4365	0·7733
47	0·4151	0·4253	0·4342	0·7756
48	0·4130	0·4231	0·4318	0·7778
49	0·4109	0·4209	0·4295	0·7801
50	0·4089	0·4187	0·4273	0·7823

RATE OF DISCOUNT

BIBLIOGRAPHY

Below is a concise reading list covering the subject-matter of this book. Detailed bibliographies, satisfying both the practitioner and theorist, and exhausting most facets of capital budgeting, are to be found in the works marked with an asterisk.

The works listed are pre-eminently a selection we would recommend to businessmen and those responsible for the analysis of investment and financing decisions in practice. Students interested in the pure theory of capital budgeting should find that any one of the more detailed bibliographies, supplemented by a perusal of recent contributions to such publications as the *Journal of Business* and *Journal of Finance*, will readily introduce them to the present position of theoretical analysis and the generally more academic aspects of the subject.

Capital Budgeting

ALFRED, A. M., and EVANS, J. B.   *Appraisal of Projects by Discounted Cash Flow.*   Chapman & Hall, 2nd edition, London, 1966.

BIERMAN, H., and SMIDT, S.   **The Capital Budgeting Decision.*   Macmillan Co., 2nd edition, New York, 1966.

GORDON, MYRON J.   *The Investment, Financing and Valuation of the Corporation.*   Homewood, Ill., Richard D. Irwin, 1962.

MERRETT, A. J. and SYKES, ALLEN.   **The Finance and Analysis of Capital Projects.*   Longmans Green, London, 1963.

ROBICHEK, ALEXANDER A., and MYERS, STEWART C.   *Optimal Financing Decision.*   Prentice Hall, Englewood Cliffs, New Jersey, 1965.

SOLOMON, EZRA.   **The Theory of Financial Management.*   Columbia University Press, New York and London, 1963.

SOLOMON, EZRA, ed.   *The Management of Corporate Capital.*   The Free Press, Glencoe, Illinois, 1959.

WESTON, J. FRED.   **Managerial Finance.*   Holt, Rinehart and Winston, New York etc., and London, 1962.

Financial Mathematics

AYRES, FRANK J.   *Theory and Problems of Mathematics of Finance.*   Schaum Publishing Co., New York, 1963.

HUMMEL, P. M., and SEEBECK, C. L.   *Mathematics of Finance.*   2nd edition, McGraw-Hill, 1956.

Empirical Studies

BARNA, TIBOR. *Investment and Growth Policies in British Industrial Firms.* Cambridge University Press, 1962.

CORNER, D. C., and WILLIAMS, A. "The Sensitivity of Business to Initial and Investment Allowances", *Economica*, 1965.

HART, H., and PRUSSMAN, D. "An account of Management Accounting and Techniques in the S.E. Hants Coastal Region", *Accountants Journal*, January 1964, and *Scientific Business*, November 1964.

ISTVAN, D. F. *Capital-Expenditure Decisions: How they are made in Large Corporations.* Bureau of Business Research Graduate School of Business Indiana University, 1961.

LAWSON, G. H. "Criteria to be observed in Judging a Capital Project", *Accountants Journal*, May and June 1964.

LAWSON, G. H. "The Cost of Ploughed-Back Profits", *The Bankers' Magazine*, February 1966.

MEREDITH, G. G. *Administrative Control of Capital Expenditure: A Survey of Australian Public Companies.* University of Queensland Press, St. Lucia, 1964.

MERRETT, A. J., and SYKES, ALLEN, "Return on Equities and Fixed Interest Securities", *District Bank Review*, December, 1963, and June 1966.

NIELD, R. R. "Replacement Policy", *National Institute Economic Review*, November 1964.

REPORT OF THE COMMITTEE ON TURNOVER TAXATION. H.M.S.O. Cmnd. 2300, March 1964.

SCOTT, W., and WILLIAMS, B. R. *Investment Proposals and Decisions.* Allen & Unwin, London, 1965.

U.K. Taxation

ASSOCIATION OF CERTIFIED AND CORPORATE ACCOUNTANTS. *Capital Gains Tax, The Provisions of the Finance Act, 1965,* 3rd edition, 1966.

CARMICHAEL, K. S. *Corporation Tax.* H.F.L. (Publishers) Ltd., London, 1966.

CHOWN, JOHN. *The Corporation Tax—A Closer Look.* The Institute of Economic Affairs, 1965.

H.M.S.O. *Investment Incentives.* Cmnd. 2874, 1966.

INDEX